BRADLEY'S
LETTERS SENT HOME

Brigadier General Luther P. Bradley

The Civil War
1861 1865

Robert D. Bradley

To all of those who have helped me - many thanks.

Especially to Traude, Kirsten and Max, who have
helped me for a very long time - with love and hugs.

Special Thanks

      KD, Cj, SO, Rob, C + JN, El, CJ+ E

      Hugs also

Bob

PREFACE

My great grandfather, Luther Prentice Bradley, was born in New Haven, Connecticut on December 8, 1822. He was the youngest child of Luther Bradley and his second wife Nancy Mona Prentice, joining two older sisters, Rebecca and Hannah Buel and five older siblings from his father's first marriage to Mary Atwater: Maria, George, Robert, Charles and Mary, all born in New Haven.

Luther, as well as my father, Prentice Bradley, devoted later years to genealogical research. I am catching up to them both in *my own* golden years, researching Luther Prentice Bradley's life during the Civil War period from 1861 to 1865. This biography primarily contains letters written by Luther to his mother and his sisters describing the war, the western theatre, and the day to day activities, experiences, observations, and the conditions existing at the time.

In four years, Civil War casualties reached 1.5 million - more than all combined wars involving American soldiers. Over 65,000 books have been written about this devastating period - fascinating, heart-moving and profound documents of the reality and horrors of war that touched every American family of that era. My great grandfather's letters evoke the same concerns and sentiments penned by many of the soldiers who wrote to their loved ones, knowing it may have been their last words and wishes sent home.

I am proud to be the descendant of a decorated career soldier who survived - along with his observations - of such an embattled period. His letters are merely a few drops in a gigantic glacier of writing which reflects an important chapter of American history. A chapter that gave a gifted and eloquent voice to battalions of common men.

My father, Prentice Bradley, donated the original letters of Luther Prentice Bradley to the archives of the U.S. Army History Institute, Carlisle Barracks, Pennsylvania. The following biography was prepared by members of the History Institute who are noted below.* Robert Dewey Bradley

* Prepared June 2010 by Mary Elizebeth Gasper, Joann Lamm, Shannon Schwaller, Jessica Sheets, and Melissa Wiford

Biography

Luther Prentice Bradley was born to Luther and Nancy (Prentice} Bradley on 8 December 1822 in New Haven, Connecticut He received his education at schools in New Haven, served for several years In the Connecticut militia, and was commissioned a lieutenant in 1850. In 1855, he moved to Chicago where he entered the book business and served in the Illinois militia.

At the start of the Civil War, Bradley recruited troops for the Union. In October 1861, he received a commission as a lieutenant colonel of the 51st Illinois Infantry Regiment During the spring of 1862, he was involved in the capture of New Madrid and Island No. 10 of Missouri, and in action against Fort Pillow, Arkansas, and Corinth, Mississippi. Bradley commanded operations against guerillas in Decatur, Alabama during the summer. In October 1862, he was promoted to colonel of the 51st Illinois Infantry Regiment.
Bradley commanded a brigade at the Battle of Stone River, as well as at Tullahoma and Chickamauga. He
was wounded twice at Chickamauga.

In early 1864, Bradley reenlisted with the 51st Illinois Infantry Regiment for three years. He served in the Atlanta Campaign from May to September 1864. In July 1864, he was appointed brigadier general of volunteers and participated in numerous battles In the South, including Texas. Bradley was wounded again at Spring Hill, Texas in November 1864. He resigned his commission in June 1865, but in July 1866 was appointed lieutenant colonel of the 27th Infantry Regiment, U.S. Army. Bradley built Fort C. F. Smith in Montana and saw action during 1867-1868 against the Sioux and Cheyenne in Montana, Nebraska and Kansas. In May 1868, he married lone Dewey in Chicago, Illinois. They would have two sons together, William and Robert.

From 1868 to 1872, Bradley commanded various posts in Nebraska and Wyoming. He was transferred to the 9th Infantry Regiment in March 1869. In 1873, he commanded infantry soldiers who accompanied engineers planning part of the Northern Pacific Railroad. Bradley then commanded two different districts in Wyoming from 1874 to 1876. In 1877, he was In Nebraska and oversaw members of the Sioux tribe who had surrendered. The following year, Bradley directed a mission against American Indians in Montana.

Bradley was appointed colonel of the 3rd InfantrY Regiment in March 1879 and was reassigned to the 13th Infantry Regiment that June. He served in Georgia, Louisiana, and New Mexico until 1886. From 1884 to 1886, Bradley commanded the District of New Mexico. During that time, he was in action against American Indians in Arizona and New Mexico. On 8 December 1886, Bradley retired at the mandatory retirement age of sixty-four. He lived most of his retirement in Tacoma. Washington, and was Involved in the community. Bradley died on 13 March 1910 and was burled at Arlington National Cemetery. A newspaper article reporting his death commented on his good character, noting that his "agreeable manner won him many friends.·

51st Illinois Infantry Regiment
(Chicago Legion, Ryan Life Guard)
Three Year Service
December 24, 1861 - September 25, 1865
(Re-enlisted as Veterans, Feb 1864)

Assigned to:

- Army of the Mississippi: March 1862 - November 1862
- Army of the Cumberland: November 1862 - August 1865
- Department of Texas: August 1865 - September 1865

Battles/Campaigns Engaged in:
New Madrid/Island No. 10, Siege of Corinth, Stone's River (Murfreesboro), Tullahoma Campaign, Chickamauga, Missionary Ridge (Chattanooga), Atlanta Campaign [Buzzard's Roost Gap, Resaca, Kenesaw Mountain, Peachtree Creek, Jonesborough], Spring Hill, Franklin, Nashville

Adjutant General's Regiment History   **Frederick Dyer's Regimental History**

51st Infantry Field & Staff   **Non-Commissioned Staff**   **Band**   **Unassigned Recruits**

Unassigned/Substitute/Drafted Recruits

Link to Roster **Link to County of Origin**

Link to Roster	Link to County of Origin
Company A	Cook County
Company B	Champaign County
Company C	Knox and Iroquois counties
Company D	Woodford County
Company E	Champaign & Vermilion counties
Company F	
Company G	Mason County
Company H	Cook and Lake counties
Company I	Rock Island County
Company K	Fulton County
	Cook County

Return to Main Page   Return to Regiment Page

http://www.rootsweb.com/~ilcivilw/reg_html/051_reg.htm

Name	Rank	Residence	Date of Rank or Enlistment	Date of Muster	Remarks
ANTHONY, Cyrus A	Adjutant	West Jersey	Jan 24, 1865	Nov 28, 1865	Prom. Captain Co. B [Aug 8, 1865]
BOYD, James S	Colonel	Chicago	Sep 24, 1865	Not must'd.	MO Sep 25, 1865; Lt. Col.
BOYD, James S	Lt. Colonel	Chicago	July 31, 1865	Aug 16, 1865	Promoted
BOYD, James S	Major	Chicago	July 3, 1865	July 13, 1865	Promoted
BRADLEY, Luther P	Colonel	Chicago	Sep 30, 1862	Dec 15, 1862	Pro. Brig. Gen., July 30, 1864
BRADLEY, Luther P	Lt. Colonel	Chicago	Sep 20, 1861	Oct 15, 1861	Promoted
COE, Albert C	Quartermaster	Chicago	Jun 9, 1862	Nov 30, 1862	Prom. Captain Co. K [Jun 14, 1864]
CUMMING, Gilbert W	Colonel	Chicago	Sep 20, 1861	Oct 15, 1861	Resigned Sep 30, 1862
DAVIS, Charles W	Colonel	Chicago	May 11, 1865	Not must'd.	Disch, Jun 30, 1865; Lt. Col.
DAVIS, Charles W	Lt. Colonel	Chicago	Oct 6, 1863	Dec 15, 1863	Promoted
DAVIS, Charles W	Major	Chicago	Sep 30, 1862	Oct 14, 1862	Promoted
DAVIS, Charles W	Adjutant	Chicago	Oct 15, 1861	Oct 15, 1861	Promoted Major
ELLIOTT, William W	1st Asst. Surg.	---	May 20, 1863	May 29, 1863	Mustered out Jun 14, 1865
GRAY, Allen W	Adjutant	Jefferson	Jun 27, 1864	Apr 2, 1864	Resigned Jan 24, 1865
HALL, Henry W	Adjutant	Chicago	Sep 30, 1862	Dec 23, 1862	Killed in battle, Jun 27, 1864
HATFIELD, Adam S	Quartermaster	Middleport	Jun 14, 1864	Mar 1, 1865	Prom. Captain Co. E [Aug 8, 1865]
HOWLAND, Henry	Quartermaster	Chicago	Sep 20, 1861	Oct 15, 1861	Pro. Brig. QM, Jun 9, 1862
HUNT, William C	Surgeon	Chicago	Oct 21, 1861	Oct 15, 1861	Resigned Apr 14, 1862
LYTLE, Francis W	1st Asst. Surg.	Troy	Sep 25, 1862	Sep 25, 1862	Prom. Surgeon 36th Reg't.
MAGEE, Thomas L	Surgeon	Prairie City	May 20, 1863	May 29, 1863	Mustered out Sep 25, 1865
MAGEE, Thomas L	1st Asst. Surg.	Prairie City	Apr 1, 1863	---	Promoted
MAGEE, Thomas L	2nd Asst. Surg.	Prairie City	Nov 25, 1862	Nov 25, 1862	Promoted
McWILLIAMS, John G	Major	Chicago	Mar 24, 1861	Not must'd.	MO Mar 6, 1865 as Capt.
MENTANDEN, James E	Major	Chicago	July 31, 1865	Not must'd.	MO Sep 25, 1865 as Capt.
PASHLEY, John S	1st Asst. Surg.	Chicago	Oct 28, 1861	Oct 15, 1861	Res. Nov 16, 1862, MO to date July 26, 1862; abs't without leave
PRATT, George	Quartermaster	---	Aug 8, 1865	Not must'd.	Mustered out Sep 25, 1865, as QM Sergeant
RAYMOND, Lewis	Chaplain	Peoria	Oct 1, 1861	Oct 15, 1861	Resigned Nov 6, 1864
RAYMOND, Samuel B	Lt. Colonel	Chicago	Sep 30, 1862	Dec 15, 1862	Resigned Oct 6, 1863
RAYMOND, Samuel B	Major	Chicago	Sep 20, 1861	Oct 15, 1861	Promoted
ROSE, Rufus	Major	Chicago	Oct 6, 1863	Dec 15, 1863	Resigned Mar 24, 1864
SCOTT, John H	1st Asst. Surg.	Metropolis	July 13, 1865	July 25, 1865	Mustered out Sep 25, 1865
STEVERS, James B	Adjutant	---	Aug 8, 1865	Sep 1, 1865	Mustered out Sep 25, 1865
WEEKS, Jerome F	Surgeon	La Salle	May 15, 1862	May 16, 1862	Resigned Aug 19, 1864

Roster of Field and Staff 51st Illinois Infantry

Name	Rank	Residence	Date of Rank or Enlistment	Date of Muster	Remarks
ANTHONY, Cyrus	QM Sergeant	---	Dec 23, 1863	Feb 8, 1864	Prom. 1st Lt., Co. G [Jun 27, 1864]
BARBER, Richard F	Serg. Major	---	Dec 8, 1863	Feb 12, 1864	Vet. Prom. 2nd Lt. 13th US Colored Infantry
CASEY, Timothy	Serg. Major	---	Sep 20, 1861	Sep 24, 1861	Died Oct 4, 1863; wounds
EDWARDS, Jesse J	Serg. Major	---	Dec 23, 1863	Feb 8, 1864	Mustered out Sep 25, 1865
FITZGIBBONS, Richard	Prin. Musician	---	Sep 20, 1861	Dec 24, 1861	Mustered out Apr 4, 1865
GRAY, Allen W	Com. Sergeant	---	Dec 23, 1863	Feb 8, 1864	Prom. 1st Lt., Co. G [Sep 12, 1863]
JAMES, Benjamin F	QM Sergeant	---	Dec 23, 1863	Feb 8, 1864	Prom. 1st Lt., Co. B [Apr 11, 1865]
LANGGUTH, George W	Prin. Musician	---	Aug 23, 1862	Sep 24, 1862	Mustered out Jun 16, 1865
LAUX, Carl	Hospital Stew.	---	Feb 6, 1864	Feb 8, 1864	App. Hosp. Stew'd, US A.
MOORE, George T	QM Sergeant	---	Oct 10, 1861	Dec 24, 1861	---
NESMITH, George W	Serg. Major	---	Dec 23, 1863	Feb 8, 1864	MO to date Jun 30, 1865; was prisoner
PARSONS, Jacob B	Hospital Stew.	---	Sep 20, 1861	Dec 24, 1861	Discharged May 14, 1865
PRATT, George	QM Sergeant	---	Dec 23, 1863	Feb 8, 1864	Mustered out Sep 25, 1865
SARGENT, Asher	Com. Sergeant	---	Dec 23, 1863	Feb 8, 1864	Mustered out Sep 25, 1865
SHIRTS, Jacob H	Prin. Musician	---	Nov 1, 1861	Dec 24, 1861	Mustered out May 11, 1865
STEVERS, James B	Serg. Major	---	July 20, 1865	---	Promoted Adjutant [Aug 8, 1865]
THOMAS, Calvin H	Serg. Major	---	Dec 23, 1863	Feb 8, 1864	Vet. Prom. 1st Lt. Co. F [Nov 25, 1863]
YORKES, Henry	Prin. Musician	---	Nov 3, 1863	Nov 23, 1863	Mustered out Sep 25, 1865

Name	Rank	Residence	Date of Rank or Enlistment	Date of Muster	Remarks
BELL, Charles F	3rd Class	---	Oct 5, 1861	Oct 15, 1861	Deserted Feb 12, 1862
BLATHERWICK, John H	2nd Class	---	Oct 5, 1861	Oct 15, 1862	Mustered out Jun 30, 1862
BROOKS, Edgar	3rd Class	---	Oct 5, 1861	Oct 15, 1863	Deserted Nov 20, 1861
BROWN, Frederick A	3rd Class	---	Oct 5, 1861	Oct 15, 1864	Deserted Apr 19, 1862
CALKINS, Albert	3rd Class	---	Oct 5, 1861	Oct 15, 1865	Mustered out Jun 30, 1862
CLARK, William B	2nd Class	---	Oct 5, 1861	Oct 15, 1866	Mustered out Jun 30, 1862
HILL, Reuben C	3rd Class	---	Oct 5, 1861	Oct 15, 1867	Mustered out Jun 30, 1862
JONES, David L	2nd Class	---	Oct 5, 1861	Oct 15, 1868	Mustered out Jun 30, 1862
KETCHUM, John L	2nd Class	---	Oct 5, 1861	Oct 15, 1869	Mustered out Jun 30, 1862
KINGSBURY, Joseph	1st Class	---	Oct 5, 1861	Oct 15, 1870	Mustered out Jun 30, 1862
McCLAIN, David	1st Class	---	Oct 5, 1861	Oct 15, 1871	Mustered out Jun 30, 1862
McLAIN, Milton	3rd Class	---	Oct 5, 1861	Oct 15, 1872	Deserted Apr 19, 1862

Roster of Field and Staff 51st Illinois Infantry

ROBERTS, George C	2nd Class	---	Oct 5, 1861	Oct 15, 1874	Mustered out Jun 30, 1862
SHUPE, Aaron	1st Class	---	Oct 5, 1861	Oct 15, 1875	Mustered out Jun 30, 1862
SIMMONS, William	1st Class	---	Oct 5, 1861	Oct 15, 1876	Mustered out Jun 30, 1862
SMITH, Solomon	3rd Class	---	Oct 5, 1861	Oct 15, 1877	Mustered out Jun 30, 1862
TAFT, John W	1st Class	---	Oct 5, 1861	Oct 15, 1878	Mustered out Jun 30, 1862
TIDMARSH, William	Leader	---	Oct 4, 1861	Oct 15, 1879	Mustered out Jun 30, 1862
VANSLYKE, Edwin Y	3rd Class	---	Oct 5, 1861	Oct 15, 1880	Mustered out Jun 30, 1862
WHEELER, Lewis S	3rd Class	---	Oct 5, 1861	Oct 15, 1881	Mustered out Jun 30, 1862

Name	Residence	Date of Rank or Enlistment	Date of Muster	Remarks
DOYLE, Joseph	St Joseph	Aug 2, 1862	---	---
GRAY, Theophilus	Time	Oct 15, 1864	Oct 17, 1864	---
GREEN, John	Stonington	Dec 3, 1864	Dec 9, 1864	---
PALMER, Champion J	Holland	Dec 3, 1864	Dec 9, 1864	Mustered out Oct 25, 1865
WILSON, George	Chicago	Dec 1, 1862	---	---

Name	Residence	Date of Rank or Enlistment	Date of Muster	Remarks
ALLINGER, Peter	---	Sep 26, 1864	Sep 26, 1864	---
BARRY, Thomas	---	Jan 5, 1865	Jan 5, 1865	Substitute
BENNETT, Matthew J	---	Dec 30, 1864	Jan 7, 1865	Substitute
BLINN, Edward N	---	Jan 7, 1865	Jan 7, 1865	Substitute
BRADY, James	---	Jan 6, 1865	Jan 6, 1865	Substitute
BROUGHTON, Nathan	---	Jan 5, 1865	Jan 5, 1865	Substitute
BROWN, Charles W	---	Oct 4, 1864	Oct 4, 1864	Substitute
BROWN, Leonard A	---	Jan 5, 1865	Jan 5, 1865	Substitute
BURKE, Nathan or Matthew	---	Jan 6, 1865	Jan 6, 1865	Substitute
BURKE, Thomas	---	Jan 5, 1865	Jan 5, 1865	Substitute
BYAN, James	---	Oct 6, 1864	Oct 6, 1864	Substitute
CASEY or CAREY, John	---	Jan 4, 1865	Jan 5, 1865	Substitute
CLARK, William	---	Aug 22, 1864	Aug 22, 1864	Substitute
CORCORAN, Michael	---	Oct 12, 1864	Oct 12, 1864	Substitute
CRAWFORD, Thomas	---	Jan 7, 1865	Jan 7, 1865	Substitute
DAVIS, Daniel	---	Jan 5, 1865	Jan 5, 1865	Substitute
ELCHLER, William	---	Jan 4, 1865	Jan 4, 1865	---
FLANWARY, Michael	---	Jan 7, 1865	Jan 7, 1865	Substitute
FRENCH, John	---	Jan 4, 1865	Jan 4, 1865	---

Roster of Field and Staff 51st Illinois Infantry

FROMAIN, Francis	---	Sep 21, 1864	Sep 29, 1864	---
FULLER, Phillip	---	Jan 9, 1865	Jan 9, 1865	Substitute
GILL or MAYGILL, Edward	---	Jan 5, 1865	Jan 5, 1865	Substitute
GRADY, William	---	Jan 5, 1865	Jan 5, 1865	---
GRISKILL, William	---	Sep 26, 1864	Sep 26, 1864	Substitute
HALEY, John	---	Jan 5, 1865	Jan 5, 1865	Substitute
HARBRECK, Jacob	---	Dec 20, 1864	Dec 20, 1864	Substitute
HARRISON, William H	---	Oct 7, 1864	Oct 7, 1864	Substitute
HENDERSON, William	---	Jan 9, 1865	Jan 9, 1865	Substitute
HICKS, John	---	Jan 5, 1865	Jan 5, 1865	Substitute
HIGGINS, James	---	Jan 5, 1865	Jan 5, 1865	Substitute
HOWARD, Albert	---	Jan 5, 1865	Jan 5, 1865	Substitute
IVERY, George W	---	Sep 20, 1864	Sep 26, 1864	Substitute
JUDSON, Charles	---	Dec 22, 1864	Dec 22, 1864	Substitute
KING, Milton G	---	Oct 7, 1864	Oct 7, 1864	---
LARKIN, James	---	Jan 7, 1865	Jan 7, 1865	Substitute
LEONARD, Charles	---	Jan 7, 1865	Jan 7, 1865	Substitute
LIEB, John	---	Jan 5, 1865	Jan 5, 1865	Substitute
LYMAN, Peter	---	Jan 5, 1865	Jan 5, 1865	Substitute
LYMAN or SEYMOUR, R	---	Jan 9, 1865	Jan 9, 1865	Substitute
MAZINGLE, William	---	Oct 13, 1864	Oct 13, 1864	Substitute
McCOY, James	---	Dec 30, 1864	Jan 7, 1865	Substitute
McGRAW, Michael	---	Jan 7, 1865	Jan 7, 1865	Substitute
McGUIRE, Frank	---	Jan 7, 1865	Jan 7, 1865	Substitute
MOORE, John	---	Dec 7, 1864	Dec 9, 1864	Substitute
MORAN, Edward	---	Jan 7, 1865	Jan 7, 1865	Substitute
MORAN, Patrick	---	Jan 7, 1865	Jan 7, 1865	Substitute
MURPHY, James	---	Jan 7, 1865	Jan 7, 1865	Substitute
OWENS, Francis or Thomas	---	Oct 12, 1864	Oct 12, 1864	Substitute
RIGHT, Robert B	---	Sep 28, 1864	Sep 28, 1864	---
ROGERS, James	---	Jan 7, 1865	Jan 7, 1865	Substitute
RYAN, Henry	---	Jan 7, 1865	Jan 7, 1865	Substitute
SAWYER, Henry	---	Jan 5, 1865	Jan 5, 1865	Substitute
SCHULTY, Thomas	---	Oct 1, 1864	Oct 1, 1864	---
SCOTET, John	---	Oct 13, 1864	Oct 13, 1864	Substitute
SHAY, Cornelius	---	Dec 24, 1864	Dec 24, 1864	Substitute
SMITH, Charles	---	Oct 10, 1864	Oct 10, 1864	Substitute
SMITH, John B	---	Jan 5, 1865	Jan 5, 1865	Substitute
ST CLAIR, Charles	---	Oct 13, 1864	Oct 13, 1864	Substitute
STEPHENS, G W	---	Oct 15, 1864	Oct 15, 1864	---
STRATTON, Michael	---	Jan 7, 1865	Jan 7, 1865	Substitute

CHRONOLOGICAL EVENTS

51st ILLINOIS INFANTRY REGIMENT

December 24, 1861 - Organized and Mustered at Camp
Douglas, Chicago. Illinois. February 14, 1862 - Moved
for training to Cairo, Illinois.
March 4, 1862 - Moved for training to Camp Cullum, Kentucky.

Attached on April 1862 to 2nd Brigade, 4th Division, Army
of the Mississippi. Attached on September 1862 to 1st
Brigade, 1Sl Division, Army of the Mississippi. Attached on
November 1862 to ISI Brigade, 13 Division, Army of the
Ohio.
Attached on January 1863 to 3rd Brigade, 3rd Division, Right
Wing, 14th Army Corps, Army of the Cumberland.
Attached on October 1863 to 3rd Brigade, 3rd Division,
20th Army Corps, Army of the Cumberland.
Attached on August 1865 to 3rd Brigade, 2nd Division,
4th Army Corps, Division Of Texas.

SERVICE AND OPERATIONS

March 7 - April 8, 1862 - New Madrid & Island # 10, Mississippi River

March I3 - 14- New Madrid

April 8 - Tiptonville

April 13 - 17 - Expedition to Fort pillow,

Tennessee April 17 - 23 - Moved to Hamburg Landing, Tennessee

April 29- May 30-Advance & Siege of Corinth, Mississippi

May 3 - Action at Farmington

May 8 - Pursuit to Booneville

June 12 - Recon to Baldwyn

June 12 -July 20 - Hold at Corinth July 20 - Move to Tuscumbia/ Dacatur

July 20 - September 4- Guard Railroad from Hillsboro to Decatur

September 4 - 12 - March to Nashville

September 12 - November 6 - Siege of Nashville

November 6 - December 26 - Bivouac at Nashville

December 26 - December 30 - March to Murfreesboro

December 30-January 3, 1863 - Battle of Stone's River

January 1863- Occupation of Murfreesboro

March 4- 14- Expedition to Colwnbia

June 24 - July 7 - Tullahoma Campaign

August 16 - Occupation of Middle Tennessee

Cwnberland Mountains & Tennessee River Skirmishes

August 16 - September 22 - Campaign at Chickamauga

September 19 - 20 - Battle of Chickamauga

September 24 - November 23 - Siege of Chattanooga

November 23 -27 - Campaign at Chattanooga-Ringgold

November 23 - 24 - Orchard Knob November 25 - Mission Ridge

November 28 - January 15, 1864 - March to Knoxville

January 15 -March 30 - Occupation of Chattanooga & Cleveland

February 10 -March 30- Veterans on Furlough

May I - September 8 - Atlanta Campaign

       May 8 - May 11 - Skirmishes at Rocky Ridge

       May 8 - 9- Skirmishes at Buzzard's Roost Gap

       May 14 - 15 - Battle of Resaca

       May 17 - Battle at Adairsville

       May 18 -19 - Skirmishes near Kingston

       May 19 - Skirmishes at Cassville

       May 22 - 25 - Skirmishes at Dallas & Pumpkin Vine Creek

       May 25 - June 5 - Battles at New Hope Church & Altoona Hills

       June IO-July 2 -Operations at Marietta & Kenesaw Mountain

       June 11 - 14- Pine Hill

       June 15 - 17 - Lost Mountain

June 27 - Assault on Kenesaw

July 4 - Ruff's Station & Smyrna Campground

July 5 - 17 - Chattahoochie River

July 18 - Buckhead & Nancy's Creek

July!9 - 20 - Peachtree Creek

July 22 - August 25 - Siege of Atlanta

August 25 - 30 - Flanking attack on Jonesborough

August 31 - Sept I - Battle of Jonesbo rough

September 28 - Move to Chattanooga, to Bridgeport, Ala., back to Chattanooga, Oct 28

November - December - Nashville Campaign

November 24 - 27 - Skirmishes at Duck River & Columbia

November 29 - Battle at Spring Hill

November 30 - Battle at Franklin

December 15 - 16 - Battle at Nashville

December 17 - 28 - Pursuit of Hood to Tennessee River

December 28 - March 1865 - Bivouac at Huntsville, Ala

March - April - E. Tennessee to Nashville until June

June 16-22-New Orleans

July 28 - 31 - Camp Placider, Texas

September 25 - Mustered out at Camp Irwin

October 15, 1865 - Discharged at Chicago

CIVIL WAR ORGANIZATION AND RANK

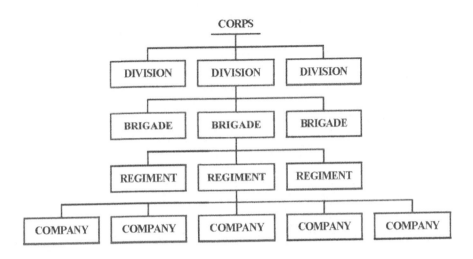

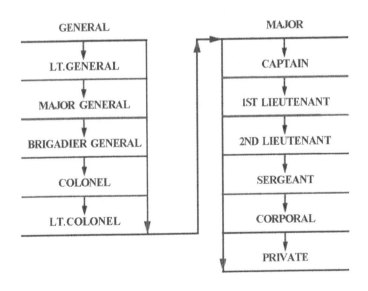

INTRODUCTION

Introducing the Bradleys

Let me begin this introduction with a profile of the Bradley family in the early 1800's. William came from England and settled in New Haven, Connecticut in 1644. Many generations later Luther Prentice Bradley was born in New Haven December 8, 1822 to Luther Bradley and Mona Nancy Prentice. He had two older sisters; Rebecca and Hanna Buel. Luther and his first wife, Mary Atwater had five children; Maria, George, Robert, Charles, and Mary.

Luther	b. 1772	d. 1830
Mary Atwater	b. 1773	d. 1815
Maria	b. ____	d. ____
George	b. 1800	d. 1834
Robert	b. 1802	d. 1824
Charles	b. 1807	d. 1 865
Mary	b._	d. _

Nancy Mona Prentice b. 1787 d. 1876		
Rebecca	b. 1817	d. 1884
Hannah Buel	b. 1820	d. 1894
Luther	b. 1822	d. 1910

In 1827, when Luther Prentice was five-years-old, the family consisted of his mother Nancy, his father Luther, brothers George and Charles and sisters Rebecca, Hanna Buel and Mary. Robert died in 1824 and Maria is missing in genealogy records.

Research showed the Bradley family was neither rich nor poor, but lived comfortably. All the children went to an elementary school in New Haven. The boys went on to schools of higher learning while the girls may have been home-schooled beyond elementary grades.

Luther's father died in 1830 and brother George died in 1834. His only remaining brother, Charles, went to Washington College (now Trinity University) in Hartford, but fell ill and left school in 1830. He later finished his education and earned a degree at the New York Theological School. Eventually he would become Secretary of State in Connecticut and earn a Masters of Arts from Yale University and a LLD from Hobart College. In 1849, Charles W. Bradley was appointed by President James Polk to be special envoy to China. His commission was also signed by James Buchanan, then Secretary Of State and future President of the United States, succeeded by Abraham Lincoln just months before the Civil War began.

Luther was well-read, and had a comprehensive education. His letter writing shows interest in nature, flowers and trees, water, weather, and crops grown and processed. Growing up in the shadow of his older brother, Charles, and a family whose New Haven roots spanned 200 years, Luther was poised and confident. The New Haven Historical Society records list the Bradley's as the largest land owners in the 1650's.

After completing his basic education, young Luther Prentice served in the Connecticut militia, as did his father and grandfather, Phineas Bradley, who was a lieutenant in a Matross Artillery Company from 1778 to 1779, and an artillery captain until 1781.

Luther (senior) was a major of the Connecticut Militia in the war of 1812. After moving to Chicago in 1855, the younger Luther ran up the ranks in the Illinois Militia as a captain, then a lieutenant colonel in the "Chicago Legion." He recruited troops from the Chicago and surrounding areas after joining the 51 st Illinois InfantrY Regiment as Lt. Colonel Bradley in 1861.

From October 1961 until October 1865, Luther served in the Union forces in the western theater. He was promoted to Colonel on October 15, 1862, and to Brigadier General on July 29, 1864. In the battle of Chickamauga on September 18, 1863, he was seriously wounded in the right arm and right hip, and wounded again in the left shoulder in the battle of Spring Hill in Tennessee on November 29, 1864. With his arm in a sling, Luther came home to Chicago in June 1965, stayed for several months and then went east to New Haven in late August. He mustered out of the service in October.

He met Ione Dewey in Chicago and courted her for several months. Though nineteen years her senior, he was determined to win her favor. She had a beautiful soprano voice and sang in the Chicago Symphony and in the Unity Church Choir. Discouraged by employment prospects, Luther reenlisted in the army and was assigned to posts in the western frontier to fight Indians. Back in Chicago shortly thereafter, the story ends happily as he wins the lady and marries Ione on May 14, 1868. As a couple, they return to assignments in the western frontier.

During his years as commander f many western posts, Luther and his new wife entertained scientists, historians, geologists, geographers and such artists as Thomas Moran, with whom he was very friendly These remote outposts had a very active social life. One book on frontier life with the army mentions the pleasures of hearing Mrs. Bradley sing "Robin Adair" in her beautiful soprano voice. They partied, danced, and enjoyed many a gay evening entertaining important visitors from the east, as well as high ranking army officers and politicians from Washington, etc.

My grandfather told me many stories about growing up on the frontier. He rode horseback with the Indian braves, and sat by the fire - many times in laps of the Indian Chlefs as they were smoking and waiting to talk to the General. They, too, participated in the festivities of the fort and he remembers listening to hls mother sing and the Indian Chiefs expressing their wonder over her voice.

Several times, my grandfather expressed his admiration of the Indian's riding skills and how they could lean from their ponies to scoop up something on the ground. Of course, this was done riding bareback and when my grandfather attempted it, he fell off his horse. He remembered watching a visitor from the East trying to ride and fire a pistol at the same time. The man ended up shooting himself in the foot.

During the fall of 1971, my great grandmother returned to Chicago to visit family and friends. On the night of October 8, 1871, she and her 4 sisters and the rest of her family spent the night up to their waist in Lake Michigan. It was the night of the Great Chicago Fire that destroyed a vast amount of the city. After my great grandfather retired from the army, he and Ione moved to Tacoma, Washington, and lived with his brother Robert. In April 1906, they went to visit friends in the Bay Area ofCalifornia,just north of San Jose. Ione woke up after midnight with her bed shaking her across the floor. Luther was downstairs and came running quickly to her rescue, managing to calm her down. Tis disaster became known as the infamous San Francisco earthquake of April 18, 1906. In less than fifty years , my great grandparents live through some of the countries most horrific disasters, which included

THE GREATEST disaster of the 19th century, the very uncivil CIVIL WAR.

I hope you enjoy the remarkable letters of my great grandfather, Luther Prentice Bradley. It's been my privilege to not only research this small segment of personal history, but to share my interesting family with you.

Please enjoy   Robert Dewey Bradley

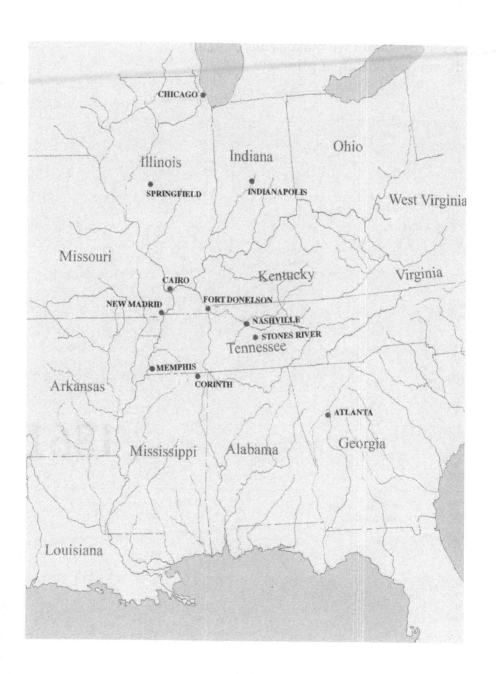

No sacrifice that we make is anything to
the success of a great principle

1861

Chicago, August 1st, 1861

My very dear Mother,

Yours of the 26th of July with Mary's letter reached me yesterday. I am sincerely glad to know, through Mary and Buel, that you are in good health. And I hope it will be very long before you are threatened with any serious illness. I return with this, Tibbie's letters sent me by sister Mary. I can already perceive a great improvement in Tibbie's writing. Her foreign travel and intercourse are developing her mentally, and I can see that she is going to return to us a cultivated woman. She has a good warm heart and it is pleasant to see how she cherishes her home love.

My dear Mother, I am grieved to think that I have given you pain by anything that I have written home or that I shall do so, by anything that I may do in the future. I wrote to Mary and Buel that I had serious thoughts of going into service because I have been considering it ever since our domestic troubles first took dangerous shape. I had no

intension of alarming you and although I had no settled plan of operation, I thought it right to prepare you for the change in case I should fully decide upon it. I have not yet made any arrangement for going into service, and, although I do not yet know in what connection I shall act, I cannot deny that I intend to take part in the struggle the coming Winter. Within the next twelve months the question will be decided I think, one way or the other. If I aid at all in the settlement of the question I must act soon. I am not apt to make up my mind hurriedly, Mother. I am glad to think that I inherit your calm, deliberate temperament, and after thinking over this matter more seriously, I think, than I ever did anything in my life, I cannot axcape the conviction that I ought to give whatever service I can render to the old government under which I was born, and under which I have lived safely and peacefully. I don't know what it is Mother - whether it is the term you use - "fratricidal war" or whether it is an expression in a former letter, that gives the suspicion that you do not enter cordially into the struggle in which we of the North are now engaged. Surely it cannot be that Charles has influenced your opinion in the matter. As for my erratic Brother's position, I am grieved and shamed that it should be so unpatriotic. If anything were wanting to decide my action in this unhappy struggle it would be his disloyalty to the flag which has sheltered him abroad and which has protected him on more than one occasion of difficulty and danger.

I admit that there have been complications of the question which has caused domestic trouble, upon which we of the North could honestly differ. I do not agree at all with the extremists of the northern party. But, when it comes to the question of sustaining the institution of slavery, or constitutional government,

I am on the side of the Government against anything else. The question in my mind is just this. The South claims the right of any state to break the Union any time without asking the consent of the majority. <u>That principal established, it will end in the breaking up of our northern states, sooner or later, into separate confederacies</u> and thus end the experiment of free government which our fathers struggled to establish and which we have claimed as a success. My dear Mother, I hope we do not differ in opinion on tis matter. If we do not, no sacrifice that we make, is anything to the success of a great principal..

Ever yours lovingly.

Luther

Chicago, August 13th, 1861

My dear Mother,

I wrote you last month explaining fully what my feelings were in regard to the present difficulties, and what I felt it my duty to do. I cannot see the matter in any other light now. There is but one course for a loyal man and that is to stand by the government and carry through the rebellion. As I have nothing to give but my services I feel bound to give them. I know, Mother, that this will pain you, and it is the sorest trial to me to know that I am deliberately doing what makes you unhappy, but I hope you will be reconciled to it. And more - that you will give your free consent to it, as a matter of duty on my part. I shall not go into the work with good heart unless I have your approval. Do not think, dear Mother, that I am wanting in thoughtfulness or love to you, whatever befalls me you will be first in my thoughts and heart.

And do not, I beg you, think too seriously of the dangers I may be exposed to, in the field or camp, -of the latter I have no fear. I am in perfectly good health, and am quite disposed to take good care of myself. I am offered a captaincy in a regiment forming in the western part of the State. And my friend, Col. Loomis has offered me the post of Major in his regiment.

The Col. Is a friend in whom I have every confidence, and the Lieut. Col.

Chadbourne is my most intimate friend here. Personally, no connection could be pleasanter to me.

I shall go to Springfield with Loomis this week, and if the Governor chooses to commission me, I shall probably accept and enter on my duties soon. The regiment is in camp and will remain there some time for instructions. As soon as I settle definitely where I go, I will write fully all that you would like to know. Ever dear Mother,

Yours lovingly,

Luther

Chicago, Sept 13th, 1861

My dear Buel,

Yours of the 4th enclosing letters from Rebecca and Ami was dully received. The letters were all most welcome, -R's especially if things are valued for their rarity, hers should bear a premium over any others. Tell her I will write in a days or two. I see by your letter that you are not yet reconciled to my going into service. I appreciate your feelings, I believe, and fully sympathize with them. But I have long since made up my mind as to what my duty was in the matter and having made up my mind to it, <u>as a duty,</u> nothing but some misfortune that would unfit me for service will deter me from doing a soldier's work in whatever place I am best qualified to fill. I am only sorry now, that I did not take part in the struggle earlier. I have had the same conviction from the first that I entertain now. But from consideration to my Mother's and Sister's feelings alone, I have waited till the necessity is demonstrated beyond a doubt, for all who are able and willing, to stand by the principle involved in the contest. As to the justice of tat principle, the religious of it, I have no doubt and I would no stop to argue with any one who did doubt it. I cannot believe that you doubt it any more than I do. Yet a remark in your letter looks queer. You say "any thing short of a religious believe in the justice of the war, would make a man of sagacity most guilty in engaging in it". My mind will not be troubled by any responsibility of that kind. If it be my lot to go down in the struggle I shall have no regrets for the manner of my death.

But enough of this - I wrote to Mother that I had declined the position offered me in Col. Loomis' Regiment, as I had something else in prospect more satisfactory. There is an effort now being made to raise a regiment in this city and vicinity and I think it will be successful. I fso, it will be composed of better material, both in officers and men, than the majority of the forces and it be pleasanter serving with it for that reason. As soon as I am <u>located</u> permanently I shall write you all about it. This Chicago Regiment has been a favorite project with me. I have been working for its success all Summer and hope to see it in the field soon. About the socks and flannel shirts, I shall need them §QQQ. I may go into camp in a week, so you had better not undertake knitting the socks as I might be ordered off before they were finished and might be difficult to get them to me. I can buy them. The shirts I should like if you can make them at once. Do not make more than <u>four</u> undershirts, remember, of colored flannel, anything but <u>red.</u> Also two pairs of drawers of the same.

I shall be very glad of the "Housewife" Rebecca proposes to send me. It will be very useful. I shall take plenty of plain, comfortable clothing. Shall be allowed all the baggage I want.

Please tell sister Mary that I will write her next week. Have been very busy of late and neglected my correspondence

Give my best love to dear Mother and all the others.

Yours ever

Luther

Chicago, August 31st, 1861

My dear Mother,

Your letter of the 21st with Buel's and the foreign letters, was duly received. I am glad you are able to write me a few lines occasionally for it shows you are in comfortable health. I knew, my dear Mother, that my determination to go into service would be painful to you and that you would hardly give your consent to it. But with this strong influence to hold me back I could not convince myself that it was not a clear and settled duty. Certainly no other motive would lead me to disregard your wishes. I thank you that you do consent to it, tho' reluctantly. I should have small heart for the work if it met your active opposition.

I have declined the offer made me by Col. Loomis of which I wrote you.

Other propositions were made me, - more attractive – for a position in an indepen- dent regiment now forming under the authority of the War Department. This will delay my departure a little as the regiment is not yet full. Without being committed to this particular regiment, I have the option of uniting with it when ready. If anything else offers meantime, I am at liberty to take it. As soon as I am settled into a position I shall inform you immediately.

Our people are waking up to the magnitude of the rebellion and are making a grand effort to do their share in putting it down. Illinois has now in the field, 30,000 men. In another month she will have 45,000 and before the first of January, if necessary, 60,000. The western column under Fremont is going to play an important part the coming winter.

You all ask in your letters if there is nothing you can do for me in the way of outfit. My wants will be few for I shall take nothing but plain com- fortable clothing, and as little of it as I can be comfortable with. I shall want some flannel shirts and woolen socks. If you can make me a small stock of these, they will be highly prized. The shirts should be of a kind of flannel that will not shrink much, and the socks, of course, of mixed yarn. I return Charles' letter with this.

With love to all, ever dear Mother,

Yours lovingly,

Luther

Camp Douglas, October 11th, 1861

My dear Mother,

I am writing you from my new quarters in Barracks. We came in on the 8th with part of the Regiment and are receiving daily accessions from the city and country. I have charge of the Regiment at present, the Colonel being engaged in recruiting. We have a fine camp ground, containing some fortY acres, surrounded by a fence ten feet high. The barracks are built around three sides in continuous apartments each containing one company with separate rooms for officers. The men have good bunks and straw mattresses. Directly back of each company quarters are the mess rooms and kitchens. The front of the ground is occupied with regimental and staff officers quarters. Everything about the camp is complete and comfortable. Our daily "order of exercise" is

6 A.M Revielee and Roll Call
7 " "   Breakfast
8 " "   Camp Cleaning
9 " "   Guard Mounting
10 " "   Squad Drill
12" "   Dinner
3 P. M. Drill
5 " "   Supper
9 " "   Tatto - Lights out

We are making good progress in recruiting and hope to fill up by the end of the month. We are particularly fortunate in our officers. They are tip top lot and a credit to any regiment. Col. Tucker, the Commandant of the camp says the Regiment promises to be the best that has been sent out from this State. It has this advantage - that all the officers are well drilled to start with.

Last evening as I was standing out on the parade ground, a young fellow in a private's uniform came up to me and saluting, asked, if I was a brother of Doctor Bradley of Ningpo. I answered "yes" and asked if he knew him. He said he had been four years mate of one of the P & 0 Companies' steamers and had often met the Doctor on board and made his acquaintance. He is a fine, hearty fellow and says he enlisted in the Legion thinking that I must be a brother of the Doctor's, as Charles had told him he had a brother living in Chicago. It is singular that I should be indebted to him for a recruit.

My own labor and responsibility is considerable and must increase the further we get into the work before us. I am by no means confident in my ability to fill my position well. I know just enough of military matters to feel my own deficiencies. I shall try hard to do my duty in all positions but no man can tell how he will behave until he is tried. I have no particular fear for my own person but when I reflect that the safety of hundreds of men may depend on my courage or coolness in some critical moment, I am sometimes a little staggered. However, I shall not be dismayed even by that. I will try and do a soldier's dty in any position I may fill. I will write you, dear Mother, as often as I can under circumstances not always favorable. Just as I am writing the drums and fifes are tearing away under my window enough to craze any one.

Give my best love to all the dear ones at home and tell them to remember me often in letters.

Ever yours affectionately

Luther

My dear Buel,

If I do not write you weekly, semi-weekly, or monthly, do not I pray you think that I am negligent or forgetful.

I rise at 6, and though I am constantly busy, the day is not long enough for my work. I certainly never had so many demands on my time and sometimes, it seems as if we were having about as hard work in camp as we could have in the field. I can tell you, -the enlisting and organizing a force of thirteen hundred men is no small job. And the next hardest thing to that is drilling and equipping them. It is a business that requires a perseverance and patience worthy of success in any calling. We have now about five hundred men and receive daily, accessions from the country. We hope to be full and in the field in a month from this time. I have been two weeks in camp and am already well browned up so that when I go in town they hardly know me. I was never better in health or spirits in my life.

Camp life is by no means monotonous. There is not an hour in the day but some special duty or service (attended, of course, with some display of music or parade) furnishes a healthy excitement and exercise. To day I am acting as officer of the day. I go on duty at 9 A.M. and remain 24 hours. This officer has under his sole charge the guards and police of the camp. He is to see that guard is properly detailed and posted by the officers of the guard, is to visit them occasionally through the day, and make the grand rounds at midnight to see that the guards are doing their duty and the camp all safe. We have about three thousand men in and post a guard of one hundred fifty. This has been an unusually busy day with us. We have had a grand parade and review in honor of the new flag just raised on the parade ground.

I made my first appearance in full uniform on horse back. We had quite a brilliant staff. Cols. Webb and Brackett of the Regular Army; Cols. Tucker, Malmberg, Cumming,

Stuart, Baldwin and Bradley of the volunteers. The parade passed off well, but a fierce shower came on just as we were in the midst of it and we got a good ducking slightly tarnishing our fine clothes. I am very tired but am filling in the hour before midnight (when I make my last tour of the grounds) by writing to you. Don't you think I'll be tired tomorrow morning, and sleepy too, when the drums beat at 6 o'clock.

You'll want to know how we live in camp. Well, we live pretty well. We have our own cooks and waiters who cater for the officers' mess of twelve, and get up a very presentable spread. There isn't much silver to be sure. Our mess chests furnish the table furniture, all plain and serviceable and the darkies furnish the pots and kettles.

We have a good sized mess room with kitchen adjoining and in the same building, offices and sleeping rooms. Davis, the Adjutant and myself room together, sleeping on our camp cots with a blanket for a covering and a blanket for a pillow. We sleep well and soundly, too.

I have written my light out, so good night. Give my best Love to dear Mother, and to all the others.

Ever yours,

Luther

Camp Douglas, Nov. 30th, 1861

My dear Buel,

Yours of the 17th reached me in good time and was welcome as all your letters are. I am sorry to hear that Louie is so ill. I cannot think there is any danger for the little fellow is so stout and strong. Mother's comfortable health is a cause for gratitude to us all and I fully appreciate it. Assure her of my constant thoughts and love. You must not think that, busy as I am, you all are not ever present in my mind. I believe that I am with you in spirit oftener than usual, for, the purposes and possible contingencies of this war ars calculated to make reflecting man <u>think</u> of what he is leaving behind him in engaging in it. Don't let this make you apprehensive for the future. "Sufficient for the day is the evil thereof". There is everything to regret for some. You need have no fears for our personal comfort here. Our Barracks are entirely comfortable for soldiers. They are tight enough to keep out storms and that is all that is necessary and we are supplied with stores for cold weather. We have already had one severe snow storm and good solid cold weather following it but it did not trouble beyond the inconvenience of marching in the snow. I find that we are all getting toughened gradually by exposure. When I got to town for my occasional evening visit I find the warm houses more uncomfortable than our barracks. Healthy men soon become inured to any common degree of cold and exposure so as not to suffer much. We have in camp a Battalion of German Calvary under common tents and they are as healthy and heartY as any men we have and, this with the thermometer at 20 degrees and snow 10 inches deep.

<u>Measles.</u> the meanest disease for adults, has made its appearance in Camp. There are about 100 cases in the hospital, all doing well. We shall probably have it with us all Winter. With this exception the Camp is healthy

I shall be very glad of the woolen socks knit by the pretty sister of your Rector. Munson is going East next week and he will bring them on his return. Many thanks for your thoughtfulness. I can't help wishing I was in the southern expedition. It would be just the service to suit me with the voyage and descent on the Coast. It was a grand success and we hope much good from it. Our destiny will be down the great Mississippi, I hope. It will be a real expedition rivalling in numbers and power anything ever set afoot. Gunboats, flatboats and munitions of war being collected in large quantities at St. Louis and Cairo.

Capt. Foote of New Haven commands the naval force and it is said to be very powerful. I am inclined to think that the troops that want fighting will find enough of it in this river campaign. By all accounts the river is fortified very strongly at various points, the bold bluffs and the windings of the stream affording unusual facilities for this. The heavy batteries can only be carried by landing troops and attacking their supports or assaulting them with the bayonet. It will be tough work and the men who talk about eating early green peas in New Orleans are fools. We find no deception but clear concept of what is to be encountered. They are more likely to find black peas further up the river that they can't digest so easy. The 51st is to form the third regiment of the Douglas Brigade, which was started here about mid-summer. The First and Second Regiments and in Missouri. The officers are all from Chicago and knowing us well have desired us to join them and Halleck the new Commander of this Department has so ordered, wishing to bring Regiments from the same localities together in Brigades rightly judging that they will co-operate with and support each other better than those who are entire strangers to each other. The arrangement is very satisfactory to us as we know the First and Second to be fine Regiments and ably officered. Major Sanger, of the Second, was in China in '60 and knows Charles having dined with him at Ningp. Write me soon again and give my best love to dear Mother and all the others.

Yours ever,

Luther

Camp Douglas, December 7th, 1861

My dear Mother,

I have just received a letter from Mary in which she says she has heard that our regiment was ordered to Kentucky. This is a mistake. The 2nd Douglas regiment encamped here is ordered to Missouri and will leave in a day or two to join the 1st now at Tipton, Mo. I wrote that we were to unite with these regiments as the 3rd of the Douglas Brigade. Col. Stuart, a prominent lawyer and politician of this City and an attached friend of Douglas, started the Brigade about mid-summer intending to raise four regiments. He has put two in the field and has urged us to make the 3rd. we are very glad of the chance for they are fine regiments and well officered. Col. Webb of the regular Army commends the 1st. the officers are nearly all Chicago men. There is no probability of our being ordered off until next month. The Government cannot arm us before January and we shall remain in Camp till the arms arrive. We shall probably be in the field in time for the campaign down the river, or through Kentucky and Tennessee. Of course, we are anxious to get to work as soon as possible hoping to reach some decisive result before next summer. The Western Army that operates on the River will be very strong and it must tell. I think the confederate Army will be very hard pushed next Spring both East and West. But I cannot see that we are likely to bring the War to a close until we succeed in maintaining ourselves permanently in the cotton States.

I think the hardest fighting is to be there. It is evident that the Government does not look for a speedy termination of the War by their building permanent camps of instruction in the various States. Our camp for instance, is an institution. It was originally built for four thousand men, but is now enlarged to double that capacity and the finished barracks are all full. We shall have ten thousand here before the close of Winter. We have a City in numbers and intelligence. I would like you to take a stroll round the Camp with me some evening and take a look into some of the barracks in one you will find a prayermmeeting under the direction of the chaplain, or some other "man of prayer", in another, a singing school, in another still, a debating club and perhaps a fiddle with a crowd of dancers, more energetic than graceful.

After 9 o'clock, lights are out and the sentinels commence challenging and calling the hour and half hour. Sentinel No. 1 at the Guard House commences the call and it goes round the Camp through seventy stations. As I am writing the guard back of my quarters sings out <u>Beat No 7-11 o'clock and all's well"</u> Now and then I hear some Dutchman on guard sing out "All's v-e-1-1." one night a waagish fellow improved on the Teuton in this wise, "eleven o'clock and <u>"all's better as goot."</u> You would think sometimes that the tower of Babel was being rebuilt here to hear the confusion of tongues. Every nation is represented and the jargon is sometimes confounding. Our Western agricultural population is made up largely of the class of emigrants many of whom had had a military training in the old country and this class furnishes a large part of our recruits.

We have a large number of cases of measles in Camp, something like a hundred. We are to have a siege of it probably and shall be disappointed if it does not go through all the regiments here. It is fortunate perhaps that it is developed so early for now we shall not fear it in the field when it would be a very serious matter.

Do you hear from Tibbie lately? I shall try to write her soon. I have written her twice but have not yet received a letter from her. Give her my best love when you write next.

With best love to all, dear Mother,

Yours ever,

Luther

I am just beginning to realize the
magnitude of this rebellion

1862

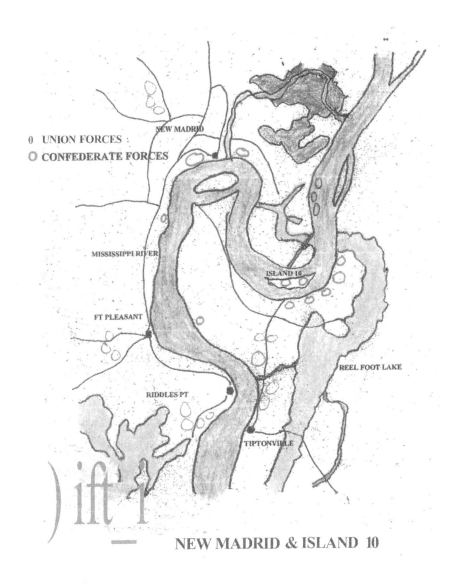

NEW MADRID & ISLAND 10

Head Quarters, Chicago Legion,
51st Regiment Illinois Volunteers.
Camp Douglas, January 3, 1862

My dear Mother,

A Happy New Year to you and all the dear ones at home.

I wish I could make the greeting in person but that cannot be at present. I hope before another year comes round that I shall join you again, safe and sound. May the New Year be a healthful, happy one to you all.

We are here, in <u>winterquarters</u> so far as the weather goes. Today it is snowing equal to anything you ever saw. Our parade ground is a pal in of "untrodden snow." It is too stormy for any out-door work, so we are making ourselves comfortable in barracks. We haven't had anything so nearly like leisure day since we came into Camp. We have been peculiarly favored with fine weather this season. It has been by far the mildest and sunniest I have known since I have lived West. Up to Christmas, we had but an occasional cold or stormy day. Now, however, we must expect to catch it. This country is as famous for cold as for any thing else and we are sure to pay for the fine times we have had but we are wel l prepared for the change, with good warm barracks, heavy boots and clothing and overcoats that will turn any storm. I dare say you think we are in a pitiable state with our llilY bunks

and rough board houses with the general lack of small comforts. I would like to convince you by a personal inspection that it takes but little to make one healthful and contented if he is disposed to make the best of things. We have a few grumblers. They are common to every place but ours are of a class of men who have seldom lived as well as they do now.

Gentlemen bear <u>roughing</u> better than beggers, as experience proves-either from pride of character or because a long course of good feeding has put them in better condition to bear a few privations. We are all right at present Mother but doubtless the time will come when we shall have to come down to the <u>minimum</u> of comforts.

You will want to know something of our prospects for service, or of moving from here. As yet we know nothing about it. We have some six thousand in Camp ready service except that they are not armed. The State authorities tell us that we are to have our arms this month but we do not consider it certain at all. I think we are quite as likely to lay here for two months longer as to move. Judging from appearances no considerable movement will be made in the West within that time. We much prefer remaining here to going into the field at mid-winter with new men. Old troops can bear the exposure much better. Our Regiment promises well and is making good progress in drill and discipline. We have good material and are working hard to bring it into condition for effective work. It is pleasant to know that, in the opinion of others, we are succeeding. The Adjutant General has spent considerable time in Camp and when last here he told a gentleman connected with another Regiment that the 51st had the best set of Officers he had seen in the State of Illinois, a very good thing coming from that source.

Dear Mother, write me a few lines if you are equal to the effort.

With best of love to you and all,

Yours ever,

Luther

My dear Buel,

I have not written to you for some time owing to constant press of duties here in Camp. Much of the time the Colonel is absent and in consequence, my work is increased so much that I have no leisure. When I fail to write as often as you think I ought, remember it is for this reason. I feel that my first duty so far as my time goes, is to the Regiment. And I must attend to this, at the risk of neglecting other matters which may seem of equal importance. You may think I am wrong in this but I hope not. The responsibility of training and commanding a thousand men with the prospect of taking them into battle where their lives may depend upon their discipline and skill for which heir officers are responsible, is a fearful one. Any one who assumes such a position without appreciating this, is very far from being a good officer. I feel a greater anxiety about the lives of the men who may have to look to me for guidance in some critical time than I do about my own. I know that you feel desirous that I should acquit myself well, and so far as my own opportunities and abilities go, I mean to do it. You ask if, in the event of my getting sick or wounded I will not send for you to take care of me, I very cheerfully promise to do it. Next to our dear Mother there is no one I would rather have with me in that event. You must not think that in any case I should lack any attention that the surroundings would permit. Fully one half the officers of the Regiment are old personal friends, on whose friendship and attention I can always count. If there is any thing the 51st is remarkable for it is the character of its line officers. They are fine hearted gentlemanly fellows on the best of terms with each other and with the field staff. We have been more than once complimented on the good conduct of our men, for which credit is due to the company officers for the influence they exert over them. While other Regiments in Camp have been insubordinate and mutinous, ours has been uniformly steady and obedient. In proof of this the 51st is the only Regiment allowed ammunition and we have twice been called out with ball cartridge to arrest mutineers in other Regiments. You must not think that this shows a bad state of discipline in the Camp. New troops are almost always uneasy and not infrequently dissatisfied with their officers, for which dissatisfaction they have frequent cause. Most of the officers in volunteer corps are entirely ignorant of their duties when they are brought together and don't take care of their men because they don't know how, Col. Cummings has been in St. Louis the present week. Gen. Halleck told him that he had heard of our Regiment and that he would very soon arm and give us marching orders and that we should have a good position. We do not care now to leave here until the Spring campaign opens though we have been impatient to get away all Winter. We are more comfortable than we should be at St. Louis or Cairo the present depots of the Illinois troops. We are daily improving in discipline and drill, and shall be in good order when the real work comes.

I send you some photographs and will send some to the others. They are poor things so my friends say and I accept their judgement. I will try and have some better ones taken before we leave. I would send you a large one but I know it would be impossible to get a decent looking picture. This is the second lot I have had; the first ones were execrable.

Give my best love to Mother, Mary, Rebecca and the children.

Yours ever,

Lt. Col.

My dear Buel,

I wrote to Mother the day after our arrival here. We reached here Saturday night, 24 hours from Camp Douglas.

The Regiment is in fine order and impatient to go forward. I am more pleased with the men than ever. They conduct themselves well and are called here, a fine Regiment.

We have received our arms and ammunition and are ordered to hold ourselves in readiness to move at any moment. Our destination will probably be up the Cumberland. Fort Donnelson having fallen, the next important place to strike in that section is Nashville. The recent victory won by the Western troops is a great thing for the North. We have taken one of their strongholds with 15,000 prisoners. Their loss of men will be a severe blow and the moral effect of the victory will be immense. Four thousand of the prisoners arrived here yesterday on their way to Alton the depot for prisoners of war. They were a motley lot, half clad and half fed, lean cadaverous looking rascals. They were mostly Tennessee and Mississippi Regiments and a more unsoldierly looking set were never seen excepting perhaps, Falstaff's ragged rascals. There was not a <u>uniform</u> in the lot. A few had woolen blankets, the balance had pieces of carpet evidently taken from floors instead. I went among them as the steamers lay at the Levee and talked with a good many. They all said they had had a hard time, no pay, or clothes and but little to eat they talked savagely of some of their Generals, imputing to them cowardice and cruelty as well as deception. Many of them from Alabama say they were forced to join the Army and that their sections are at heart, loyal. I send you a Southern Shin plaster and postage stamp which I bought of them. Day before yesterday I went down the river on a reconnaisance with Col. Buford of the 27th Illinois. Col. Buford was ordered to reconnoiter in the neighborhood of Columbus to see if any movement was afoot there. It was thought that they might make a move on Bird's Point or Paduca as so large a force had been seen from those places to attack Fort Donnelson.

We went down to Lucas Bend, 3 ½ miles above Columbus, accompanied by three steamboats and the gunboats Caroudelet and Cincinnati. We landed and visited two plantations but got no information further that that they had heard that Gen. Polk was marching on Paduca. We could hear their guns plainly at Columbus. They saw us, for after we put about at dusk, we could see lights of one of their gunboats following us. She watched us for about 10 miles and then returned. We returned on the Carondelet, one of the heaviest gunboats and were handsomely entertained by her officers. This craft was in the fight at Fort Donelson, and is badly cut up but the enemy could not get through her iron plates. Capt.

Walk has a 120 lb. shot in his cabin which came aboard during the fight and lodged in some heavy timbers without injuring any one.

Cairo is full of wounded men and officers just from the Fort. I find a great many old friends among them, some of whom left Camp Douglas within a month. The hospitals are full and private houses are taken to provide quarters for the severe cases. All accounts from the enemy and from our own side, agree that our troops fought with great steadiness and determination. We outnumbered them but our line extended 8 miles round the Fort and at the place where they sallied out to cut their way through, they greatly outnumbered us. Will write again soon.

Yours ever,

Luther

My dear Buel,

Yours of the 16th and 19th of February came to hand some days since. I had written to Mother, Mary and yourself soon after we reached Cairo so I delayed answering these a little, especially as I have been entirely busy getting the Regiment into the new Camp.

I wish you could see us. We have camped on the bank of the Ohio, directly opposite Cairo in a fine old Kentucky forest. We cleared off about twenty acres of small trees and brush and after leveling off the ground have a fine Camp and drill grounds. It is a picturesque spot. Our eighty large Sibley tents make a fine show and when they are lighted up at night with camp fire burning and the band playing it is really a pretty sight. We have plenty of society here. On our right are Delano's Cavalry and the 2nd Battalion Illinois Artillery; on our left the 42nd Illinois, 80th Ohio and the 3 rd Michigan Cavalry. Officers of the different Regiments visit us every day at Guard Mounting or dress parade. Our fine band offering inducement at these times by their excellent music. We were inspected yesterday by the U.S. inspecting officer who pronounced us ready for the field with the exception of five teams, we having but ten. Our tents are roomy and very comfortable. Mine is a Sibley eighteen feet diameter with a three foot wall. It is made of heavy duck and is impervious to water or wind. We had a rattling shower last night with thunder and lightning equal to anything I have seen but when the thunder woke me I found my self as comfortable as I should have been at home. The lightning has a singular look seen through tents. The air seems all ablaze and everything inside is brought out as clear as in day light. We are having fine spring like weather, soft and balmy as May. The forest around us is alive with birds all singing their best. Buds are swelling on the trees and the grass is taking on a visible green. Everything betokens Spring, and with it, dry weather and good roads, - the latter of which are all important, for without them the Army can't move. I dare say you stay-at-home people can't see why the Army need wait for the roads to dry up. Just follow a single Regiment of a thousand men once in a rain or over soft ground and you'll understand. The tramp of the men and horses with the fifteen or twenty four and six horse teams and six ambulance soon make mud and mire of decent ground.

We had a little episode in Camp life last night. About two o'clock Col. Duff, aid to Gen. Cullum came over the river and rousted us out saying that information had reached headquarters that Clay King, a notorious Kentucky Guerilla was out in this neighborhood with his band. They feared he would make a dash at some of our Camps. He ordered us to send out scouts and notify the commandants of other Regiments near us. We immediately turned out Company "K" and sent them out two miles as pickets, but the night passed without any further alarm. Our boys were in high glee and behaved well.

You say truly that Illinois has won all the glory in the late fight. The 11th, 12th, 18th, and 20th fought nobly as their thinned ranks testify. Companies A and B of the 12th were sent forward as skirmishers. Crossing the brow of a hill they encountered two Mississippi Regiments and received their fire. They came out with 12 and 20 men respectively. The Commandants of the 11th, 12th and 20th, Ransom, Ducat and Marsh are Chicago men whom I know well. Ransom was badly wounded. This was his second battle. He was wounded in each. I think the Western men furnish better stuff for soldiers than the Eastern. They are mostly from the farming districts, tough, hard fellows, used to hunting and a free, wild life. They have more self-reliance in danger that men unused to adventure, more dash, of what the French call "elan". I do not think they are any better men but their training makes them better soldiers. I have seen and made the acquaintance of another gentleman who knew Charles in China, - Col. Murphy of the 8th Wisconsin. He was Consul at Shanghai for several years. I have not yet received the pictures of Rebecca and the children which you mentioned she would send. Tell her not to forget it and send them soon.

We are daily expecting orders to move but yet they may not come for weeks. A force of several thousands is held at this point for some purpose known to the Generals - we shall know more in time. Some fine morning orders will come to break Camp and away we shall go up the River or down the River, just as the tide of battle turns. I shall notify you immediately of any change. After it comes I cannot tell how often I can **write** to you or hear from you. **With** best love each and all of you.

Yours ever,

Luther

Camp near New Madrid, Marcl\'.l.4th,1862

My dear Buel.

We are resting today after a fatiguing march and fight yesterday. Night before last I received orders to be ready to march at day break with one day's rations and forty rounds of ammunition

I am now in command of the Brigade, consisting of the 22nd and 51st and 1 Rifles. We form the 2nd Brigade of the extreme left Gen. Pope's Army. The morning opened dark and threating after hard rain during the night. We marched out of Camp in the gray of the morning and found everything astir for miles around. Columns in motion in all directions while in the direction of the town we could hear heavy firing between our siege batteries and the rebel forts and gunboats. I had never heard any large guns before and had no idea of the grandeur of the sound. Thunder does not equal it. The boom of sixty-eight pounders, with the whiz of the shells is musical as well as alarming - really alarming as we found later in the day. We reached our position in the left wing about 8 o'clock and found the center engaged with the enemy. Constant discharges of small arms and rounds from the field batteries. We stood quietly until 11 o'clock when we made a flank march three miles to the east and took up a new position quite near the town and within range of the upper fort. Gen. Pope's design seems to have been not to reconnoiter at all points, draw the fire of their forts and batteries with a view of ascertaining their strength and hoping, perhaps, to open a favorable chance for a general attack. On the last page I have drawn a sketch of the country around Madrid with the positions.

At 11 o'clock the Rifles were ordered in to draw the fire of the fort and I was ordered to support them with the right wing of the 51st leaving the left under the Major to follow if necessary. The ground before us was a large cornfield with the stakes standing. It afforded some cover the skirmishers. To the left was heavy timber, a road leading to the town divided them. As the Rifles deployed in the field I marched into the road opening a full view of the fort and gunboats lying with their broadsides toward us less than a half mile distant. My column had just got fairly into the road when we saw a puff of smoke rise from the fort and slap came a 32 pounder right in our faces. It struck the ground thirty feet ahead of us and imbedded itself in the mud, fortunately. If it had bounded it would have gone through us for the range was exact. I immediately filed to the right into the cornfield but they saw us and in a moment we heard a report and the sing of a shell. I sang out to the men to drop and down they went as flat and snug as a bevy of quail while the shell went over our heads and burst a short distance in the rear. About this time the Major came up with the other wing forming to our left and rear. A second shell soon burst a little ahead of us. Seeing they had our range exactly, I moved to the right and front to get out of range. For three quarters of an hour we had this-moving continually through the tall corn to deceive them as to our position. All the while the Rifles were skirmishing in our front. I certainly never expected to get out of that field with all the men. I was not much scared but I felt a terrible anxiety for the men. No one can realize the responsibility until they have a body of men under fire. The object having been attained, an aid-de-camp came in with orders to retire. As we march out the men moved a steadily as they would on parade. We left the field at a point quite distant from where we entered. As we came out, Gen. Paine met us and said, "Colonel, have you lost any men". I answered, "No". "Well, I am glad" said he, "they behaved admirably. You have done all I expected". Soon after Constable's battery came up and engaged the fort for an hour, we retiring out of range. About the middle of the afternoon firing ceased all around and we returned to Camp. I think we shall never be more exposed than we were yesterday. And yet we all escaped. It shows at least that the men may be under heavy fire without being hit. We gave the rascals a bad scare for last night they evacuated the town, crossing the river in steamers, and leaving everything behind them, - guns, ammunition, tents, baggage and even their beds and blankets.

Major Raymond was out last night in command of the Brigade pickets.

Towards morning he suspected something was going on and neared the town with a few men. Getting into position in an old mill where he could overlook the fort he saw they had vanished. Pushing on with his party he was among the first to enter and secured a flag and several other trophies. We shall very likely cross the river in pursuit. Will write as soon as we get orders.

With constant love to dear Mother and all of you,

Yours ever,

Luther

HEADQUARTERS CHICAGOLEGION

51 st Regiment Illinois Volunteers

Camp near New Madrid, March 19, 1862

My dear Mother,

I wrote you last, I think, from Bertrand. We left there onthe afternoon of the 9th, march to Sikeston, camped out in a hard rain without tents and left again at 7 on the morning of the 10 th, reach New Madrid, twenty miles at 3 P.M. Our tents and baggage did not come up until the 13th so we were entirely out of doors for four nights. With the exception of the first night in the rain at Sikeston, we got along very well. The climate here is very mild. Our present weather is about equal to your June and but for the frequent rains would be delightful. We had a smart skirmish on the 13 th and narrowly escaped a great battle. The rebels were in strong force in the town supported by two large, well built, well armed forts and eight gunboats on the River. It is most unaccountable how they should evacuate such a place without a stubborn resistance. Our whole Army was out on the 13th and although there was nothing decisive in the way of fighting the rebels were undoubtedly intimidated by the show of force. They fled with the greatest haste, abandoning guns, stores, private baggage and everything. They must have been in a curious state of alarm, judging by the condition of their Camp. Officers' trunks were found in their tents half packed with uniforms folded ready for packing but abandoned at the last moment The body of an officer lay in one tent having been placed in a box for sending home. Whoever was marking it had left it with the name halffinished, the brush lyingon the box with a large blot where it had stuck. If our gunboats could have come down, the whole rebel force here would have been captured, but as they commanded the River from Island No. 10 down, we could not prevent their leaving on their steamers.

It was Gen. Pope's intention to attack with his whole force on the 15th.We should have taken the town and forts, but with heavy loss. The forts must have been carried by storming and the lower one was extraordinary strength having eighteen large guns with plenty of ammunition and being surrounded with a ditch fifteen feet wide and ten deep with abattis work entirely around it. Gen. Paine said that with five thousand men we could have held it against any force that could have been brought before it and I believe it.i cannot understand the policy of the rebels in evacuating their strong places one after another and I must say it makes me distrust their pluck. At Island No. 10 a few miles above here they are making a stand. The Island is said to be very strongly fortified to prevent the descent of our gunboats and for two miles above the Island on the Kentucky side they have got the shore lined with forts. Commodore Foote came down three days since with six gunboats and seven mortar-boats. Since then there has been the most tremendous cannonading. I don't think Sebastapol could have surpassed it. We are only three miles from them in a straight line but the country between here and the River and for miles up and down is a dense swamp so we cannot reach it. Com. Foote has got the heaviest mortars ever made and their roar is like thunder. Gen. Pope had advices from him last night that after two days fighting he had demolished most of the shore batteries and should attack the Island immediately. We are in hopes to see him here soon. The movement of this Army is dependent on his successes. If he cleans out the river above here we shall probably move South. Pope's Army must number twenty-five thousand and is constantly increasing. I am in command of the 51st, Col. Cummings being put in command of 2nd Brigade of Gen. Paine's Division. This arrangement suits me for it gives me the entire control of the Regiment. I find no difficulty in handling it for I am readily supported by all officers and I believe I have their confidence as well as that of the men. It is a laborious and responsible position and a faithful officer cannot escape care and anxiety. I am as hearty and full of work as any man in the Army but you need not be surprised to see me looking older when I return. This life necessarily roughens a man and will leave its mark on all of us. We are quite out of the world so far as any news goes. We get no papers and but little information of any kind beyond the operations in our immediate neighborhood.

I wish you would send me papers frequently, both New Haven and New York. I haven't seen a New York paper since the first of March.

Give my best love to Mary, Rebecca, Buel and the children. Writ e me as often as possible and direct until furthers orders to Cairo.

Yours ever,

Luther

HEADQUARTERS CHICAGO LEGION

51st Regiment Illinois Volunteers

Camp near New Madrid, March 31, 1862

My dear Buel,

I feel inclined to scold somebody. I wrote to you on the 15th and written to Mother and Mary since but have heard nothingfrom you in that time.

I should scold if I did not think you had written and the letters failed to reach me.

There is great complaint through all the Regiments of the "Army of the Mississippi" that letters are lost. We frequentl y get those belonging to other Regiments and ours are, no doubt, miscarried. Cairo is distributing point for this Army as well as Grant's and Buel's, altogether one hundred and fifty Regiments. You can judge of the amount of business involved in making up and distributing their mails when I tell you that our letters average two hundred per day. Of course, such a load of work thrust upon an unimportant office ill-prepared for it must occasion great confusion. You must write me often calculating that part of your letters will not reach me. I will write every week to some of you.

We are still in Camp impatiently waiting for Com. Foote to open the river and give us escort to Fort Randolph or Memphis. The Commodore has not succeeded in silencing No. 10 and the batteries on shore. For this reason, I think, the gunboats cannot fight well down stream. The strong current makes them partially unmanageable and disturbs the aim so much so as to lesson the effect of their shot materially. Col. Bissell with his engineer Regiment is now cutting a channel through the bayou which makes out from the river above No. 10. By which the gunboats can go round the island and attack it and the batteries in the rear then will make short work of them. We shall not move South independently of this but that is not the policy. This point is to be held to prevent reinforcements from coming up. We are to make clean work as we go along, capturing or destroying any place likely to make hereafter. There is an uneasy feeling creeping through the Army at this delay there is to be a great battle fought in Mississippi for which the forces are now mustering under Grant and Beauregard. Perhaps it will be the decisive battle of the War. Of course, we want to be there and if we were released from this point could be there in time for the fight. Gen. Halleck has sent word to Pope to send all the troops he could spare to Gen. Grant by way of Cairo. Pope sends back that he has noneto spare but if an Q!'.Qfil comes to that effect he must send them and in that event Gen. Paine will try to have this Division selected.

We had a great review of the Army by Gen. Pope a few days since. The 51st was on the extreme left of the line. As Pope rode up he asked Gen. Paine what Regiment That was and remarked "they make a very soldierly appearance.· After the review the Officers commanding Regiments were invited to meet the Generals and their staffs, at Paines's Head Quarters. Gen. Pope said to us that he was very much pleased with the appearance of the troops and added "I don't care where you go, you can't find a finer looking lot of men than we have got in this Army" the General is proud of his Army and well he may be. It is composed of the young blood of Ohio Indiana, Illinois, Michigan and Wisconsin and there is a deal of dash and spirit in it. In the fight here when the 10th and 16th Illinois lay in the trenches supporting our siege battery, they had their flags flying from the top of the ridge of earth that sheltered them in full view of the large fort, making a fine mark for the rebel guns which were dropping shot and shell among them with a good deal of effect. Gen. Stanley saw a number carried away dead and wounded and ordered the flags to be lowered but the men said "No, General, the flag flies wherever we are". "Very well", said he, "if you take the risk I won't say a word".

I wish you were here to take a ride through and around New Madrid and see how the rebels have desolated it. Every house, tree, fence, or hedge that could afford the least shelter to an attacking force is burned to clear the range for their guns in the forts. You will see beautiful gardens, planned with exquisite taste and filled with flowers, orange and lemon trees and choice shrubbery with nothing left to guard them but the charred timbers of the house, or a few posts of the fences. The people have fled and what few houses are standing are deserted. I send you in a paper, a crocus which I picked while riding out on Sunday. I have a bunch of them in my tent, as yellow and fragrant as any you ever saw. The timber around here is full of the mistletoe which you know historically and poetically, but may not have seen. It looks oddly and prettily growing in green bunches on the limbs of the bare trees. I will try and get a sprig to send you.

With best love to dear Mother and all the others,

Yours ever,

Luther

STEAMER ALECK SCOTT, MISSISSIPPI

RIVER, April 9th, 1862

My dear Buel,

We are returning from three days campaign in Tennessee victo rious and rejoicing.

We have four thousand prisoners and have taken a large number of cannon, rifles, muskets, stores, etc. without the loss of a man.

Three days since our Division - the 10th, 16th, 22nd, and 51st Illinois with Houghtelling's battery went board transports and dropped down the river eight miles, landing on the Tennessee side. Our gunboats had just silenced a heavy battery here and a force of rebel troops had retreated about two hours before we landed. We started in pursuit and marched rapidly, but could not bring them to a fight. Three times they put their guns in position but retired as soon as the head of our column showed. We left our landingplace at 12 o'clock. At 3 P.M. I was ordered by Gen. Paine to halt the 51st. rest a short time, and reconnoiter towards the river and immediately follow the column.

We threw out skirmishers and after advancing a mile came to the river, in the vicinity of Island 10. The celebrated floating battery lay directly under the river bank within fifty feet of us.We could have taken it in thirty minutes but orders were peremtory- not to engage.

General Paine reached Tiptonville at dark but owingto our delay we were an hour or two later. We halted at 7, about a mile from the town and within half that distance pf the rebels encampment. Our pickets were in sight of each other all night. Our rapid pursuit and show of force alarmed them and they surrendered next morning without strikinga blow. Our prisoners outnumber our force by nearly five hundred.

The march was a hard one. It had rained the previous night and the roads were awfully muddy. We made the fifteen miles between 12 N. and 7 P.M. we have bivouacked three nights without tents; the second night in a severe rain storm lasting all night. Have not had my boots or coat off for three days and nights. I am as tired as I ever want to be. I have slept sweetly on the ground with just myblanket for a bed and covering. I dare say you think you have slept well but you don't know the luxury of sleep until you can drop down beside a tree, draw your blanket around you and go off without caring for anything in the world but just <u>sleep</u>. waking up in the morning with dirt in your eyes and sticks in your hair, but with the conviction that you never had slept so well in your life.

I have got a fine horse belonging to the Colonel of the 1st Alabama which the Quartermaster has turned over to me, for use, also sundry rifles, knives, etc. in haste. Love to all,

Luther

Steamer •Meteor" April 14, 1862

My dear Mother,

We are moving down the river with the "ARMYOF THE MISSISSIPPI". Yesterday's sun rose on a grand and novel sight. Twelve gunboats, two mortar boats and thirty-four transports laden with troops and supplies. As I write there are thirty-seven boats in sight coming down in a long line two abreast. The day is one of the blandest and clearest and the Great River is as smooth and shining as glass. The steamers are decked with flags with their decks filled with troops and bands playing. It is a sight worth seeing at any cost we are now twenty miles above Fort Randolph, a strong work on the east bank of the River. The gunboats are steaming ahead to engage the Fort if the rebels make a stand there, which I doubt. We have reports that all the Forts above Memphis are abandoned or the forces there will be taken, beyond a doubt We are strong enough to beat any force they can muster on the River. Our Army will number 25,000 ofthe troops. Gen. Pope leads the flotilla of transports in the Perry. Next comes our Division which is now the leading Division of the Army having the right permanently assigned to it. The Taylor and Thompson carry the 1st Brigade and the North Star and Meteor the 2nd.

We do not anticipate much trouble in clearingthe River this side of Memphis. The recent victories near Corinth should decide the fate of every place north of Memphis. If the rebels fight us they must do it at a disadvantage for we outnumber them and can out fight them for we have the prestige of victory and perfect confidence in our success. If there was any incentive needed to make us do our duty it would be supplied by the gallant conduct of the Illinois troops at Donnelson and Pittsburgh. We are proud of our men, proud of their valor and proud of their success and we do not intend that their well earned laurels shall be tarnished by any conduct of ours. Our Division is composed entirely of Illinois troops and our general is an Illinois man, a good officer and a gallant, fine-hearted gentleman. We feel the utmost confidence in his skill and judgment. His courage is undoubted.

I hope to writ you next from Memphis. When we get there we shall feel our work is nearly done. With best Love to all.

Ever yours,

Luther

P.S. You will think this a short letter but the up boat is just off.

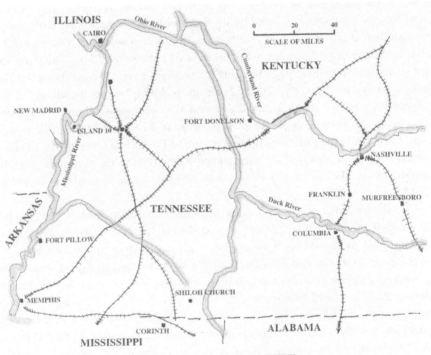

ILLINOIS

CAIRO

Ohio River

SCALE OF MILES
0   20   40

KENTUCKY

Cumberland River

NEW MADRID

ISLAND 10

FORT DONELSON

Mississippi River

NASHVILLE

FRANKLIN   MURFREESBORO

TENNESSEE

Duck River

COLUMBIA

ARKANSAS

FORT PILLOW

MEMPHIS

SHILOH CHURCH

CORINTH

ALABAMA

MISSISSIPPI

WESTERN THEATER

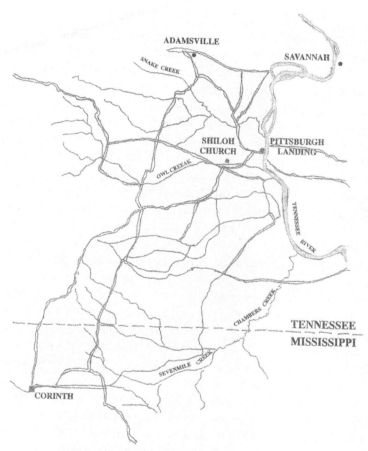

CORINTH / SHILOH AREA

Camp 18 miles from Corinth, April 23, 1862

My dear Mother,

Here we are, right in the enemy's country but four miles from the scene of the great battle of the 13th• I wrote to Buel the other day from the Steamer telling her the Pope's Army was leaving the Mississippi to join General Halleck by his order, at Pittsburgh. We reached this point four miles from Pittsburgh yesterday morning and are now encamped on the road to Corinth, eighteen miles distant. We are not, I think, to form part of Halleck's Army proper, but to act independently as a flanking force, unless attacked. Pope has the extreme left of thewhole line resting on the Tennessee River. Pope was the first ordered to Huntsville, Alabama but protested against being sent so far from the scene of active operations and was afterwards assigned his present position. We are in the face of the enemy and sooner or later shall fight him. I know, my dear Mother, that you will be anxious and alarmed for my safety but do not let it make you unhappy. You would not have me shrink from danger when my duty tells me to face it. I may not be in a battle again, I may be. If I am undoubtedly my position will be an exposed one for I shall try not to have the 51st do discredit to the flag or to the good name the Illinois troops have now. At the same time, I assure you, I will take the best care of myself that I can. By this I mean that I will not foolishly expose myself anywhere. I have great confidence in Gen. Halleck and I hope he will defeat the enemy without a serious battle. The last battle was a soldier's fight purely. The Generals had little to do with it except to blunder into it. It was won by the steady pluck of the men.

The next one should be a strategic victory as ours was at Tiftonville. Taking the enemy prisoners without losing a man. We had a tedious time of it on the steamers. From the time we left Madrid to go down the Mississippi until our landing here was ten days. It was pleasant enough in some respects as such a trip could not help being. But the discomforts were considerable. We had a thousand men on a moderate sized steamer. At night every square foot on each deck was covered with sleeping men and for six days it rained <u>constantly</u>. keeping us wet nearly all the time as the steamer leaked through all the decks and the sides of the boat. The Western boats afford no protection being unlike an Eastern steamer as a summer house is like a prison. We started with four days cooked rations expecting to land at the expiration of that time. But return trip up the river prevented this andwereduced to what could be cooked on two common stoves. However, we got through it and were glad enough to land here yesterday. The beautiful country in which we are camped goes far to make up for any discomforts we have suffered. I have seldom seen anything finer than this part of Tennessee. It is a rough country with plenty of <u>rock and iron</u>, well wooded and watered. And for picturesque beauty is not surpassed by any thingI have seen. There are few sights more striking than the hills, valleys or timber of a fine country dotted over with the white tents and the colored flags of any army. Add to this the constant moving of masses of troops with the attendant parade of mounted m n all "with music and banners", and you have a scene which good home bodies seldom see. There is much in this wild, free like that is charming to a msn of vigorous life. Changing residences sometimes every week, picking out the prettiest place you can find to pitch your canvas houses, always with an eye to safety and conveniences of life, wood and water. I ca understand now how the Gipsy Tribe is kept up. The Tennessee River is about the size of the Connecticut but navigable for a much greater distance. The scenery on the eastern side is mostly bold and rugged with occasionally a high mountain covered with fine timber. It reminds me of some parts of the Housatonic Valley.

Let me tell you one thing Mother, which will comfort you. Beauregard will not attack <u>us</u> because we have got an <u>Army</u> here and it is commanded by Generals. No more surprises and no more defeats. We outnumber him and can beat him any day when Halleck gives the order. There are but two results for him - retreat or defeat - both disastrous. The saddest part of this sadbusiness is the sorrow and grief it brings to the hearts of t ender women who have to mourn the fall of some husband or son or brother. As I was entering Tiptonville, the morning after our march after the rebels, riding at the head of the Regiment we passed a fine mansion and a black boy came out with a request for "the officer" to come in. On the Portico stood a group of ladies, some of them young and pretty, so I jumped off instantly and walked up to the house. I introduced myself and was politely received. The eldest of the party, a lady of about fifty, and without mistake a lady, came forward and with a good deal of feelingsaid that she had a son in the rebel army at Island 10. He was about all she had to endear her to the world and she wanted to know what would be done with him if he was captured. She half apologized for him by saying that the state of public opinion at the South was such that no young man could stay at home without losing his social status. I assured gentle Mrs. Rivers that her son was safe from all harm if he surrendered and that if it was our good fortune to capture him I would see personally to his comfort. When we took the force under Gen. MacKal prisoners on that same day, I enquired for young Rivers among the rebel officers but could not find him. He undoubtedly escaped with some of the scattered parties who separated from the n main force. I could not but think of you as I talked to this anxious Mother and

I promised to befriend her rebel son all the more readily because I know what would be your feelings under the same circumstances. I afterwards took tea with them and found them good stiff secessionists and I couldn't help tellingthem that I had a good deal more respect for southern women than for southern men. They aired their sentiments boldly while <u>the men</u> talked Union when they were caught while their acts were all the other way. Good night, dear Mother and with best love to all.

Yours lovingly,

Luther

HEADQUARTERS CHICAGO LEGION
51ST Regiment Illinois Volunteers
Camp 18 miles from Corinth
Sunday, April 27, 1862

Dear Buell,

Yours of the 15th with Tibbie's came to hand yesterday. I wrote to you on the 17th from the river and to Mother on the 24th just after we landed here giving such particulars of the trip as I thought would interest you. We are camped in a beautiful country four miles from the last battle ground. I have not visited it being too busy to leave camp for anything.

We received orders last night to prepare to move today. The Brigade will march this noon and encamp six miles in advance on the Corinth toad. The rebels are in force in front of us and sending out scouting parties are engaged with them every day. Yesterday a scouting party of Gen. Buel's captured 400 of t hem. Pope's Army forms the left wing of Halleck's line. Paine'a Division has been doubled since we reached here. He now has eight Regiments and twobatteries. We are Brigaded with the 22nd, 27th & 42 nd Illinois under Gen. Palmer. Col. Cummings

is sick and unfit for duty.I do not think the rebels will fight us this side of Corinth, if they do there. I don't know how strongly they may have fortified that place but if they fight us in the open field we shall beat them badly. You need have no fears about the grand result. We have the best General in the country to direct us and he has as fine an Army as ever marched and they feel like making this a decisive battle.

I wrote you about the part our Division took in the operations around Island 10. I suppose you have the letters before this. I send with this a map of the Island and the surrounding country which is the most correct of any that I have seen. I have been all around it by land and water and can vouch for its accuracy. I have marked out the course of the river below the Island. The route we marched on the 7th and the place where we captured Gen. MacJall and his Army. When we reconnoitered in the neighborhood of the Island, we halted the Regiment at the corner near the letter F going up to the river with two companies of skirmishers. At that time the Floating Battery lay directly at the bank at the end of the road. The steamers you see entering the bayou are the identical ones on which we crossed the river. You will see where I have marked the position of the Camps on the night of the 7th• This little affair, though masking little figure in history and of moderate importance in the results is one of the most credible of the war. It is purely strategical, a well conceived plan, consummated by a rapid march.

Give my best love to dear Mother and all the others. Will write from the next camp.

Yours ever,

Luther

HEADQUARTERS CHICAGO LEGION
51st Regiment Illinois Volunteers
Camp 4 miles east of Corinth,
Monday, May 5, 1862

My dear Buel,

I don't know whether you received all my letters at home. If you do you are largely in by debt. I have written to some of you from every camp. Generally as often as twice a week. I think some of your letters must go astray for they are very infrequent. There is something wrong in the pen and paper line. The trouble is not confined to Head Quarters either. The whole Regiment is concerned in it. We send off, by careful estimate, four times as many letters as we receive. This for a regiment that is in active service in the field and is doing pretty well. Your letter of the 15th is the only one from home in three weeks. You will see from the date of this that we are a little nearer Corinth than when I wrote last. We have been in daily expectation of going into battle for a week. And the day before yesterday we had what used to be called a battle, two or three hours fighting with 4,000 of the rebels with 60 to 70 killed and wounded on both sides. Saturday at 11 A.M. Paine's Division, eight regiments and two batteries and four squadrons of cavalry left camp on a reconnaissance, taking the road to Corinth via Farmington, three miles east on the Memphis and Charleston R.R. Our route gave us a march of nine miles which brought us to Farmington, a small village of twenty or thirty houses. Just before entering the town we came on the enemies pickets and some sharp skirmishing ensued. We drove them in, killing a number and having several wounded ourselves. On emerging from the timber where the skirmishers were posted we came on the rebel camp and half a mile back saw them, some four thousand strong, on the rising ground to the right. They had a strong battery, well posted and it took us an hour to dislodge them. Gen. Paine moved cautiously for he didn't know what force they had at hand. He finally gave the order to advance. When the right wing went forward, the rebels scattered. The 51st was on the left supporting Hescock's Battery and escaped without a scratch. We were within about 400 yards of the rebel battery and they sent shell and grape at us smartly. Hescock lost four men, wounded. When the right wing advanced, the General ordered us (with the battery, four companies of the Rifles and two of cavalry) to go through the town and seize the railroad. He accompanied us, leaving the rest of the Division under Gen. Palmer. We had just got in sight of the rebels again, back of the town and had fixed bayonets by the General's order, when an orderly came galloping up, bringing an order from General Pope to retire. This did not please us for we had got the rascals in a position where we were pretty sure of their Battery and part of them. We retired a mile and bivouacked.

The other Divisions are now comping up. I do not believe there is to be any great battle at Corinth. I think they are now evacuating it and I can only account for Gen. Hallek's failing to attack them by what I know to be his policy, not to fight them in any stronghold when he has got to beat them at great cost of life but to watch them until the opportunity offers: <u>then bag them</u>. This may not be a brilliant policy but it is a humane one and I am sure, the mothers and sisters of the North will thank him more for having a care for the lives of his men than for winning the most brilliant victory as most victories are won. For the last twenty hours it has rained incessantly and we are without tents, the old Camp not being moved up yet.

Camp life is all well enough in dry weather or under canvas but when the rain catches you with no shelter but such as you can make with a few bushes, perhaps in a swamp for your lines must be preserved, lead where they will the ground wet and muddy, it is anything but fun. The last discomfort to a tired and hungry man, just in from a long march, is to bivouac in a rain. It is a curious to see the expedients resorted to escape a soaking but they don't avail. You are sure very soon to find your self what Mrs. Pecksniff calls "a darned, damp, unpleasant body". Happily the rains are the exceptions and the sunny days the rule, so that in the responsible position and a faithful officer cannot escape care and anxiety. I am as hearty and full of work as any man in the Army but you need not be surprised to see me lookingolder when I return. This life necessarily roughens a man and will leave its mark on all of us. We are quite out of the world so far as any news goes. We get no papers and but little information of any kind beyond the operations in our immediate neighborhood.

I wish you would send me papers frequently, both New Haven and New York. I haven't seen a New York paper since the first of March.

Give my best love to Mary, Rebecca, Buel and the children. Write me as often as possible and direct until further orders to Cairo.

Yours ever,

Luther

Camp near Corinth, May 20, 1862

My dear Buel,

Yours of the 3d and 8th with Mary's are received and as always kindly welcomed. There are some wants which nothing but home letters will satisfy and those wants I often feel. Once in a while when the mail brings letters for almost everyone but me, I confess to a feeling of disappointment such as I have seldom felt before. Cut off as we are from all society and from almost all the surroundings of civilized life, letters are the links which bind us to home. I thank you for writing me so regularly and beg you not to tire of it for my sake. One of my steadiest correspondents is Mrs. Livingston, my kind and appreciative sister. She always addresses me as "Brother John" and her letters are full of pleasant chat of home affairs and cheerful anticipation for the future. She never fails to remind me of her firm belief that I am to return and resume my old place in Chicago Society.

I wrote to Mother on the 13th and to yourself shortly before that date. I am almost incessantly busy and seldom get time to write till after Tattoo when the Camp is quiet. What with reconnaissances, skirmishes, marches, picket duty, etc. There is actually no leisure and these, added to the regular routine duties of Camp crowd the hours and the days so fast that you can't possible keep up with them. I am often startled by someone saying "it is Sunday" when I hadn't thought of its being later than Thursday so rapidly does time slip away. I wrote to Mother of a battle we had on the 9th with a large rebel force under Bragg, Price and Van Dorn. They took us completely by surprise as we were moving forward our Camp to ground we had thoroughly reconnoitered the day before. They came very near trapping us but by activity and hard fighting General Palmer succeeded in bringing us off.

We had eight regiments and 12 guns. The rebels had 30 regiments and 40 guns. We get the report of their numbers from prisoners we took and from our men taken prisoners in the battle and since released because they cannot feed them. Our Brigade, the 22nd 27th, 42nd and 51st lost their knapsacks containing all the blankets and extra clothing of the men.

The day was very hot and when we first got on the field and saw there was to be a fight we ordered knapsacks unslung to relieve the men not supposing we would have to retreat. Soon after the regiments were ordered to different and distant parts of the field and for four hours were fighting to get their heads out of the noose they had run them into never once going near the place where they had left their baggage and as we retired, of course, the rebels took possession of them. And I imagine they had a rare time over them as they contained letters, miniatures and all the little trappings which men away from home are apt to cherish and preserve. We are now occupying the very ground from which we were driven on the 91h just one hour's march from Corinth. The right of our line now joins Buel's line and there is a continuous wall of steel around the town from east to west. We have thrown up strong earthworks in anticipation the Beauregard will attach us. Orders were issued last night to be prepared to fight at any moment as the rebels were expected to attack our whole line this morning. The attack, however, did not come. The rebels are known to be short of rations and they must soon fight or evacuate Corinth. The latter course would demoralize their Army, perhaps destroy it, so it is expected they will attack with the hope of defeating us and capturing our stores. If they can defeat us they are welcome to them.

May 21st • I laid this letter aside last evening and before I had time to take it orders came to march at day light with one days rations. So we made ready and this morning went out with our Division and Crittendens on a reconnaissance to look at the country between us and Corinth, with a view to a further advance. We had a little sharp work with the enemy's pickets in driving them in but had none hurt.

I shall send Mary a couple of hundred dollars by express tomorrow. Fifty of this she will pay to you. I want you to accept it from me and use it in any way that your tastes or needs direct. I have wanted to send you a remittance before this but my expenses are heavy and I have not been able to get ahead of them 'till now. One would think that a field officer's pay would allow him to live liberally and bring something out at the end of the War. But there are more who will come out short than ahead. There are a hundred calls on his purse and many of them it would be simply inhuman to deny.

With best love to all'

Yours ever,

Luther.

Camp Boonville, Miss. June 3d, 1862

My dear Mother,

We are now 20 miles south of Corinth, following the rebel Army.

The papers will have told you all about the evacuation of the rebel stronghold and of their precipitate flight.

I confess I am disappointed at the turn things have taken. I was confidently hoping that we should bring them to a fight and capture or scatter this nest of traitors. Gen. Halleck would not attack until the last preparation was made and the rebels would not wait for that. I think the General has lost a great opportunity. He may have a plan of fighting them to better advantage. The rebel army has broken up into half a dozen columns and they are retreating by as many different roads besides a large number carried by railroad. Pope's Army is divided into two columns, and is following Hardee, Van Dorn and Price. Our progress is necessarily slow as the rebels burn all the bridges in their rear. The bridge over the Tuscumbia detained us a whole day. I have no idea where they are going or where we are likely to overtake them. It is not probable that they will, or can, make a stand for a long time yet though we may overtake and fight separate bodies of them. They are dispirited and demoralized and I am convinced if we could get at them we could easily break them up or capture them. I am writing on a log at a little past day light in the morning to send my note back by the quartermaster. I have had no opportunity to write for a week. Have not had my clothes or boots off in that time and cannot say when I shall have a chance to send back again. Do not be anxious for me. I am entirely well and have escaped all danger and sickness. Let this re-assure you. When I can find time and conveniences I will write you particulars of our part of the work before Corinth. The place was not given up without a good deal of fighting. There was a series of battles between bodies of from 5 to 20,000. The 51st was in four of these affairs.

We are marching without tents or anything but rations so that our conveniences at present are very small.

With love constant and true for my dear Mother and Sisters and all friends.

Yours ever,

Luther

HEAD QUARTERS, CHICAGO LEGION,
51st Regiment Illinois Volunteers. Camp 30
miles South of Corinth June 9, 1862

My dear Buel,

On the 20th of May I received my last letter from you and the only other home letter since that data is Mary's of May 29th, which came to hand yesterday. There is an evil spirit in the mail bags which either devours or spirits away my letters. I feel provoked and angry at times to think that my correspondence should be lost. At a time too when it is of more value than ever before. I wrote you last on the 22nd of May and since then have been so constantly on the move that I have had neither time or opportunity to write save a h urried note to Mother. On the 28th we made our last move on Corinth taking position within a half mile of the rebel works. We had severe fighting here, the rebels contesting th e ground with great spirit, coming out in strong force and engaging our battles until they found we were too strong for them. Our brigade was in reserve but our plucky general carried us up to the line of battle hoping to receive orders to engage. We were under fire for half a day but none of us were hit. Bullets sprinkled round us freely and I was told a shell burst a few feet over my head but I did not know it at the time. At five P.M. the firing ceased and we laid out our lines and threw up entrenchments. By morning we had a line of works with redouts and rifle pits strong enough to hold the whole rebel army in check if they had tried to turn our left. Our part of the line has had harder fighting than any other for the reason that the rebels have always had a heavy force on their right to prevent our flanking them and attacking the railroad in their rear. On the night of the 29th the rebels evacuated Corinth.

The morning of the 30th being ushered in by a tremendous explosion followed by huge fires and bursting mines. You will have seen all about Corinth and the circumstances attending the retreat in the New York papers. I did not get a chance to go into the town as we were ordered off in pursuit but the works that I saw in front of our line were very strong.

We overtook the rear guard of the rebels at Tuscumbia River, ten miles from Corinth. Here they burned the bridge and planted batteries to prevent our rebuilding it. We skirmished with them for a day to ascertain their strength and finally threw across a footbridge pushed over two regiments and drove them from their position. The same day we got a bridge up that would pass artillery and the balance of the army. We pushed on to Danville, Rienzi and Boonville, t wentymiles from Corinth and here we lay one day while the cavalry were reconnoitering. Our next advance was about ten miles on the line of the Mobile & Ohio Railroad after a body of rebels said to be lurking in the neighborhood. We came on them after a march of five miles but they would not stand. We had a running fight of four miles, killing and capturing fifteen and drove them across Twenty-Mile Creek, a little north of which we now lay. The whole of Buel's Army is joining us and we must have fifty or sixty thousand men massed together here. What the future of this army is to be none of us can tell. I hardly think we shall be sent in pursuit of the rebels through the State at mid-summer though we should undoubtedly, stand the heat as well or better than they. Yet we shall suffer severely. It is thought that as we now hold the Mississippi River, the Gulf, and the Atlantic Coasts, that if a chain of posts is formed across the northern line of the Cotton States, hemming them in, that we shall only have to wait for the rebellion to die out. If this policy should be pursued we are in hopes to be sent to Memphis to spend the Summer or such part of it as the War lasts. I confess I should have no objections to laying up for a while. We have had hard work for nearly four months; for the last month, extremely hard, almost constantly on the march, leading a most harassing life; always on the alert and subject to sudden moves at mid-night or mid-day for a reconnaissance or skirmish; moving generally without tents or baggage and with a limited supply of rations which are sure to give out before the teams overtake us. It is not an uncommon thingto be reduced for a couple of days to hard bread and coffee. For two weeks now we have been without tents or baggage of any kind, sleeping on the ground with only a blanket. For all this we are healthy and in good condition for work, Q!1)y <u>tired</u>. Our men are actually in better health than when we lay in camp with all the comforts we could collect around us. This is shown by the Surgeon's report and it is the experience of all the Regiments in our Division.

I am thinking if the War should end this Summer, what a play spell I'll have on the Sea Coast. I can tell you, the men who come out of this War will have earned a long respite from labor and an indulgence of the lazy part of their natures. No more harassing or wearing work was ever done by men and you needn't be surprised to see me looking older If I return, than when you saw me last. It is nearly two years since I have been home and as the hot weather is on us I have a cont inual longing to get among the cool sea breezes again. God grant that the War may be brought to a speedy close and those who survive it's perils be returned to their homes and fri ends.

I sent you fift y dollars on the 22nd of May. Did you receive it? Give my best love to dear Mother, Mary, Rebecca and th e children. Remember me also to Mr. and Mrs. Baldwin, Mary and Fanny.

Yours ever,

Luther

HEADQUARTERS CHICAGO LEGION,
51st Regiment Illinois Volunteers,
Camp Big Spring, near Corinth,
June 27, 1862

My dear Buel,

Yours of the 8th by way of Chicago came to hand a day or two since the last before that, dated the 3rd was received about the middle of the month. You do not mention having received the Fifty Dollars I sent you enclosed in Mary's letter. It has reached you before this, no doubt. I am glad if it will add to your comfort and shall enjoy the thought of that more than any use I could put it to myself. I am grieved to think of Mother's ill health. A severe cough at this time of year is part icularly distressing. I hope it will soon wear off and leave her comfortab ly well. Give her my best love and assure her of my constant thought. I wrote her but a short time since. You ask if the papers you send reach me. I answer as the boy did "Always. sometimes. never". Once in a while a stray copy of the Times comes along bearing the tracings of your pen on the brown wrapper, but the arrivals are so infrequent. might almost deny ever receiving any. I thank you for sending them and hope you will continue it. We seldom see New York papers here and there is always matter of interest in them which we do not get in any other form. Mary sends the Palladium and it reaches me with tolerable regularity.

So you have got a new sensation for your quiet town, - a soldiers' hospital. am glad it is located in New Haven for aside from the wholesomeair and pleasant sights so necessary to the poor fellows. It will give you all a new idea of the horrors of war and of the dangers and sufferings of those who engage in it. Take good care of the sufferers no matter where they come from and remember that the women of the West are as ready to do all kind offers for us as you can be to do for them. I am glad Mary is engaged in the work. She never did a more Christian act in her life.

I am glad to know that Mrs. Livingston has written you. She has often spoken of you and expressed a desire to see and know you. She is a very good friend to me and her letters are always full of pleasant assurances that I am kept in remembrance by my Chicago friends. Keep up the correspondence if you can. I send you and old letter of hers which I happen to have in my folio that you may see the style in which she writes me. You need not take alarm at her allusion to my fair friend, Helen. It is a favorite notion of Madame's that she is the fairest and best of all the women in our acquaintance and she insists on my believing this;

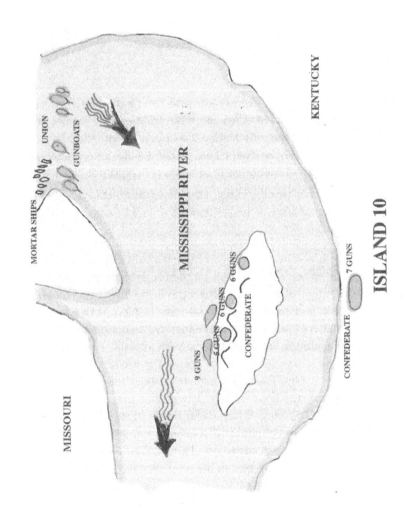

MISSOURI

MORTAR SHIPS

UNION
GUNBOATS

MISSISSIPPI RIVER

9 GUNS

5 GUNS
6 GUNS
6 GUNS

CONFEDERATE

KENTUCKY

CONFEDERATE
7 GUNS

ISLAND 10

a fancy in which I have not indulged her yet. Mrs. Booneer and Mrs. De Forest whom she mentions are my old Bridgeport friends. The Forsyths are a southern family, near neighbors of ours and intensely "secese".

I am sorry to hear of Stone's failing health and wish you would remember me kindly to him if you write. I saw him last in New York some two years since when he was looking extremely well. I hope he may speedily recover.

We are still camped on the wooded hills of northern Mississippi. It is intensely hot through the day but cool through the night, always requiring a blanket on my cot and often a double one. We are working hard still thou we are in camp. The Generals seem determined to make soldiers of us and they'll accomplish it if drill and study can do it. "General Orders" issued since we came into Camp lay out the days' work as follows: rise at Revielle, 4 A.M.; breakfast, 5; Drill 5:30 to 7; Guard Mounting, 8; Officers' School, 9 to 10; Field Officers' School, at Brigade Head Quarters, 10:30 to 12; Dinner, 12; Officers School 4 to 5 P.M.; Battalion Drill, 5 to 7:30; Dress parade and supper consumes the balance of the day, when you smoke a pipe and go to bed. This is the round from week to week with an occasional tour of picket duty. It is a little monotonous after the stirring life we have led for the last days.

There is a good deal of speculation as to the destination of this Army. It does not seem probable that so large a force will be kept here through the season. The country is all quiet and is likely to remain so. There are rumors that we are to go to Alabama, to Tennessee, and to Richmond. This is all speculation, however, but I am expecting every day, the order to move. Pope is a good soldier-an ambitious and enterprising fellow and he won't be content to sit down here through the Summer months. I would like to go to Virginia and compare our Western troops with the Eastern, side and side in a campaign. Our Regiments are small in numbers beingthinned by death and disease but they are in excellent condition and able to do all that any men can.

You speak of the possibility of my coming home for a short visit. It would delight me but it is not possible from present appearances. When our work is done, we'll come home and stay till you are tired of us. Till then wait with love and patience. Give best love to all and remember me to Mr. and Mrs. Band the girls.

Yours,

Luther

Camp BigSprings, July 8, 1862

My dear Mother,

I have just received Buel's letter of the 28th June in which she gently complains that my letters are not more frequent. I know how anxious you must be for news direct from me and I try to keep you informed of all my movements and assured of my safety. If I do not write as often as you wish or as often as I ought bear with me. I think of you constantly and if I could talk with you it seems as if I would never stop. But writing letters takes time and that just now is so entirely taken up with necessary and imperative duties, that I can hardly get time for an hour's gallop my way of relaxation from work. I <u>will</u> write as often as once a week to some of you, more than that I cannot promise. But if anything unusual occurs or is likely to occur, affecting me, I will write immediately. I am <u>well</u> and from the experience of the campaign we have been through and inclined to think that fatigue and exposure won't hurt me. Certainly they have had a fair chance if they were disposed to do it. It is a matter of congratulation to myself that I have been able to keep up when so many strong men have broken down. I can see now the benefit of accustoming ones self to work, and hardy sports as furnishing a stock of steady and elastic strength on which you can draw at need. I assure you I take the best care I can of myself under the circumstances and for the rest I must trust to GOD and a good constitution. I fear you have been needlessly anxious, Mother, at what I have written about ones toils and privations. I did not intend to give you the idea that we were being reduced to great extremity but only to give you and idea of a soldier's life in the field. I am now living in comparative comfort having all my baggage and my old cook, black Foster, whom we left at Farmington when we made the march south of Corinth. Of the staples of Army food, bacon and hard bread, we have plenty. Potatoes, flour, rice, etc. we have about half the time, but fruit, fresh vegetables and the like luxuries we know only by tradition. Occasionally we get a few better things of some enterprising sutler who has brought them from the far regions of the north, and holds them at such fabulous prices that we think he must have brought them from the Indies. Butter, 50 cents per lb.; ice, 25 cents; poor claret wine $2.00 per bottle and son on. Coffee and sugar we have, of course, - they are the soldier's chief solace. Of late we have found blackberries, tolerably plenty and they garnish our tables with their round black bodies occasionally. I went out about five miles on the 4th of July morning with the Adjutant and picked a fine lot. We ate our fill and brought home a lot in a basket of leaves. You cannot realize how barren a country this is. There is nothing in New England to match it and the people are a miserable "do-nothing" set, living upon corn bread and bacon and apparently caring for nothing else. Of fruits, flowers and the things pleasant to eye and taste which surround our northern houses they know and care nothing. A rare exception to the common rule is a house with some little flowers growing in front of it, - a violet or dwarf rose. We, at once set the occupant down as a Christian. The only things attractive about these places are the children, always abundant, in fact, they seem indigenous to the soil. The houses are almost universally of logs with a mud and stick chimney built on the outside. They are built like two houses connected by a covered passage way between. The logs are laid up unhewn, with huge cracks between, filled up with chips and clay though, sometimes they forget the chinking and daubing. The spinning wheel and loom are found in almost every house. Here they spin their cotton and weave the historical "butternut". Vile looking stuff it is, and is used, I've no doubt, because it won't show dirt. The Negroes are a more tidy and generally smarter looking set than the poor whites.

We have bad news today from the Potomac. It is report that after six days of fighting, Mclellan is driven back a number of miles. It may not be true but if it is, it will be as great a disappointment to us as to the men engaged. We have watched the movements of the Potomac Army with as much interest and anxiety as any men in the country because our own movements are in great measure dependent on theirs. If we have met with a severe repulse, there it will delay the day of settlement for which we are all anxiously looking. I don't allow myself to be depressed by any disasters. I know that we are going to win this battle and all others, but it grieves me to think of so much suffering and bloodshed in accomplishing the end. And it should not be. I wish they'd give Pope command there for a month and I wish he'd had command at Corinth. I believe the country would have been nearer a peace. Well, we must trust and wait confidant that it will all come out right. With best love and an intense longing to see you all, and hopes of a long continuance in comfortable health for your dear self.

Yours lovingly,

Luther

My dear Buel,

Yours of the 4th has just reached me by way of Chicago. It is full of good things but the lock of baby's hair was "non-est".

Your frequent letters are a great comfort to me and I beg you that I will not weary of writing. Mary's of the 7th came to hand yesterday and yours of June 22 and 28th and July 2 are received. I wrote you last on the 27th of June and to Mother on July 8th.

You'll almost feel like scolding that I have not written you in three weeks but it's the same old story, -busy! busy! For two weeks I have been sitting on a General Court Martial every day from nine to three and this with the necessary regimental business has just about fagged me out. I tell you I am tired! When I lop down on my blanket I can't help wishing that I was off in some quiet nook for then I could take my fill of sleep. I believe I could lay dormant for a week. Don't let this worry you now. It's just as it should be. Hard work brings sound sleep. Only in this case it don't bring quite enough of it. You must dismiss the thought of my coming home for the present. It is impossible for an officer to get leave of absence unless he is sick and the case so extreme that he is likely to die. Very stringent orders have been lately issued in this matter called out by the abuse of leaves of absence on the part of officers. Gen. Halleck has issued an order that all officers and men now absent whose leave has expired, must report on the 19th or be declared deserters. I am fearful the Colonel and Major will be caught. They are both considerably over due, and I am expecting them daily. We move from here tomorrow into Northern Alabama. I do not know the exact point we occupy, but we are to relieve General Thomas who joins Buel. Our location will be on the Tennessee River about forty miles from here. Our force consists of nine regiments of infantry, one cavalry, and two batteries. I am glad of the change for this country has lost all charm. I was never more than tolerable and the absence of all thrift and cultivation makes it as dull as possible after the novelty has worn off. On the Tennessee we shall have, at least, the charm of water and probably the neighborhood of towns as they are frequent there.

I shall write you immediately on my arrival at the new Camp. Meantime direct to me at Corinth.

We are to hold one of the chain of posts established across the country with little prospect of anything to do for the present. I am told that the guerrilla parties are showing themselves in that neighborhood and I hope it is true. It needs the occasional crack of fire arms to steady ones nerves. I have just read in the New York Tribune an article on the "Unhonored braves who die on picket." It is so true of our own experiences in the swamps in front of Corinth, at the Tuscumbia, and at Twenty Mile Creek, that I send it to you. All he says of the dangers and toils of picket duty are literally true. In face of the enemy watching a chance to strike it required the most sleepless vigilance and often the most stubborn courage. The pickets are the guardians of the Army and the duties are so sacred that sleeping on post is punishable with death. I shall not soon forget the last day I was on in front of Corinth. I had command of the pickets in front of our lines consisting of ten companies from the different Regiments of the Division. It was a dark, gloomy day and it rained heavily nearly the whole twenty-four hours. The picket line was rather more than a vile from our Camp and half that distance from the rebel works. I was cautioned by the Officer who I relieved to be careful for the line was constantly under fire and he had lost an officer and three men. The line lay through a wooded county for a mile and a half, part of it a heavy swamp, almost impassible in the storm and here and there on open field. The rebel pickets were so near that we could see them plainly when they dogged from cover to cover.

It is very much like Indian fighting. The whole game consists in keeping yourself covered and tryingto catch your enemy exposed. The lines are like this

Videttes

* * * * * * * * *

Picket Posts

The videttes are within sight of each other and are relieved every two hours from the picket posts. If attacked in force, they fall back on the posts and the reserves are advanced. On the day I speak of the rascals seemed particularly alert. We could not show a head without drawing fire. In the afternoon we noticed them reinforcing and pushing forward their lines so we prepared for them and a good chance offered. We opened a cross fire on three points that had been very troublesome. We got a volley in return and after half an hour drove them from their advanced posts, carrying three bodies. We got through the day without losing a man but the next day the rebels got so bold, General Stanley sent out a battery and drove them back with grape and canister.

I don't know when I have felt a greater sense of relief than when I marched my men out of that swamp after being twenty-four hours under fire.

Give my best love to dear Mother and tell her to keep up good heart for my sake. With love to you all and kind wishes to all friends.

Yours ever,

Luther

Decatur, Ala., July 30, 1862

My dear Mother,

I have not written you for ten days having been constantly on the road since the 21st. I wrote in my last that we were under orders for Alabama and supposed to be destined for a point some 30 miles from Corinth. When we received definite orders we found it quite another matter. Our Division is detailed to guard the Memphis & Charleston Railroad from Inka to Decatur - 60 miles - and is not scattered along that line. I was assigned to the easterly end of the line and consequently, have had the longest march and probably shall have the hardest work. I have charge of 15 miles of road and have had to divide the regiment up into four parts to station them at Bridges which have been burned and which we have to rebuild and protect. Of all the work which a soldier can do, this is the most disagreeable and unsatisfactory. We have to watch the inhabitants of the country as well as the guerrilla parties from the mountains. The road runs between the Tennessee River and Cumberland Mountains sometimes touching the River and generally within 4 or 5 miles of the mountains. Guerrilla bands infest the latter making frequent sallies into the low country, burning bridges, houses of Union men and attacking small parties of our troops. have two posts from which they drove off some Ohio troops last week but my men are fortifying and will hold them against a pretty strong force. I have four companies of the 51st and three of the 71n cavalry here. I have taken possession of a large strong brick Bank and camped my men in a vacant lot adjoining. In case of an attack in any force we shall occupy the Bank and defined it. I have no fear of an attack however. The guerrilla bands are not strong enough for us and unless some strong column of the Southern Army should enter the valley we are pretty safe.

Decatur is a fine old town of about 1,000 inhabitants when it is peopled. I judge there are not half of that number here now. The residents are intensely "secesh", bitter and malignant, as indeed, are all the Southerners I have seen with but one or two exceptions. At Tuscumbia I dined with a pretty young lady of genuine union sentiments. Her name is Molly Creamer. She said she <u>knew</u> the Northern men were not such rascals and brutes as had been represented. She told me that her loyalty to the North had cost her all her social position and acquaintances; she being now as thoroughly tabooed as if she were black. There is no doubt that all the culture and wealth of the South is against us. The influence of these beings in poorer classes among whom I have not doubt there is a good deal of loyal feeling if it could be safely let out. But there is the most complete system of terrorism prevailing here. Men are compelled to enlist under the conscription act or leave the country, remaining here at the risk of their lives. Only this morning ten men came in here for protection who had been driven out of the mountains by the Guerrillas. They brought their long deer rifles with them and offered to enlist. I shall send them up to Huntsville where they are raising a Union Regiment.

Fires are occurring every night either dwelling houses or cotton. The little town of Trinity which I passed on the way here was burning every house having been fired by a roving band that passed the same afternoon.

We have made one of the hardest marches of the war - 125 miles in a southern climate in the month of July. We made the march in seven days having halted a day each at Tuscumbia and Cortland. The heat was terrific at times and on the first days marching when Gen. Morgan kept us on the road until afternoon there were at least a thousand men so prostrated by it that they had to be left behind. Most of them caught up with the column at night. After this day we made our marches from 5 to 9 in the morning and the same hours in the evening. We had but two men sick when we arrived here, but all were foot sore and weary. Many a poor fellow's feet were so blistered that he could not wear a shoe. And almost every man walked with evident pain at every step. However, they trudged along the last day cheerfully, singing some patriotic song whenever we passed a town or plantation, the whole Regiment joining in the chorus.

The Tennessee Valley through which we have passed is a beautiful country. It is much like the best parts of New England. Bold mountain scenery and fertile valleys abounding in fine plantations. I have had some funny glimpses of southern life.

With best love to all,

Yours ever,

Luther

Headquarters, Decatur, August 3, 1862

My dear Buel,

Your letter of the 21st and Mary's of the 19th July reached me here on the 1st. I took possession of this town on the 29th July and am holding it for the protection of the Ferry and Railroad, with four companies of the 51st and three companies of the 7th Cavalry. Our Division is covering sixty miles of the road from Iuka to Decatur, and the 51st is holding the bridges at Mallard and Fox Creeks and at the village of Trinity. From this point to Mallard Creek is 15 miles and we have to patrol the track for this distance every day to guard against the attacks of guerrilla bands. The road has been guarded by Ohio troops since we occupied this country. Last week the Guerrillas made a raid from the mountains in strong force and attacked all the posts within twenty miles of here, capturing five companies driving off the balance and burningthe bridges. We came up just after the mischief had been done and have since been busily employed re-building. The road will be in running order today and I expect an attack on it soon. The rebels swear we shall not hold it and they are collecting in considerable force in the mountains. We have little fear of them though they out-number us two or three to one. They are a cowardly set, imperfectly armed, relying on superior numbers for success. I have built rough forts at all my posts of earthwork and cotton bales, tak ing cotton whenever I could find it on plantations and pressing slaves to do the digging. If these rascals will compel us to come down here and defend their own property, they must furnish the labor and materials to do it. At this point we have a stockade of heavy logs pierced for rifles and large enough to hold all our force. It commands the ferry and railroad and is proof against any thing but artillery. I think the Guerrillas will be lots to attack usfor they have a wholesome dread of our arms. On our march up here they were watching us and I expected an attack. We have a train of 25 wagons to protect and they could have taken us at a disadvantage. One body of six hundred lay within ½ mile of us one night but they did not trouble us. This is a fine old town of about 1500 inhabitants containing an abundance of wealth, aristocracy and treason. The cultivated class at the south are all disloyal, many of them malignant and bitter. They visit us and appear friendly enough, inviting us to their houses and plantations but I know they hate us and are only civil because they dare not be otherwise, so I have as little to do with them as possible, declining their favors but treating them politely and giving them to understand that we are watching them and shall arrest and punish them if we find them aiding Guerrilla parties as we know some of them do.

A fine old gentleman, Gen. Garth called on us the day before yesterday and spent nearly the whole day, seeming really disposed to be friends with us. He is quite an old man with white hair and beard, of commanding appearance and most courteous manners. He owns a number of plantations and a fabulous amount of "negros". Being wealthy and influential he can set public opinion at defiance, if it runs counter to his notions and in some things does do it. He denounces the Guerrilla system as barbarous and shameful, and tho's a secessionist aids the poor men who are driven from their houses because of their loyal sentiments. He invited us to visit him at his plantation a few miles out, and, I have no doubt, he would receive us with true southern hospitality. You can have no idea of the persecution practiced on loyal men here. Northern Alabama was strongly Union from the first and voted by a large majority not to secede. Many of the men who originally opposed secession have joined the movement because the sate went out. But there are still a large number of loyal residents chiefly among the poorer farmers in the mountains. Since the guerrillas have organized they have hunted, robbed and murdered these men because they refused to join them. There are some twenty or more now here who have come in for protection and I am supporting them by levying contributions on the planters until I can find some way of disposing of them. I have already sent twenty-five of them to Huntsville where they are organizing a Union Regiment of these refugees. I am just beginning to realize the magnitude of this rebellion. As the boys say it's a "big thing". You may set down the Southerners as a disloyal people. They have stake their all on success and they'll win it if possible. The North today is not making half the effort or half the sacrifices that the South is. We have got the whole population to fight for the conscription act will bring out the last man. Unless the northern men speedily reinforce their armies they will find them outnumbered and overpowered.

We are camped on the banks of the Tennessee, a beautiful, placid stream which flows as peacefully as ever though its waters of late have often been stained with blood. The valley named after it is as beautiful as any I have ever seen. On one side is the river and on the other the Cumberland Mountains, from five to ten miles distant. Here you see real southern life - fine plantations with splendid mansions and every evidence of taste and wealth.

Flowers grow luxuriously. Mother would go into ecstasies at sight of them. Most of them are varieties that we do not grow. Some of the most curious are of great size and beauty. For instance, they have a sensitive plant bearing a beautiful flower are large as our peach tree. Fruits grown here to perfection. Peaches, plums, figs and pomegranates are abundant. The figs are now opening the second crop this year and look beautiful on the trees as do the pomegranates.

The cotton fields are a novel and pleasant sight. They raise the staple in large fields, frequently a hundred acres and over. It is cultivated with great care, the fields looking as clean as a garden, and when in bloom are covered with a mass of pink and yellow flowers. It is an odd sight to see the "field hands" at work.

Hundreds of men, women and children in the same field, plowing and hoeing, - some of them got up in the most grotesque and extravagant style, - the African tastes for colors and finery sticking out everywhere. I never saw anything more comical than the southern "threshing machine". The grain is laid on the ground to the extend of an acre or more and the darkies, men and women, mount horses, mules and anything that has four legs and race over it until the grain is beaten out.

To see them at it - thirty or forty at a time with animals of all sizes and colors some jogging along soberly, others running like mad, as though it was the best fun in the world-it would tickle you in spite of yourself. We thought at first it was a negro circus. We have seen more of plantation life in our march of 125 miles from Corinth than we could in 1,000 of ordinary travel. Our route has taken us through an unfrequented country and over more plantation roads made for local travel. This has brought us in immediate contact with the planters and their people.

Many of the finest residences are off the regularly traveled roads; therefore not visible to the common traveler. I have enjoyed the weeks experience very much.

I am glad to see that our people are moving so earnestly to raise the new levy of 300,000 men. I am glad, too, that my old Capt. Tolles is to have a command in one of the new Connecticut regiments. He is a man of merit and will make a fine officer. Chicago has taken new life and is sending some of the best blood there into the Army. A number of my intimate friends are joining the Regiments and Batteries raising under the new call. The Chicago Board of Trade has raised and equipped a full Battery and is now raising a Regiment at its own expense. My weak-backed colonel still remains at home under the plea of disability. I am disgusted with him and so, from what I hear, are his friends at home.

With best love to all.

Yours ever,

Luther

My dear Buel,

Yours of the 10th and 13th came to hand last week. I wrote to Mother about the time I received yours and have thought of writing to you every day since but have had no leisure. On the 24th the companies of the 51st were concentrated at Decatur, being relieved on their posts by the 27th Illinois. I have also a section of the 9th Wisconsin Battery. So we are now strong enough to go into the mountains and fight the guerrillas on their own ground.

On the 23rd we had a sharp skirmish with the rascals. They tore up the railroad track and run the train off within four miles of town. Expecting an attack the guard sent for reinforcements each way, a part of the 51st being yet at Fox Creek. Owing to the length of time it took for the courier to reach us and for us to get to the train we failed to save it. It was attacked by 600 rebel cavalry, the guard captured and the train burned. We reached the scene just in time to see their coat tails streaming out behind as they hurriedly sought their cover in the mountains. By sharp marching we succeeded in flanking them and got in a telling fire but we could not bring them to a stand though they outnumbered us considerably. We had two men wounded and the enemy carried off five wounded on horses.

We lost eleven men taken prisoners on the train. Our surgeon, Dr. Weeks, was taken also on the cars but the rebels released him on finding he was a non-combatant.

One of the rebel officers asked Dr. Weeks if there was a Col. Bradley at Decatur and said "tell him I have got his letters and dispatches". The scamps captured our mail on the train. Just fancy their reading your letters aloud to a select audience of rebels in some quiet hole in the Cumberland mountains.

If you could look in on me now you'd think soldiering was not such bad fun after all. The regiment is camped on the river, the tents pitched in a large field just outside the town and everything looking comfortable and pleasant. My own quarters are in a good brick house, built on a high bank directly over the river. From the door or windows you have a beautiful view of the river stretching along miles east and west, a sight worth halting anywhere to see. The Tennessee is one of the loveliest streams I have seen and in one thing it is peculiar, - the water has the beautiful green tinge you see in the Niagara.

I must answer your often repeated question about the "Times". I have received quite a lot and many thanks for them. There is good reading in the paper but I do not attach much importance to its political opinions. Raymond is a clever man but not a very broad one. I hope you won't think the Union is going to smash because he blows up the Generals and takes the President and Cabinet to task. He likes to stir up the political waters and fancies himself riding on top. In a shallow stream there is always plenty of fuss and foam as it dashes among the stones. It is your <u>deep</u> water that runs smooth and still. I am getting a contempt for this small fry of Journalists who are continually worrying the men who are delegated to manage affairs because they don't conduct them according to their notions. If they would drop the pen and take the sword they would perhaps earn a right to abuse their superiors. And I have as little sympathy with the opinions of our brother, that ours is the most corrupt government in the world. No man who knows the military and financial history of the old countries can say that. We are not without reproach but any of the old ladies across the water may sit down in our houses without soiling their skirts. It is a humiliating thing to say of ones government and every man who thinks thus must take part of the blame to himself. If a government is corrupt so are the people who support it.

You speak of Mother's sending me a line in a letter of yours. <u>I did not receive it</u> much to my regret. Do have her write me a few lines in your next letter. Matters are looking serious in Tennessee. The rebels are concentrating large forces there and our troops are marching in from all quarters. Two divisions of the "Army of the Mississippi" are en route to Nashville and we may have orders to move any day. In the course of the present week, 30,000 fresh troops will cross into Kentucky from Illinois and Indiana and in a few weeks more, the hosts will gather who are to crush out this internal rebellion. I tell the rebels here that the "cart of Juggernaut" is rolling down this way and they must look out for the wheels. I want to see a Northern Army sweep over this country like a great wave, that the natives may see what we are, <u>they don't know us yet</u>.

Give my best love to dear Mother, Mary, Rebecca and the children. Kind regards to Mrs. Ramsdell and Emily.

Yours ever,

Luther

My dear Mother,

We are again in Camp after a hard march of 150 miles. On the 4th Gen. Palmer came up to Decatur with the 27th and 42nd Regiments and crossed the Tennessee taking the road to Athens. I crossed the next morning, burned the ferry and flat boats and followed with the Division train of 200 wagons. We were just a week on the march making from 15 to 30 miles a day. It was intensely and infernally hot and we suffered badly. Some of our strongest men gave out. For three or four hours at midday it was as painful as anything you can imagine. It was hard work to make the men keep up but we had to force them to it for they were in danger of being shot if they got separated. Several of the 10th Michigan were shot by Guerrillas while loitering in the rear. I never had a more painful duty to perform than forcing along some of my poor fellows who had expended just about their last pound of strength. I saw one of them laying by the road side one hot noon and called to him to get up and come on. He said he couldn't. I then ordered him to join the regiment for we were the last in the column. He held up his bare foot and said "Colonel, look at my feet". He had worn out his shoes and his toes were raw. It was more than I could stand so I put him on my horse and carried him the rest of the day and for the next three days marched myself and gave Charley (NOTE) to my over-tired men. We have made a successful march through the enemy's country fighting them every day since we left Athens. Our loss is probably 30 or 40 of which the 51st has but two. The rebel cavalry have attacked the train every day with greater or less force. Sometimes as many as 2,000 but they have not got a pound of our stores. Twice they shot the mules on the road hoping to throw the train into disorder but the wagons were promptly upset and burned with their contents. While crossing the river at Columbia they made a bold dash on us thinking they could cut off the rear of the train but the 42°d and 51 st had been left as rear guard and were all ready for them. We had a sharp skirmish for an hour, killing several, capturing a load of flour and meat and driving them out of the town.

We were fired upon from one house but only from one for the General told the leading men he would shell the town if it was repeated. Most of the towns we have passed through are bitterly hostile but in the pleasant burg of Franklin we were greeted with miniature Union flags from the windows and smiles and pleasant words from the fair occupants.

I must say this much for the people of the South. With all their bitterness and hate for us I have never received a rude or insulting word from any non-combatant and when I see the stories about Southern women openly insulting our men, I can't but think the insults are provoked by some unmanly conduct on their part. In Decatur we enforced very stringent rules which very much incommoded the citizens yet they treated us with uniform politeness and when we left many of the solid men came to bid us "goodbye", following us to the river bank with well expressed wishes for our health and safety. And yet we had treated them with all the severity allowable under orders. We had taken their cotton, corn, cattle, mules or whatever we needed, giving them receipts not worth a rush to them because they were avowedly disloyal. My observation has convinced me that there is a latent feeling of regard for the old Union among the intelligent men of the South and though they are secessionists and hope to see it successful they will yield a ready obedience when they see it must fail and they are beginning to see it now. If we are wide awake for the coming Winter we shall put the rebellion in process of settlement. What we want is unity of purpose. We have men enough and material enough but we have too many opinions. Let us beat the rebels and discuss matters afterwards. We hear that Pope, the redoubtable Pope, has been beaten. He had better have staid with his Western troops or, perhaps he had better have taken them with him. I'll warrant he'd have given something to see the "Army of the Mississippi" coming up to join him when he was fighting the bulk of the rebel Army on the field of his first defeat. Palmer's Division was ordered up here to reinforce Buel but he had left the Kentucky before we arrived so we are halted here to await events. Bragg has gone into Kentucky and quite likely another week will see us on his flank. The rebel generals are playing a bold game, transferring the War to the boarder States and even menacing the Northern States. A brilliant success on the boarder would tell well for them but a defeat that will ruin the Army that suffers it.

We are camped on a high hill in the suburbs of Nashville, a beautiful city situated in a most charming country. It is rough and hilly and reminds me of the best parts of New England fully equating that favored land in a natural beauty and in the intelligence of its population.

There is no telling when th is will reach you. Communication is cut off with Louisville.

With best love to all

Yours ever,

Luther

Nashville, September 24th, 1862

My dear Buel,

I wrote to Mother on the day after our arrival here, telling her of our safe transit from Alabama. I am in doubt if the letter has reached her and if it has not you will be worrying your dear hearts to know what has become of me We are cut off from any regular communication with the North and so far as I can learn no mails are sent out. Until Buel beats Bragg and opens the line we are likely to starve for news and our friends will cherish the pleasant delusion that we are prisoners. I wrote you from Decatur that we were under orders to join Buel. Our Division was so much scattered that we did not get under way soon enough to effect the junction, Buel having left before we arrived here, much to our disappointment. This stoppage of the mails is as bad for us as for you. I have received no letters for nearly a <u>month</u> and am as ignorant of what is going on among you as you are of my whereabouts. I shall try and get this into the hand of some citizen going to Louisville. If I do not succeed in that it must take its chances with the rest. As for the news we have none. We are almost as ignorant of the state of affairs North as the residents of Hamden or Milford. The last Northern paper in our Camp is of the 26th August. We hear rumors of battles in Maryland in which the rebelsare worsted and we are all on tiptoe to get particulars. If it proves true we shall be jubilant over it. Our own position is safe though not without its menace. We have Palmer's and Negley's Divisions here and the City is strongly defended with forts and earthworks, the hills surrounding it giving us every advantage of ground. It is rumored that Breckenridge is marching up here with a strong force and it is not improbable. At any rate we are looking for him and shall be glad to see him. I believe we can beat any force the rebels can bring against us and await the opportunity to add one more to the list of Union victories. Would to God but one more were needed and we would win it speedily. I am looking hopefully as ever for the termination of this war; it cannot last much longer. The South is impoverished and the people are getting tired of it. The burdens fall especially hard on the poorer classes but the rich are feeling them keenly enough. All the articles of household consumption are difficult to obtain even at high prices - Coffee ranges from 60 cents to $1, flour, 20 cents to 30 cents per pound, sugar, 40 cents to 60 cents per pound, bacon 30 cents per pound. Shoes and boots bear the same relative price. Cotton cloth 30 cents per yard, sale 12 to 20 cents per bush. Coin of any kind is very scarce and the only local currency is shim plasters. They are of no account except to use from day to day. Everybody issues them and every body takes them 'par necessite'.

When we have beaten the Southern Armies we have used up the Rebellion and the balance of the people will submit without much trouble. Not that they are loyal but they see that secession is a failure. As for "dying in the last ditch" and all that, they are not a bit more fond of it than other people.

The people in the country through which we lately passed are undoubtedly hostile though they seldom showed it openly. Once in a while we meet a little honest sturdy patriotism. While passing through Athens we came on a fine mansion with a group of ladies standing in the door. As the Regiment passed a stately matron of forty or thereabouts walked down the lawn, waved her hand to the colors and said "that is my flag". Simple as it was, the manner and the words made an impression on us. In the pleasant burg of Franklin we found the Stars and Stripes flying over a private house and a party of ladies at the gate waving miniature flags. The circumstance was so novel that the General stopped and talked with them. He found they were daughters of a Surgeon, now in Buel's Army. They said they had been threatened with violence for their loyalty but they would avow it and show it when they could. Gen. Palmer offered to take them to Nashville but they declined. He then called together a lot of the citizens and told them if any harm came to that family he would come back and batter the town about their ears.

A more beautiful country than that lying between Athens and this point is not easily found. It reminds me of the better parts of New E ngland. It is fully as rough and more fertile. Fine towns and plantations are plenty and the people are evidently wealthy and cultivated. Nashville, the "Rock City" is a very pretty town and the country around it is unsurpassed.

We are camped on College Hill, one of the heights outside the city. On our right is St. Cloud Hill covered with tents. On our left the Cumberland and in front, the City with Capitol Hill in the distance, crowned with the noble State House.

Nashville is a city of wealth and fashion. There is every evidence of taste and cultivation and the people have an air of undoubted gentility. In peaceful times it would be a charming place to live in.

Give my best love to dear Mother, Mary, Rebecca and the children.

Yours ever,

Luther

Nashville, September 29, 1862

My dear Mother,

I have written home twice since we arrived here but as we have no mail communication, - and but little of any kind with the North it is quite probable my letters have not reached you.

The rebels have possession of the railroads and are in strong force north of us, so that it is difficult to get anything past them.

We are in daily expectation of a decisive battle being fought in Kentucky which shall open the routes again. This letter is to b e concealed in a lady's dress and I hope it will make the journey safely. If my letters have not reached you, as I surmise, you must be indulging in some anxious speculations as to my condition and where-a bouts. I hope this may go through safely to relieve any anxieties you may fell. I have had no word from any of you in just a month. Our mail is floating about somewhere waiting an opportunity to join us. If the rebels do not get hold of it we shall have a good time reading the letters on of these days. We are cut off from all news, whatever, -neither letters or papers reach here - and we are living upon rumors. We left Decatur on the 5th of the month to reinforce Buel at this point but he had left for Kentucky before we arrived. So we remain here for the present with Nehley's Division to garrison and place. Our march from Alabama was tedious and painful.

It was hot, amost beyond endurance and as we were on a forced march our men suffered greatly. Here we are very comfortably situated, though we are working hard building fortifications and are restricted to a diet of bread and fresh beef. Salt meat, coffee, sugar, etc. are not obtainable except in small quantities and rarely. I paid 40 cents per pound for very coarse and very brown sugar the other day. Coffee is $1 and other necessaries in proportion. We hear of battles in Maryland in which McClellan is victorious but we have no particulars. Also, that part of our old Army under Rosecrans have beaten Price at Iuka.

There are rumors of a force under Breckenridge marching on this place and it is quite probable an attack will be made. The rebels seem bent on reclaiming Nashville but we are strongly fortified and I think we can hold it against any force they can bring. I have only time for half a sheet but I send that full of love for you all.

Yours ever,

Luther

Nashville, November 12, 1862

My very dear Mother,

Your note of October 20th came to hand last evening enclosedin a letter from Munson brought through from Chicago by our Sutler. I cannot tell you how welcome it was. It is the first line from home in two and a half months. I thank God that I am once more in communication with you and know that you are alive and well. Your anxiety about me is, no doubt, great, but it can scarcely exceed mine for all you dear ones at home when I am cut off for months from all tidings of you. Communication by rail is at last opened to within forty miles of here and wagon trains are now running under strong guard to connect with the cars. Our Brigade had the honor of being the first to bridge this gap, taking a train of 300 wagons through in one day, loading them with rations the second day and returning the third. For two months we have been on short rations of flour and fresh beef and subsisting entirely on these, no coffee, sugar or tea. But now we are gain supplied liberally. Our long blockade is *ended,* and it is hardly within the range of probabilities that our communications will again be interrupted. An Army of 100,000 men under Rosecrans is on the way here. The advance, under the hero of Corinth, came in yesterday and in the afternoon he reviewed the garrison of Nashville - 20 regiments of infantry, one of cavalry and six batteries. The day was a fine one and the spectacle imposing. We were under Rosecrans at Corinth and as he rode up to the regiment he called out "How are the 1st" and breaking through the formal reserve of a review he shook me by the hand and laughed and chatted for some little time, telling us about the battles of Iuka and Corinth and seeming pleased with himself and with us. This General is a rising man and thus far a successful one. We have great hopes of him and after his splendidconductat Corinth can follow him with confidence and alacrity. We discard the idea of winter quarters and expect in a few days to enter on a sharp campaign through Eastern or Southern Tennessee or wherever Bragg may mass his forces. It is rumored that our Division is to have the advance of which we shall be proud. Ours is a fighting Division, as a day on the battle field will prove. We are nearlyall Illinois troops who have served together all Summer and in whom long service has begot confidenceand respect. I t hink there is not a Regiment in the command that would hesitate to follow or support another anywhere or anyhow. If we are ordered forward and come in contact with the enemy, you may look for

Palmer's Division to make its mark. It is made up as formerly of the 101L 16th - 22nd - 27th - 42 nd 51st - 60 th Illinois - the 10th - 14th Michigan-Houghtelling's and Bebee's Batteries. Col. Cummings has resigned, the resignation to take effect on the 30th of September. On receipt of the resignation I called a meeting of the officers to fill thevacancy when they made me Colonel on the first ballot without a dissenting vote. When I received my commission I shall mount the eagles and shall have realized all the ambition for rank that I have every felt.

Majoy Raymond is elected Lieut. -Colonel and my old, substantial friend, the Adjutant, t he Major. I feel no little pleasure in receiving the vote of every officer of the Regiment for the command when I know that I have offended some of them by off icial acts and I am proud of the confidence thus expressed by a set of officers of more than ordinary intelligence. I believe there is not one of them but would follow me today into any place of danger, promptly and cheerfully. I am sensible of my own unfitness for this work of fighting a Regiment. What it needs is a special education and much experience to fit a man for. No one can learn in a single year. Howeve,r I will try to do my duty with the aid of a strong hand and stout heart. have written you some four or five times since we have been in Nashville. Whether any of the letters have reached you or not I do not know. I have had a trust to chance to get them through. Some I know have been captured. Today, we have had a jubilee over the arrival of our mail the first since September first. I had a good hand full of letters, among them yours, Mary's, Rebecca's, and Buel's for August and September. You don't know how much all you kind words and wishes cheer and comfort me. It is my constant thought and solace that you will always think kindly and justly of me and that whether I meet with success or censure, I am equally sure of your confidence and love. You must wait a while longer for my return. I cannot get away if I wished. I did send in my resignation in August not because I wished to get out of the service but because I was so much disgusted with the conduct of Col.

Cummings that I determined to break all connections with him, if I could, even at the sacrifice of my position, trusting to my influence with the Gov. to get another, but the General decidedly refused to let me go and I had to wait my time.

With best love to each and all of you.

Yours lovingly,

Col.

CAMP OF PALMERS' DIVISION,
NASHVILLE, November 22nd, 1862

My dear Buel,

I am sitting in my tent alone this rainy night thinking of home. For some days my mind has been full of you and my heart is yearning to see you all. I am not homesick bu I _do_ want to see you. As the cold weather comes on ones thoughts go back to home and its comforts for the cold pinches us and the rain soaks us. Summer with its flowers and green fields is gone and in its stead will come months of dreary weather with a plentiful crop of ills to vex our bodies and spirits. It seems but a week since we were marching under a blistering sun and now its hard to keep warm "O'nights".

I have learned something in the last year I didn't know before; how much discomfort a man would stand before body and spirit rebelled against the unequal pressure but I find that muscle and a little pluck will carry him through many rough places and trials to which he would succumb at home. I don't say this so much with references to myself as to many a gallant fellow serving in the ranks who hasn't half the aids to comfort that I have.

We have just returned from a three day march into Kentucky, making forty miles a day and sleeping on the ground in rain and a little snow with our feet to the camp fires, finding it hard to keep warm with the aid of the fire. If I was cold with my double blanket, my men who had but one, must have been twice as cold as I was. A degree of discomfort that must be felt to be appreciated.

What are the poor devils in the rebel army to do this Winter, shoe-less, blanketless and almost coat-less. They are pitiable objects to see most of them. If December and January do not freeze treason out of them they are tougher knots than I think them. Their conscripts are put into the field most illy equipped and they must perish in herds when the frost and rains overtake them.

We are expecting soon to take the field for the Winter Campaign in "Thomas Corps" which forms the center of Rosecrans Army and is made up of the Divisions of Rosseau, Palmer, Dumont, Fry and Negley. Our line of operations will be through Southern Tennessee toward Chattanooga unless we are detailed to Garrison Nashville or some other point, which, the Gods forbid. It's a dull like; two months of it has surfeited us. I had rather be camped in the woods with no sign of civilization about than quartered in a town where the population is hostile. You are no where so lonely as in a city without friends. But the woods are grand places to live in anyway. The fine old trees are always in good humor and good tongue, real "Talking Oaks" as pleasant and wise as he whose top "o'er-looked _text not legible_____place." I never sleep so well as under the protecting arms of one of the old monarchs. There lu the forest camps we are rid of all the temptations to wander and dissipation in which the vile towns abound. There we are thrown on our own resources for amusement - excellent resources too you must know. I think there is not in the Army a Division whose officers are more intimate or congenial than ours; certainly they are excellent fellows as well as excellent soldiers. I count largely on the success of the Division if we get into a battle, from the intimate and confidential relations existing among its officers and men. There is not a Regiment that would hesitate to support either of its fellows or follow it wherever it might go.

Some of the new Illinois Regiments are joining us among them the 88th and 89th from Chicago. They are officered by old friends of ours and we have had a pleasant time rehearsing old matters with them.

Tell Mary that Tom Henderson is in Kentucky with his Regiment. I am hoping he will join us. He ran for Congress at the late election and came within 200 votes of beating Lovejoy. I see by returns of the recent elections that there is an apparent revulsion of feeling in the Northern States. To what cause it is owing or what it means, I do not know, unless it is an indication of public sentiment on the President's Emancipation Policy. But I know that the election of avowed opponents of the Administration tends to weaken it at a time when it needs the support of every loyal man. We are all interested in this for a political organization to fight the Government will prolong the War and keep us here an indefinitely long time than is otherwise necessary. I don't care for the emancipation policy except as a military measure. On other grounds I should oppose it now, but the South is not going to fight us and maintain slavery much longer. It has come to just this, <u>the Confederates must succeed or theyshall notmake another crop with the slaves</u>. And if any party at the North prevents the Government carrying out this policy the Army will accept it and enforce it and it will be well for politicians to remember that an Army of 1,000,000 trained men is a power in the land and it will not do to trifle with it. History furnished examples enough to show that such a power is a dangerous one. I for one don't want to see it provoked.

With constant love to dear Mother and all of you.

Yours ever,

Col.

By the death of two friends, I found
myself in command of the Brigade at a
time when my own Regiment was hotly
engaged and needed all my care.

1863

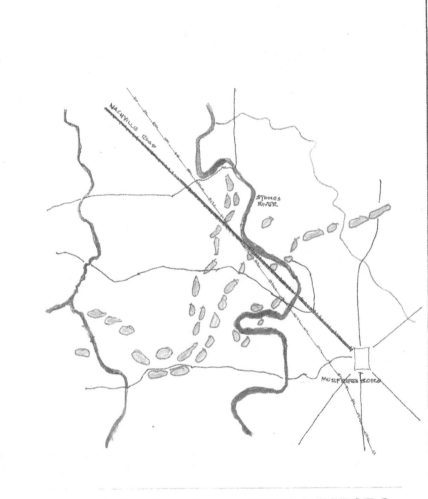

STONES RIVER & MURFREESBORO

My dear Mother,

I write you a line from the battle field to assure you of my safety. We have had three days hard fighting in two of which my Regiment has been engaged. We have suffered severely but by God's mercy I have been preserved. Our loss is sixty-five killed and wounded and is smaller than any other Regiment in the Brigade. The Brigade fought splendidly and lost two thirds it's number. On t he morning of December 30 th we formed line of battle at day light and were hotly engaged till noon. For the fi rst hour we drove the rebels but finally they outflanked us owing to the Division on our right giving way. They were new troops and could not stand the fire. From this time our Division had the whole right to protect and for three hours we fought Hardee's whole "Army Corps", holding our position until our ammunition was expanded and we had lost two third our members. Every Colonel in the Brigade fell except myself. My good horse, Charley was killed by a shell which burst at his side and carried off his legand hip. I was on his back at the time but was not touched. Major Davis lost his right arm. Lieut. Keith was killed and two captains and three Lieu's of the 51st were wounded. Both my color bearers were billed and a shell passed through the Regimental Flag. Col. Roberts commanding the Brigade and Col. Harrington,senior Colonel, being killed the command fell to me and I brought off the Regiments in good order the enemy pressing us hard. The rebel General, Brushrod Johnson with five regiments attempted to outflank and cut us off. He broke through our line and threw it into confusion. I was ordered to move up and hold the position at all hazards. After some sharp work with our rifles, I charged them with the 27th and 51st and routed them completely, killinga large number and taking three hundred prisoners. This ended the fight on our flank. My gallant Regiment behaved nobly and I am proud of them. Of all that fell in that bloody field not one showed an unmanly trait. I did not hear a murmur from one of them though they suffered from every conceivable wound. The sorest trial I ever had was to retreat and leave my wounded men on the field.

General Crittenden has defeated the rebels on the left and we shall beat them in this affair, no doubt of that. They are contesting the ground most stubbornly but we must win. Our reinforcements are coming up and tomorrow or next day will probably decide the campaign in the West. We have another fiery ordeal to pass through. How many of us will escape, God only knows, but we Will all do our duty, come what may. I have now four Regiments and a battery to manage.

The responsibility is not a light one, I assure you and I wish they were in more experienced hands. Fortunately they are so well drilled then can almost be trusted to fight alone.

Give my best love to Mary, Rebecca, Buel, Lucius and the children. Hoping we may all meet again, safe and well.

Yours ever,
Luther

My dear Buel,

You will see by the heading that I have a camp of my own. Sheridan's Division is now camped in a beautiful grove three miles south of Murphreesboro on the river which gives it's name to the bloody battle of December 31st or rather to the series of battles fought the last two days of the old year and the first two of the new. The General has named the camp after me, - a quiet compliment for which I thank him. I am now in command of the 3 rd Brigade, my seniors, Cols.

Roberts and Harrington having fallen in the fight of December 31st.

Buel, we have been through a terrible week. God grant I may never see such another. What it is to live through four days of battle in which your most intimate friends with home you have tented and messed and marched for a year are falling around you every hour, moving a midst carnage and witnessing every conceivable horror - no one knows who has not experienced it. Of all horrors the horrors of the battle field are the worst and yet when you are in the midst of them they don't appall one as it would seem they ought. You are engrossed with the struggle and see one and another go down and say, "there goes poor so-and-so. Well it will be my turn next·. Your losses and dangers don't oppress you 'till afterwards when you sit down quietly to look over the result or go out with details to bury the dead. In the series of battles ending with the evacuating of Murphreesboro, the 51st was hotly engaged two days and partially engaged in all, losing 65 killed and wounded. The Brigade loses 580 and the Division 1,700. I think the losses will exceed those of Antietam in proportion to numbers engaged. Our Army did not reach 50,000. The rebel force, I am sure, was much larger they fought with courage and desperation. On the second day they gained a decided advantage, partially turning our right and but for the steady courage of the old troops it might have proved a disaster. Our glorious old Brigade which was served together since last April made the first and last charge of the day, routing a superior force of rebels in both cases.

At one time Sheridan was forced back nearly a mile, owing to the giving way of the Division on our right, leaving our flank unprotected. We retreated to another position and for three hours fought the Divisions of Cheatham, Clairborn, Mccowan and Withers, outnumbering us certainlythree to one. Here we lost our 1,700. Every Colonel in the 3rd Brigade was killed except myself. Every commander of Brigade was killed, - Roberts, Still, Shaeffer. Roberts was the Colonel of the 42nd and has commanded the Brigade since the evacuation of Corinth. He was a man of uncommon talent and a natural soldier, was a graduate of Yale and for three or four years has practiced law in Chicago. He was a splendid looking fellow and a born !filillfil. He was shot through the breast while giving an order to one of his aids. As he fell to the ground his attendants jumped to pick him up. He roused a little and said "Put me up, boys, put me up", and died.

Harrington of the 27th fell about the same time, shot through the head. He was a good fellow too and I loved him. This night before the battle we slept together under a shelter of rails with a blazing campfire in front. It rained and we were supperless but he (Harrington) was merry over our discomforts, and talked confidently of the victory we were to win. He was a graduate of West Point and a thorough soldier. His regiment is one of the best in service. The last time I spoke to him was when my regiment marched past his at day light toward the rebel line, and he called out "the ball's opened". Thus by the death of two intimate friends, I found my self in command of the Brigade at a time when my own Regiment was hotly engaged and needed all my care. This was at the crisis of the battle on our part of the line. We were surrounded on three sides and were soon forced to retire. I brought off the Regiments in good order and I believe they were mainly the salvation of the right wing for their steadiness intimidated the enemy and in the final attack on our lines the 27th and 51st repulsed a rebel Brigade defeating them signally and taking a large number of prisoners.

I send a photograph of Col. Roberts which please preserve carefully.

With love and constant thought.

Yours ever,
Luther

(P.S.) Direct to me still as Col. Of the 51st, Sheridan's Division.

Camp near Murphreesboro
January 25, 1983

My dear Mother,

I have written a letter each to yourself, Mary and Buel this month. Unfortunately I get none from you owingto the deranged state of the mails. This is a privation, I assure you, for home letters are my chief comfort. We are laying quietly in camp, doing little work but just recruiting our energies after the hard work of the early part of the month and getting ready for another advance.

The general health of the army is good, surprisingly good, considering what it has been through. I have been nearly disabled for a couple of weeks by a lame foot beingobliged to keep to my tent most of the time. It is about well now and I shall soon be as sound as ever. My health is entirely good in every other respect and in a few days I shall be as fit for work as ever. do not think this Army will make any general advance for perhaps a month to come. The wet season has set in and it is raining almost constantly. There is no frost in the ground to harden it and the quantity of water falling makes the face of the country anything but what the geologists call "hard-pan". Moving artillery and transportation under such circumstances is impracticable.

Our wounded from the late battles are mostly removed to Nashville and from there, they will be sent to northern hospitals. A great many have died in Murphreesboro and vicinity, fully one third of the wounded die in the first hospital to which they are carried. This swells the total of "killed" largely. I have lost some of the best men whom I confidently expected to recover. Major Davis has so far recovered from his wound as to start for Chicago. He will remain there a while and then go home to Massachusetts. I have given him a letter of introduction to Lucuis and he promises to stop in New Haven and see you. You will remember he is an old and intimate friend as well as brother officer and I bespeak your kindest attention to him. He is a good and gallant fellow. My Regiment is sadly reduced in officers from killed, wounded and sick, having scarcely one to a company. The senior Captain is in command and two companies are commanded by Sergeants. am likely to remain in command of the Brigade for what I see. I would much prefer returning to the Regiment and shall try to arrange to do so byand by. The increased command brings new duties and much greater responsibilities and though I would not shrink from my responsibilities that fairly fall to me I don't care to undertake what many men of greater experience fail in. An ambitious man would think it a great chance and any man might be proud to command the old Brigade but I think too much of it to want to hazard its success on my slender experience.

The importance of our late victory is becoming more apparent to us every day. It has produced a great effect in all this part of the country, not only on the rebel army but on the quiet and malignant rebels who stay at home. They had counted so largely on success that defeat was a double disappointment. They are losing confidence in their leaders, and talk less confidently of the future than they were wont. If Burnside can win a decided victory in Virginia I am sure our western men will settle the matter at Vicksburg and success for us in these quarters will go far to discourage the already desponding soldiers of the Southern Army. Among the prisoners we have taken, the feeling is almost universal that they are fighting in a hopeless cause and a great many openly express the wish that the Union could be restored and peace return. The discipline in the rebel army is most rigorous and despotic, and thousands of unwilling men are forced to fight in a cause in which they feel little interest, knowing they will be shot by their own friends if they falter. On the last day of the fight, I took 117 prisoners with 60 of my own men. After they had surrendered and thrown down their arms and while we were in range of the enemies guns, they were in terror lest they be shot by their own men, saying their officers would make their comrades shoot them when they saw them surrender.

With best love dear Mother,

Yours ever,

Luther

Camp near Murphreesboro
February 1st, 1863

My dear Buel,

Yours of January 17 th reached me yesterday and greatly rejoiced my heart. It was the first letter from home since December and today I have Mother's Mary's and Rebecca's of later date. I am set up again in the social line and begin to feel that I am not alone in the world.

There is no change with us since I wrote last. We are laying quietly in camp, going out occasionally on a reconnaissance or forge expedition and are quite likely to stay her for a month to come the rainy season has set in its full force and it is impossible to put any Army into the field until the heavy rains are over. The rebels have withdrawn to Alabama in the neighborhood of Chattanooga. We shall find them there when we want them and shall whip them to a certainty.

I believe there is not a man in this Army who would not go into another battle with increased confidence. As the smoke of the last battle clears away we begin to see more clearly what we have gained and what we might have gained had the General's plan been carried out as it might have been. Thank God none of the blame rests on Sheridan's Division though we shared in the disaster and suffered our heaviest losses in trying to avert it. In the Army our reputation has not suffered and Sheridan is prominently mentioned for promotion. I send you two letters from a Cincinnati paper written by Capt. Bartlett of Rosecran's Staff. They are very correct in the descriptions of the battle field and in matters of opinion may be supposed to reflect somewhat the feeling at Headquarters.

For myself I can say that I am satisfied with the conduct of my Regiment and with the conduct of the Brigade and Division. Others may have done better but we did all we could do and another time shall do better still.

As you are interested in the particulars of the battle I will send you the official reports of Rosecrans and Sheridan when they are published. They will give you the statistical facts more correctly than you will get them elsewhere. If I express a confidence in our ability to beat Bragg's Army even at odds, do not think I underrate them. The Southerners are unquestionably a fighting people and I have great respect for their soldierly qualities. They are well officered and far better drilled and disciplined than our Army. They show great spirit and dash and perform their revolutions steadily and quickly. If there is any one thing in which they are inferior to us, it is in that stubborn qualify which will make a beaten man fight even when the chances are all against him.

And in one think I am satisfied we are entirely their masters: -the use of the bayonet, the real infantry weapon. They can't meet us with that partly because they are not so well drilled in it use, and more, because their temperaments do not suit that kind of work. The officers of the rebel army are generally intelligent and capable and very much in earnest. They represent the wealth and power of the South and of course, have everything at stake, but the rank and file of the Southern Army, I am satisfied, would willingly see the war ended and the old order of things restored, but for the stern discipline exercised over them. I am confidently in hope that the Spring will see us in possession of all the rebel strongholds west and south and the rebel Armies practically in our hands. If that magnificent failure the "Army of the Potomac" will win a victory or two in Virginia, I think we shall see "the beginning of the end". The new year has opened will for us and I think 1863 will bringus out of our troubles. I don't relish the idea of spending another summer in the far South. All my inclinations are against it. I have constitutional and social antipathies to overcome in doing it but it looks now very much as though bacon and corn bread were to be our staples for another season.

I believe I wrote you or Mother that I had been lame since the battle having hurt my right foot and taken cold in it. It troubles me still. I cannot get on a boot or shoe and am obliged to wear an old moccasin. It is improving slowly and I am now able to ride.

Give my best love to Mother, Mary, Rebecca and the children.

Kind regards to Mr. and Mrs. Baldwin, Mary and Fannie.

Your ever,
Col.

Camp of the 3 rd Brigade
Salem, February 23, 1863

My dear Buel,

Yours of the 14 th and 17th are received. You are so faithful in writing to me that I must strain a point to write you tonight though it is but a few days since I sent you a long letter. This must necessarily be short as I am reduced to half a sheet of paper. First, about the rumor that my Chicago friends are urging my claim for promotion. I have heard nothing of it and can assure you there"s no more chance of my being made a Brigadier than a millionaire. You may dismiss the thought from your mind at once. There are already hundreds of candidates most of whom have some claims, political or other. I do not want the position and would not lift my finger for it. Indeed, if it was offered me I should be very likely to decline it. I have no "fitness" for it, or if I have, it will take longer than one year to bring it out. At any rate I would rather have the reputation of beinga good Colonel tan a boor Brigadier. I do not know either Major King or St.

Clair Morton. The latter is now a General havingcommand of the Pioneer Brigade, made up of men detailed from the volunteer regiments.

The bodies of Cols. Roberts and Harrington were sent home to their friends. Roberts was not married. Harrington leaves a wife and child.

I have received letters from Mrs. Livingston in which she says she had written you since the battle. Major Davis was at her house and was leaving for the East. I suppose you have seen him before this. My foot is nearly well.

You want to know how my tent is furnished. Well, in the center stands a mess chest; in one corner, my camp cot covered with three blankets and a hair pillow; in the other my field desk; a cracker box on end serves for a wash-stand and two crouched sticks driven into the ground with a pole laid across for a clothes, similar one for saddles, bridles, etc., four camp stools and a sheet iron stove make up the equipment. It's not very luxurious, not very warm or very dry but it does pretty well.

Give my best love to Mother, Mary, Rebecca and the children.

Yours ever,
Col.

CAMP SHAEFFER, March 23rd, 1863

My dear Buel,

This has been almost the busiest month I have known since I came into service. On the 4th we started on a long march going as far south as Columbia on Duck River in pursuit of Van Dorn.

Returning about the 16th I was sent out with my Brigade in pursuit of a body of rebel

cavalry who were hovering round our lines and after drivingthem off had to change camp, attend reviews, etc., so that I have not written except a hasty letter to Mother a few days since. Yours of the 3rd I received on my return from Columbia. I note especially what you say about Wm. Austing. wrote you my own thoughts and opinions without thinking or wishing that they should influence yours. Your defense of him does not alter my opinion in the least. I have seen too much of the horrors and curses of rebellion to judge lightly such offenses as his. I admit all you claim for him as a good fellow and good brother. I respect his devotion to his sister and pity his misfortunes, but I denounce his treason. Do you properly estimate what he has been doing? He has been killing loyal men who were defending the flat he pretends still to love. Is there any greater offense against moral or civil law than shedding blood in a cause which is against your convictions and conscience? I have had friends shot by just such men as he. I may be shot by such one myself.

Will that make the matter any better? Bring the thing home to yourself as it has been brought home to thousands of others. Suppose the expected battle had come off at Corinth and I had been shot by one of Wm. Austin's men as some one would have been. What would you have thought of his position? Would you have taken him back to your confidence and esteem? This is a fair question for if he was not been the means of killing me he <u>has</u> been the means of taking lives just as good as mine. I give you my word, If I had been living in a southern city when the War broke out they might have hung me up to a lamp post before I would have gone out to fight against my friends. You say my judgment of him is unjust; I would like to see you judge him from a stand point like Stone River battle ground or the hospital at Murphreesboro and see how much we would differ.

I have had two letters from Major Davis since he reached home. He has much to say of his hurried visit among you and hopes to review it with me sometime. Dr. Warren, a distinguished surgeon of Boston gives him some encouragement that he may yet have the use of his hand, tho it will be a long time, I fear, before he can handle a saber. He is anxious to return to us and I am sure we are all anxious to see him.

We had a grand review of the Division yesterday by Rosecrans, McCook, Thomas and a lot of Brigadiers. Rosecrans said to Negley in my hearingthat "Phil Sherridan" had "the finest Division in the Army". I know that it hasthe reputation here of beingthe best fighting Division. I hear occasionally from Chicago that my chances for promotion are beingcanvassed. I wrote you that I hadnoambition this way and if at any time you should see my name in connection with the matter I want you to understand that it's none of my work. I have said this to all my friends who have mentioned it to me and I don't thank any of them to push my name. There have been too many appointments through political influence and I shouldn't feel it any compliment to be included with them. Gen. Rosecrans told me yesterday at the review that hehadrecommended me for Brigadier. I told him he must be mistaken, it was probably some other man but he said "no it was you". I don't know who procured this unless it was Sherridan. If I am promoted through the influence of Army Officers , all right.

This is between ourselves: I would not give a fig for it and do not expect it. If I can carry my eagles out with credit I am satisfied. You tell meyou are collecting notices of my Regiment and myself. Have you seen McCook's official report that contains a neat compliment for our charge on the enemy done under his own eye. If you find it, book it.

Give my best love to dear Mother and all,

Yours ever,

Luther

Note in Aunt Buel's hand
"I did book it"

Camp of Third Brigade
April 1st , 1863

My dear Buel,

As I have an opportunity to send north by private hand, I enclose fifty dollars to be forwarded with letter by express from Louisville. I want you to use it for your own comfort in any way that suits you, either in dress, books, or play in the Spring vacation. If your economic life needs no stimulus, put the "rag" in the Savings Bank where it will not waste, if it does not grow. wish my means were but equal to my wishes or my deserts, and I'd surround you with all comforts and luxuries.

I have just returned from Salem, doing out post duty again and am settled in Camp after a month of marchings and scoutings. How long a respite we have I don't know. Our future is uncertain in this,. that it is doubtful whether we go after the rebels, or they come after us.

Certainly we shall solve the doubt if they don't, in due time. We are inclined to the opinion that they are approaching a crisis in their affairs and I, for one, am feeling more hopeful than ever.

All the evidence that we get from our own observation, and from scouts and

deserters, goes to show this, conclusively, - that their supplies are nearly exhausted and that in many places they are in actual want. Grant is sure to get control of the Mississippi and with the great depot of Texas cut off, they have no resources but to get into the fertile regions of Kentucky and Tennessee for subsistence. This will suit us exactly and the movement toward Kentucky from Virginia means this without doubt. If the Rebel Army is driven from Vicksburg we shall have them up here too. And as soon as Grant arrives we can fight it out. I believe the War is to be defeated here in the West and it couldn't be finished in a better place or by better men. We are amply provided with munitions, stores, and men.

I have to attend Brigade drill now. Will write you a long letter soon.

Yours ever,

Col.

My dear Mother,

It seems a longtime since I have heard from home. Buel's letter written somewhere about the last of March being the latest news I have from you. I have written Mary and Buel within a fortnight and am looking for letters from the East daily. I am anxious to hear from you and to know that you are well.

I am in wonderfully good health and am enjoying it to the full. Nothing can be finer than the climate here and for beauty of hill and valley this region is unsurpassed. The forests are out in full leaf, the numerous flowering shrubs that grow here mingling their colors with the green of the larger trees with the prettiest effect. Vegetation comes forward here with astonishing rapidity. After the spring rains cease the trees and flowers set to work in earnest and Summer is on you before you know it.

I wish you could see my camp. I claim to have an eye for sylvan scenes and seldom fail to find a pleasant spot to pitch my tents on. We are now in a fine old forest near the village of Salem. The trees are all large and stately, carrying their heads high and throwing out their arms so wide as nearly to keep the sun from the ground which is as clear from bushes and as bright with grass as an English Park. Living so much among the trees and birds I have got a new idea of Life and begin to understand why some men prefer the freedom of the woods to the civilization of the towns.

The Army is in fine condition occupied mainly in watching the enemy, strengthening its position and making itself comfortable for the approaching hot weather. I see no prospect of our moving very soon, or until some important change takes place, East or West, there is no use in our moving either. We are hurting the rebels by holding them in their present position, eating their heads off, then we should by driving them south of the Tennessee, to occupy Chattanooga or strengthen Vicksburg. Georgia will be the final stand of the rebels, the "last ditch". There they will go after they are driven from Virginia and Mississippi and we are prepared to press Bragg over the mountains whenever the time comes, believing that it will result favorably for us and in good time, well satisfied that the rebels are wearing themselves down to a poverty of men and material from which they have no power to recuperate.

If the Army remains here until June I shall ask for a short "leaveof absence" and think I can get it. I feel the want of a little change of scene and a little rest. More than all, I want to see your dear self and all "the loved ones at home". I cannot tell you what a longing I sometimes have to escape from the stir and bustle of camps and taste the quiet of home.

Do not set your heart on my coming, Mother, but rest assured I will do it unless I see clearly that I out to remain here and I will not let any trifle of duty or any hope of personal advantage keep me from seeing you this Summer. You may sometimes feel that I out to come home any way but on reflection you will agree, I know, that you would rather forgo the pleasure of seeing me than feel that I had left my post when I ought to be at it or had neglected any part of my duty. More than this, I have a feeling of pride which would prevent my leaving my command if there was any likelihood being actively engaged in the field. No man shall have the opportunity of saying that I have turned my back on the enemy or left to others the work I ought to have done myself. Don't think I am ambitious of making reputation, Mother, I care little for it and heartily wish all this strife and struggle at any end. I simply want to do my duty.

I had yesterday a letter from Major Davis. He is in Chicago and I am sorry to hear that his arm is doing but poorly. He has had the wound opened and 22 pieces of bone taken out. He writes that the arm is giving him more pain than ever before but that the surgeons tell him it is in a fairer way of recovery, these fragments of bone having kept in constant irritation and prevented its healing.

He writes very pluckily; says he shall return to the Regiment and remain till the end of the War unless the arm permanently disables him. I am impatient to see him for he is my constant companion in camp and my right-bower in the field.

We have just had a new Brigadier join our Division, <u>Gen. Lytle</u>. I expect he would take my Brigade but Gen. Sherridan assigned him to the "1st". I have asked to be relieved from the command of the Brigade by Sherridan says "No, you must keep it ". I'd rather be rid of the responsibility but I feel very much like the boy who said he's "make a spoon, or spoil a horn", which means, I'll do my best and if I win, I make something and if I lose, I don't lose much.

Give my best love to all,

Ever yours,

Luther

My dear Buel,

Yours of April 26th has just come to hand. Am glad you received my letter by express safely. I must have written very carelessly in a former letter to you the impression that anything of yours had annoyed me. Nothing was further from my thoughts, believe me. I wrote as I did simply on your account, -to urge you to take a cheerful view of my soldiers' lifeand believe me always safe and well unless you had positive knowledgeto the contrary. I shall never find fault with your sisterly solitude and anxieties. I only want you should not exaggerate my dangers. Now! Don't you ever take a notion of that kind again.

"About Books" "Barrington" which you mention, I have, having come across it in a sutler's store, and bought it, of course, on my recollection of "O'Malley" and "TomBurke". It is very Lever-ish and very Irish and well worth reading. We are tolerably supplied with the common run of cheap novels. Our sutlers and merchants in Murphreesboro paying some attention to our mental wants. If you send me anything let it be a little above the common run. There is a book in press which I shall send you as soon as I can get it, the "Army of the Cumberland" by the correspondent of the Cincinnat i Commercial, containing a history of its organization and movements, a descripti on of the battle of "Stone River", official reports of same, etc. I send you a war poem from the Louisville Journal which is a remarkable and touching thingto my fancy. I enclose also my friend Col. Tillson, one of the best men I know. Take good care of him.

I have just read Emile Schalk's remarkable military works on strategy and the science of war. He made some singular predictions (which have come true) of what would happen to us for violating well known and established rules of war. I thi nk we are learning some thing by our failures and if the war lasts longenough we shall educate our Generals.

I see that the Army of the Potomac is inn motion again having crossed the Rappahamock, as we understand, 130,000 strong. God speed them and give them victory. But if this campaign is not successful I hope it won't be tried again. These constant failures are discouraging and demoralizing. More than half of our immense army has been at work during the last year on the Atlantic Coast and yet about the only gains of territory they have made are

Yorktown and Port Royal. The Western Army has fought a string of battles, every one of which has added to loyal territory. Take 1862 and we have "New Madrid", "Island 10", "Fort Henry", Fort Donnelson", "Shilch", Corinth", "Iuka", and "Stone River". During the year we have regained Kentucky, Missouri, and a large part of Tennessee and Arkansas with the northern portions of Alabama and Mississippi. All that this Army is waitingfor now is a successful move in Virginia. Just as soon as that occurs we shall go forward. Until then Rosecrans will probably content himself

with holding Bragg in check. The rebels have moved up toward us within a week and some of the northern papers predict that we are to be attacked. Probably this move of Bragg's is to cover some other. If he should attack us here it will be in mere desperation hoping to capture our supplies and we shall fight <u>the decisive battle of the war</u>. Our men are in splendid condition and entirely confident. An eastern Surgeon traveling for the sanitary commission was through our camp a few days since and he said our troops were healthier and cleaner than any he had seen in the country.

I am now serving on a Department Court-Martial at Rosecrans' Headquarters for a week or two. It is an agreeable change from field work for a little time. I send you a little rose from Gen. Rosecrans' garden. He occupiesthe finest mansion in Murphreesboro and the garden is wonder of floral beauty. I wish I could send you a fresh bouquet such as I might pick there.

Give my best love to dear Mother, Mary, Rebecca and the children. Remember me also to Mr. and Mrs. Baldwin, Mary and Fannie.

Yours ever,
Col.

CAMP OF 3 rd BRIGADE
May 25th, 1863

My dear Mother,

It is a good while since I've written to you direct, though I write to Mary and Buel with tolerable frequency as they are so good to write me constantly. I know you would also, if you could. Of course, you see all my letters and I wish you to consider them equally yours though addressed to the girls.

I have been trying for some days to get a "Carte de Visite" to send you. An adventurous photographer having pitched a juge tent in our midst which he modestly styles an "Art -Gallery". I haven't been able to get a sitting yet but I will do it and you shall see with your own eyes that I am really well. I hope you will not be impatient for my promised visit. The girls write enquiringly when I will come. I do not think it can be before mid-summer, but as soon as I can get away you may be sure I will.

We hear most cheering news from Grant and it would seem that he had met with a real success. If he has in reality defeated and captured a large part of the rebel Army at Vicksburg , then he will probably cooperate with Rosecrans and we may expect to go forward soon. It is time and we shall all be glad to move. We have lain here nearly five months and though we have not been altogether idle or useless yet the life is too inactive for a soldier.

We take great encouragement from Grant's success and it cannot but have a decisive influence on the future of the War. Since the "Army of the Potomac " made its semi-annual failure we have been fearful that we would be obliged to remain here all Summer to hold this point against Bragg, who was concentrating troops for the apparent purpose of trying to reconquer Tennessee and Kentucky.

Indeed, two columns of men had been sent to reinforce him, <u>one</u> from Virginia had reached Knoxville, the other, from Vicksburg had reached Chattanooga when they were recalled, by the more pressing demand for their service at home. I think Bragg will be forced to retire to Chattanooga without waiting for us to drive him there.

Some of the Federal Officers captured here in the battle have recently returned. They say that while imprisoned at Atlanta they saw a great many undoubted Union men that came to them privately and announced themselves as such and offered assistance.

113

Col. Grierson says too that he met them in considerable numbers in, Mississippi. There is no doubt in my mind and has not been for a long time that there is a leven working in the South and I shall not be surprised at any time to see the Union spirit beat out again. I met today an Indiana Colonel captured some two months since on the Railroad between here and Nashville. He is just from Richmond and says that while a prisoner in Knoxville soon after his capture he was quartered at the Hotel, having the freedom of the house and while walking on the piaua one evening he saw some ladies watching him intently from the parlor windows. Presently he saw a hand extended through the blinds and, of course, he took it. When it was withdrawn leaving a roll of bills amounting to 100 dollars in <u>his</u> hand. He went into the house, found an opportunity of speaking to the ladies unnoticed and returned the money as he had enough for present use.

A significant fact, is the avowal made by prominent Methodists about here that the "Methodist Church South" is about making an effort to unite its members on a peace movement for the reason, as they say, that if the war continues, Methodism in the south is dead and they are satisfied that slavery is doomed so there is no use fighting for that any longer. This will be a movement of great importance considering the number and influence of the Methodists in rebellion.

I do not hear anything of the box yet, and I fear we must give it up for lost. I am sorry, for I should have prized anything from your loving hands.

Give my love to Mary, Rebecca, Buel and the little ones.

Yours ever,

Luther

CAMP of Third Brigade
Salem, Tenn., May 31, 1863

My dear Buel,

I am camped again in the pleasant forests of Salem, on out-post duty, that is watching for movements in Hardee's Army Corps which is posted a few miles in our front. This is the last day of Spring and as beautiful as any day you ever saw. We have flowers and ripe cherries in abundance from neighboring houses and the trees over our heads are full of mocking birds, singing their loudest and best. Forest life at this season is just charming. There is nothing in the towns to compare with it.

One year ago today we went into Corinth and started after the retreating rebels winding up inn a tame pursuit, the completest blunder of the War and throwing away the skill and labor of "the finest Army in the World" not excepting that of the Potomac. If old Halleck would return to his law clients in California he would do the country infinite service.

I have received three letters from you this month with the papers and "counterparts' for which I am much obliged. I am reading the book now and like it though there is much bad.. and some bad morals in it. The characters are well drawn and the talks are very entertaining.

Altogether it is much above the common run. You do not tell me whether you have read "Les Miserables" yet. Read it by all means, and tell me what you think of it.

I am not surprised at the complications growing out of Tibbie's foreign residence and study. It has always seemed probable to me that with such opportunities and her enthusiastic nature she would make just this choice. She has talents and ambition and I have no doubt she would win success. Personally my objection to her adopting music as a profession would be that it would be distasteful to her Mother and the rest of the family ties of which we think so much. For Rebecca's sake I hope she will come home and settle down under her protecting wind. I fear tho that she has built this "castle in the air" so strong it will not easily be knocked over. In any event tell Rebecca not to let this make her unhappy.

While writing the mail boy has brought me your letter of the 24th• I am glad to hear that Mother and the rest of you are so well. If I find you in good health when I return I shall not care if you have grown old and a little as you assure me you have. I am in the same boat, too. I'm not very grey, not very wrinkled, but you'll see that a year and a half of hard work and exposure has made a change in me. The least that canbe said of this life is, that it is a very wearing one.

I have just hada photograph taken and will send some on as soon as finished. Now if you have any sense of justice or reciprocity you'll send me yours. Remember I have never had a picture of you of any kind and if you have waited till your good looks have departed it is no fault of mine for I've been asking for it these twenty years back.

I see no chance of my coming home before mid-summer. I wrote when I first mentioned it that I would ask leave of absence when the army settled down for the Summer. That time is not yet. I cannot think of leaving while active operations are going on, -East and West which may engage us any day.

Much as I want to see you all and much as I want the relaxation from constant work and responsibility, I ca nnot think of it until it is certain we are not to have an active campaign.

Every man counts now and I have the confidence to believe that, if any fighting is to be done here, I can do more with my own men, than any one else could in my absence.

We are looking for the fall of Vicksburg. Grant has made a splendid campaign since he landed at Grand Gulph and we have the strongest hopes of his complete success. The rebels are concentrating to try and feat him and he is being reinforced from Memphis and Arkansas. God grant he may win!

Give my best love to dear Mother and all the rest. Regards to Mrs. Baldwin and family and Mrs. Beers and family.

Yours ever,

"Col"

Camp of 3rd Brigade
June 4, 1863

My dear Buel,

I wrote you a few days since from Salem. I am now back in the old camp again having been relieved on out-post on the 2nd.

I have sent you by mail Capt. Brickham's book "Rosecrans Campaign with the 14th Army corps". Brickham was a volunteer aid on the General's Staff. You will be interested to know what part my Regiment took in the battle and will see it mentioned in the "official reports" and in the narrative. I send also with this some photographs - Rosecrans is very good; mine indifferently so. Keep one for yourself and give one to Miss Fannie as you wrote she requested it. I will send one to Mother as soon as I have time to write. Please thank Rebecca for Tibbie's "carte de visiti". It is very good, I will send one of mine for Tib soon.

We are under orders to march and expect to take the road tomorrow. It is understood to be a general movement so you need not be surprised if no letters come from me for a week or so. I will write on the first opportunity to relieve the anxiety this may suggest. I presume we are bound for Tullahoma but I doubt if Bragg meets us there. According to the best information we have he has sent off two Divisions to reinforce Johnson at Vicksburg. Our Army is large and in every respect better than it was at Stone river. We have no doubt of our ability to beat Bragg's Army if they fight us.

We shall very likely have difficulty in keeping open our communications for a time.

Our supplies must come from Murphreesboro and Nashville and it will be strange if the rebel cavalry do not succeed in capturing some of our trains. The length of our communications will embarass us until we drive the rebels across the Tennessee.

Give my best love to dear Mother, Mary, Rebecca, Lucius and the children. Regards to Mr. and Mrs. Baldwin and the girls.

Yours ever,

Col

CAMP IN THE FIELD,
June 28, 1863

My dear Buel,

this is an unquiet Sunday. I am sitting on a camp stool surrounded by horses, mule teams and men by the thousand. We reached here at 9 A.M. After a fatiguing march of four days. We lie between Manchester and Tullahoma and shall move on the latter place tonight. The whole Army is concentrating her and gettingthis position the rebel position at Shelbyville is turned so they evacuated the latter place yesterday in haste and have retreated to Tullahoma. They will not fight there and I do not think they will anywhere unless we can overtake them. It is more likely to be a foot race than a fight and I expect we shall chase them south of the Tennessee. We are in a mountain region and the roads are execrable, the hills rock, and the valleys muddy for it has rained every day since the 22nd. This is in our favor though for it tempers the cruel heat. We have had some severe fighting in our Corps for the rebels disputed all the gaps in the mountains. I have been engaged but once. On the morning of the start I hadthe advance with my Brigade, a six gun battery and five companies of cavalry. I was to go out the Shelbyville road, take possession of the cross roads leading over the mountains and hold them until the Corps passed. We ran on to the rebel pickets within tow hours after starting. We drove them in and they brought up reinforcements with a battery and attempted to check us. My orders were not to bring on an engagement so I did as little fighting as possible - puttingthe Regiments and guns in position and holding the ground we wanted with skirmishers. About two o'clock I was relieved by Gen. Brannon and went on with the Division.

We are all in fine condition and anxious to get at Bragg. Not that we care to fight but we must do something to balance this disgraceful business in the East.

Give my best love to dear Mother and the rest. Will write again soon.

Yours ever,

Luther

CAMP ON CUMBERLAND
MOUNTAINS,
July 12th, 1863

My dear Buel,

I wrote to Mother a few days since from "Cowan", where we spent the 4th. I have written both Mary and yourself since we left Murphreesboro. On the 6th General Sheridan ordered me over the mountains with the Brigade accompanying us with a regiment of Cavalry. We are now 20 miles in advance of the Division and more than that much in advance of any part of the Army. have been within six miles of Bridgeport reconnoitering and our Cavalry have been to Bridgeport and find no rebels this side of the Tennessee. We shall move on soon I think and occupy the line of the Tennessee River. There are a few bridges to build north of here as soon as they are ready, the cars will bring us rations and we shall move on to "Stevenson"or "Huntsville". At present we are on ½ rations and of course are sometimes hungry. The country for miles around is as bald and barren as the top of East Rock, and we can obtain nothing to eke out our supplies, which are hauled from the Elk River. The breaking down of a wagon or two, or a rain which shall impede the travel on the roads are matters of moment to us now. If our trains should fail to reach us we can subsist ourselves a little while, for in searching the mountains we have found a grist-mill on a little stream, and miles away, in a little nook of tillable land, there are a few hundred bushels of corn, which can be converted into meal. So, if the worst comes, I can subsist my little family of 2,000 without the aid of Uncle Sam's Commissary.

I wish you were here to look at some of these mountain views through my field glasses. East and West Rock are babies to these mountain ridges. The Cumberland ridge is a succession of a great hills and little valleys, rather than clear straight mountain. It is interspersed with streams and waterfalls of exceeding beauty, and such landscapes as are seldom seen. Yesterday I chanced on a view fully equal to Church's "Heart of the Andes". And in a reconnaissance toward Bridgeport I passed through a valley about six miles long called "Sweden's Cove ", which was a little paradise, a fertile patch surrounded by high mountains. For two days past it has not rained, but since we left Murphreesboro, it has rained every day up to the 10th. thought I had seen mud and water, but the last fortnight beats all my experiences. Mud has reigned supreme. It has covered every one from the Major general to the Private, and it has stalled our teams, so that no mule power could pull them out.

Gen Crittenden with the Left Wing made but two miles in a hard days work. The rain has defeated the prime object of the campaign, which was to put Bragg off from his line of retreat by reaching Tullahoma before he did and compelling him to fight us. McCook's corps could have reached Tullahoma in time but the other corps, marching on different roads, could not. So we were obliged to follow Bragg with the hope of overtaking him in the mountains. This also, was defeated by the rise of Elk River after we had forded it, cuttingoff ourtrains, and obliging us to stop for want of rations until the rivercould be bridged. The rebels retreated with excellent speed. By hard marching Sheridan over took them at the foot of the Cumberland Mountains and had a days skirmishing with them. He was ordered by Rosecrans to cease the pursuit here. And he was afterward ordered to send a Brigade over the mountains to re counter.

Bragg's Army is all south of the Tennessee River. As soon as the brigades are build our Army will take up position on the other side of the river, and make arrangements for crossing, I suppose.

We heard yesterday of the fall of Vicksburg and of the success of the Potomac Army under General Meade. It is glorious news, and we are jubilant over it. I only wish we could have had the chance to add a victory over Bragg to the list. It seems from our news that Lee has been badly defeated, and we are in hopes that hemay be crushed before he can cross the Potomac.

Certainly, with a large river before him and a victorious army behind him, he out not to escape with his whole force.

We have had no mails or papers for a week, but we are looking for them daily, and I hope to get letters from some of you.

With best love to Mother, Mary, Rebecca, Lucius and the children.

And regards to Mr. and Mrs. Baldwin, Mary and Fannie.

Yours ever,
"Col"

My dear Mother,

I am writing home often as we have a leisure week after three weeks of hardmarching.

My camp is at a place called "University" on the top of the Cumberland Mountains. There is nothing here to denote a town but two log houses. The site was selected in 1860 and the ground laid out for a great Southern University which should furnish educational facilities for all the South and emancipate them from dependence on Northern Colleges. The plan was for each State to build a large college at its own expense, the whole to comprise one institution and to be under one management. The sites of the different buildings are selected and in some cases the corner stones are laid. The location is as fine as could be selected in the whole country. Mountains scenery of the grandest, valleys between the mountain ranges with a railroad running within a mile. It would have been a grand affair if the war had not interfered with it's completion. And it may be yet. Bishop Polk was the originator and director of the project. He had a house here for summer use which was burned by the Union people living on the mountain. Ii am very glad I was ordered on to the mountain for I could not have found a prettier place to camp. Gen. Sheridan is in the valley six miles from here with the balance of the Division. My special business here is to watch the roads toward Bridgeport and Chattanooga to see that the rebels do not advance to interrupt our pioneer parties building bridges. The repairs to the railroad are nearly finished and we shall probably move too Stevenson inn a few days. We know nothing of Rosecrans's plans for the future. I do not think we are to have any severe fighting for I don't believe the rebels will risk a battle with us. It is more than likely we shall advance and hold the line of the Tennessee until Grant's forces are near enough to cooperate in which case our Division may go to Huntsville. This, you know, is the prettiest town in the South. I would like very well to go there as it is the home of Mrs. Breck, sister of Mrs. Livingston. The rumor is quite current that our Corps is to go to Virginia and that Grant is to be transferred there leaving Rosecrans all the forces in the South and southwes.t I do not know whether there is anything in this report but under the circumstances it would not be at all strange. Grant and Rosecrans united have more troops than are needed here and I suppose all that can be spared are needed in Virginia. The change would be a pleasant one for us tho we are quite content to remain here.

We are all much elated with the recent victories as you must be at the North.

It is really glorious that all this should happen in July. The old 4th is keeping up its ancient reunion. Charleston must fall next and then we will take Chattanooga if the rebels will fight there, which I doubt. I think 1863 will see the end of the fighting in this War.

We already begin to speculate on the time when we shall quit campaigning and return to the quiet pursuits of peace. For my part, I shall lay aside the sword with a pleasure equal to any I ever felt.

With best love,dear Mother, to you and all the family.

Yours lovingly,

Luther

CAMP ON CUMBERLAND MOUNTAINS
Sunday, July 26, 1863

My dear Buel,

Yours of the 22nd came to hand today in remarkably quick time. I received yours of the 14th also a few days since. You see we are still on the mountains and not in Rome, George as the papers have it.

I am contentto stay here as long as the Army is idle for a more beautiful place could not be found. My camp is on the tip-top of the Cumberland range, 1200 feet above the surrounding country. We have cool air, fine springs and all the aids to health. The little valleys between the ranges furnish us with vegetables and fruit so that we fare very sell. The charm of the place is the magnificent mountain scenery all around us. I could take you on the bluffs where you could have a view of the mountains and valley for fifty miles. On one of these we have a signal station, communicating with McCook's and Sheridan's headquarters at Winchester and Cowan.

This army telegraph is a curious affair; the words are spelled out by motions with flags. At night torches are used, and the effect is very pretty. When the air is clear, with the aid of glasses, we can signal twelve and fifteen miles and almost as fast as the magnetic telegraph.

The position of the troops is unchanged but we are expecting to go forward to the Tennessee soon. Sheridan's Division is still in advance, one Brigade at Cowan, one on the mountains and one at Stevenson. I think we shall halt a while on the river and the attack when we cross is more likely to be on Atlanta than Chattanooga. If we go into camp for any time I shall come home without delay if I can get leave. It will be short. Twenty days at the most. I join with you in exultation's over the recent victories. They are glorious. If old Bragg had stood at Tullahoma, as he ought, we would have added a victory to the list.

My friend Ransom, lately made Brigadier, has distinguished himself at Vicksburg and is now in command of a force of 12,000 men with transports operating at Natches and other points on the River. He is a resident of Chicago and son of the Col. Ransom who commanded the New England regiments in the Mexican War.

I am not surprised to hear that the Eastern people are alarmed at the recent out- break in New York. It is a shocking affair, most disastrous and disgraceful, but it is the legitimate fruit of the teachings of the Seymous and other men of that stamp. The New York mob was an Irish out-break and the meddling of

Hughes and other prominent Catholics is most significant. Unless this mob spirit is checked, promptly, we shall have the bloody outrages of Ireland repeated here. I wish the authorities had blown every man and woman of them off the ground. A mob is the cruelest thing in the world and the most unreasonable. I don't agree with you. r opinion of the draft at all. To me it seems the fairest way to raise an army always. Of course, the burden falls heavily on some. So does every other burden of society. It is no fault of the law that it gives the rich man an advantage over the poor. No law can be framed that takes away this advantage from wealth .

Cases of individual hardship will occur under the law for conscripting and they will be magnified till they seem outrageous. But every case of hardship can be matched in the volunteer army. There are poor men here whose families are suffering and there are men who have sacrificed as many comforts, as many interests and as good prospects as any in the North, now fighting in the Army. If the draft can't be enforced by the civil authority, I hope Government will call on the Army. A few Brigades of old troops scattered through the North will make the work easy.

Mrs. Livingston writes me that she has not heard from you in a long time. I hope you have not dropped the correspondence. She enquirers after you with much interest.

The Major has not returned yet but I hear he is on the way.

We are just getting up our tents and baggage from Murphreesboro where it was stored when we marched.

You may not know I am not as nice in small matters as formerly when I tell you that I brought from Murphreesboro nothing but what I wore except an extra shirt and that I have not undressed at night since the 24th of June. I have come to the way of thinking that fresh air is about all one wants to ensure health. With plenty of that night and day, it does not much matter what you have or what you lack.

You do not tell me who Mary's persecutor is. Don't let her be cruel to him because

he is old.

You would enjoy this calm still Sunday if you were here. There is scarcely a sound heard but the singing of the birds, except now and then a strain of some old hymn from the grove where the Chaplain is holding his Sunday service.

Give my best love to dear Mother. I will answer her letter in a day or town. Love to all the others.

Yours ever,

"Col."

CAMP "ROBERTS"
Bridgeport, August12, 1863

My dear Buel,

Enclosed I forward fifty dollars which you are to use in any way you like, for yourself or others. I had intended to hand it to you in person but as I cannot come on just yet will trust it to the Express. On the 9th Inst. Gen. Lytle came up here with his Brigade and took command. I thought it would be a favorable time to ask for leave as it seemed probable we would lay here some time . So I sent up an application but the very next day after, I regretted it, for we got orders to prepare to move and I knew the request would not be granted. My application came back today. It was "app roved" by Sheridan and McCook, but Rosecrans made the endorsement that , the leave could not be granted now, but it would be in a few weeks.

We are making preparations to cross the Tennessee and shall probably move in a few days. The Army is concentrating at Stevenson and will cross in force. I presume we are to move on Chattanooga but do not think there will be any fighting of consequence. Bragg dare not fight us and he has weakened his Army by sending forces to East Tennessee. Our movement will be simultaneous with one on Knoxville so Bragg cannot recall his Divisions to repel us. I am pleased to think we are to take possession of Chattanooga for it will give us control of important railroad connections ., and force the rebel army to wander in search of another stronghold.

We are in good health and temper for work and if the rebels want to cross bayonets with us again we shall not deny them . From all indications they are not in the most confident humor.

Will write again soon. Give my best love to Mother and all the family.

Yours ever,

"Col."

HOG JAW VALLY, ALABAMA
September 3rd, 1863

My dear Mother,

We crossed the Tennessee yesterday and are now camped in a little valley with the above euphonious name.

Here we await the arrival of the other Divisions of our Corps, when we go forward in the direction of Rome. What the campaign is to be I do not know, but the whole Army is crossing and the movement equally menaces Chattanooga and Atlanta. It is probable the rebels will stand at Chattanooga and I do not see that they can fight us short of Atla nta. We shall not reach there for some little time as it will be impossible I think to ration the Army so far from the river until the railroad bridge is rebuilt. We have entire possessions of the country south of the river for considerable distance and the rebels have not attempted to contest our crossing anywhere. We have entire confidence in the success of the campaign wherever it may lead us and will give a good account of the rebels if we find them.

I have been bridge building for the last week, Sheridan having ordered me to throw a bridge over the Tennessee to cross his Division.

My Brigade cut down 1,500 trees and with the assistance of three companies of Engineers, put up the bridge 400 yards long in four days. The weather is very hot but being in a mountain region we get more air and suffer less than we did last Summer. We shall have a hot march and expect to melt some of our men. If the rebels give us another long chase as they did in July, we shall feel like annihilating them.

I received yesterday, Buel's letter of august 27th written at Westville. She tells me that you are well enough to take long walks and enjoy them . I am glad to hear this and wish I could be near to give you my arm in some of them. I hope to see you before the month is out. Rosecrans dined with me a day or two before leaving Bridgeport and voluntarily renewed his promise that I should have leave of absence after this movement was ended. I shall not delay the request after the proper time comes. I meet the "Old Chief " frequently and find him very chatty and pleasant. He possesses remarkable vivacity and exuberance of spirits making him one of the pleasantest companions I have me in the Army. He has a large vein of humor in him and indulges it freely when not occupied with weight matters.

I send you another photograph which I had taken to exchange with friends. I think it the best I have taken and hope you will like it.

Direct letters the same as formerly and tell the girls to write often: I received but <u>two</u> letters from home in August.

Give my best love to Mary, Rebecca, Buel and the children.

Yours ever,

Luther

CAMP OF THE 3rd BRIGADE,
Look-out Valley, Georgia
Sept. 8, 1863

My dear Buel,

Yours of August 27 th reached me just after leaving Bridgeport. I am glad to know that you are enjoying your Summer visit in the country and wish I could be with you for a few tramps over the hills. I am having enough of tramping and enough hill practice but I would like a little change of scene and society. I hope Mother still continues well and that she will be rejuvenated by the country air. You will see by the papers which tell all that happens in a military way and a good deal more that we are moving south again. Just a year from the time we crossed the Tennessee at Decatur going North; we crossed again at Bridgeport, going South. We built a temporary bridge and passed our Division over on the 2nd inst. After a night's halt we struck out for this valley crossing a high mountainous country with the steepest ridges I have ever seen. East and West Rocks are nothing to these spurs of the Cumberlands . It took half a day to get my battery one mile with ten horses to a gun and our teams suffered materially, some of them rolling down the mountains and literally going to smash. After great labor we got over the ridge twelve miles in extent and descended into this quiet little valley having Look-Out mountain on one side and Raccoon Mountain on the other. If there is any place on earth one would choose to be out of the way of Armies it is just this little nook shut in by high mountains almost impassable and yet here we are much to the astonishment of the few people who remain at home.

We have flanked Chattanooga being now some thirty miles south west of it and we hold the passes in the mountains leading toward Dalton where the rebels are supposed to be concentrating so that we can advance on them or keep marching south toward Rome, flanking their present position and compel them to leave that. I think the rebels will collect their forces at or near Atlanta and try to defend that point and very likely a severe battle will come off there but I do not believe it will be fought very soon. I do not believe it is Rosecrans policy to press them to a battle now but to make them retire from the neighborhood of the river so that he can rebuild the bridges and use the railroad to supply his Army. The rebels are growing weaker every day so that delays hurt them and not us. As soon as our railroad communications are resumed we can advance and fight them.

The mail boy is just leaving and I may not have a chance to send again for some days so I must close. Give my best love to dear Mother and all the others.

Yours ever,

"Col."

128

My dear Mother,

I must write you a few lines today though I use my arm with diff iculty. I arrived here last night and immediately telegraphed Lucius. I instructed one of my officers to telegraph you as soon as possible after I was wounded and have no doubt he made every effort to do so but the wires were almost constantly in use by Headquarters.

I had a tedious, painful journey over the mountains to Bridgeport lying on my back in an ambulance and when I reached here was about tired out. I had a friend with me who took the best care of me.

My wounds are doing well and a few weeks will heal them up. The ball is still in my right arm but strange enough, does not disable it.

The surgeon advises me to take a good rest here and I think I shall spend most of the week.

I will write you again in a day or two and let you know when I start for home.

Love to all,

Yours ever,

Luther

Louisville, October 2, 1863

My dear Mother,

I left Nashville yesterday and reached here safely last night. The journey did not fatigue me as much as I expected. My rest in Nashville having restored my strength inn good measure. I am getting on surprisingly well and expect to be able to take the field again in a few weeks. The wound in my hip is going finely and I can already walk pretty well with a crutch and cane. My arm scarcely troubles me at all though I suppose the ball is still in there.

I shall leave for Chicago this P.M. And reach there tomorrow (Saturday) morning. shall rest there two days and then join you as soon as possible. I should go directly east from here but I have some business I wish to attend to in Chicago and I don't know when I shall have so good an opportunity. Don't be impatient at the delay for I shall make you a good long visit when I get there.

You ought to be glad that I am wounded for it gives me a long leave of absence without any danger of permanent injury.

I intend to leave Chicago for the East on the 5th and if I am able to go through without stopping shall reach home by the 8th. I will telegraph from New York when I reach there.

With best love to all.

Every Yours,
Luther

Chicago, November 18 , 1863

My dear Buel,

I am afraid you will scold me for not writing sooner. I sent a hurried note to Mother the other day to assure here of my safe arrival here.

My friends have occupied my time constantly since I came back so that you have been neglected though not forgotten.

Our letter, also one from Mary and a little note from Tady, reached me safely. Much obliged for your prompt remembrance of me. My trip from the East was a pleasant one though devoid of interest. Mrs. Woodruff did not come out with me, she being quite ill when I was in New York. Mrs. Livingston sends her love and thanks for your gift. She is quite delighted with it.

I am as well as when I left you and shall leave for the Army the day after "Thanksgiving". It occurs here the same day a.s with you so you may remember me over your turkey.

I am going to Springfield tomorrow to see Judge Fuller, the Adjt . General who manages all the military affairs of the State. I saw him here a few moments the day after I arrived. He spoke of the Brigade very flatteringly and said he should urge my promotion at Washington. I find my friends here have already taken this matter in hand and though I do not like this way of doing it cannot well object, as they are acting in all kindness to me and, as they say, by advice of General Sheridan.

They have already got letters of recommendation to the President from Generals Rosecrans, McCook, Sheridan, Palmer and Wood. Also official reports of battles of "Stone Riv er" and "Chickamauga" in which I am mentioned. These they will put into the hands of Mr. Arnnold M.C. From this City to be laid before the President. I write you this because it will interest you to know that my friends are doing for me what I would not do for myself. The kindness and good feeling which prompts this action on the part of my friends and my superior officers is as pleasant to me as anything that could happen and I shall be content if I do not get the promotion. For all these testimonials are pretty strong I do not count upon their success. There are dozens of others whose chances are just as good who will fail of the prize. Do not say anything of this out of the family.

131

My object in going to Springfield is to make arrangement for recruits. Illinois has to furnish about 15,000 under the recent call. Of course, she wants to raise them by volunteering if possible.

I am going to make the proposition to re-enlist my Regiment for three years, upon condition that they allow me to bring it home and fill it up this Winter. I can do this if the Secretary of War will authorize it, which by the way is very doubtful. There is less likelihood of a movement at Chattanooga than I thought when at home, at least, an early movement. So I judge from what I learn here. This induces me to make the above proposition. I will write you again on my return from Springfield.

Give my best love to dear Mother, Mary, Rebecca, Annie, Tady, and the boys. Regards to all the people on Olive Street.

Yours ever,
Col.

Chattanooga December 10th, 1863

My dear Buel,

I wrote you last from Louisville, about ten days since. I spend a few days in Nashville with four of the officers of the 51st, who are sick and wounded. After leaving there I had a tedious time, the facilities for getting to Chattanooga being neither frequent, or pleasant. I stopped in Stevenson one day, and found my black boy and horses fill glad to see me. My animals have fared badly being nearly, starved for a month. "Salem" is no in tolerable condition, but "Tramp" my find black, is nearly, if not quite spoiled. He was reduced so low for want of feed that he got sick, and it will be a long time before he is good for anything, if he ever is. My boy was glad to see me and the honest fellow told me that he had dreamed about me while I was gone. I have him and Salem with

me here. I found only about fifty of the regiment here in camp, the division being absent. Those remaining are wounded and sick. I had a warm welcome from all and many expressions of satisfaction from my men at the return. I have been pleased at meeting men here, and at Nashville and Stevenson whom I did not know, but who accosted me with "How do you do, Col." or "Am glad to see you back sir, Have you got well", I'd answer, "I don't remember you, what regiment are you with", "Oh, I'm of such and such a regiment". I saw you at Chickamauga. One black fellow came up to me, hat in hand, and grinning wide. I shook hands and said, "Well Bob, how are you" - "Spec, you don't know me sir, I helped you to the hospital". Mighty glad to see yer back ". I miss a great many familiar faces, that I shall never see again. Chickamauga, and Mission Ridge, have told terribly on the Brigade. Seven Hundred men, and on hundred ten officers killed and wounded in the two battles. Johnson of whom you heard me speak as my Aid de Camp died night before last from wounds received at Mission Ridge. He was as gallant a fellow as ever drew a sword and a kind and amiable gentleman. Davis is now lying in camp quite low from a wound in the leg received at the same time. He fell at the head of the Regiment near the top of the mountain. He will recover with good care, but there is danger that his leg will be permanently injured. He is now Lt. Col. And well deserves the promotion. He sends his love to all of you.

You wonder perhaps that I can think of re-enlisting with my men, but the companionship of such men is enough to make the service tolerable.

There was enough gallantry and heroism displayed inn the late battle to redeem a hundred failures.

Citt er, the color bearer of the 27th went ahead of his Regiment at the storming of the ridge, and was shot six times , galling twice, but each time jumping up and pushing ahead, and finally coming down near the crest , with his leg broken by a grape shot. The gallant fellow is still living, and all who pray, ought to pray for his recovery. But this is only one of a hundred cases.

There is little prospect of my proposition succeeding, so you need not feel any alarm.

Love to all.

Yours,
Col.

One night during a thunderstorm, it was
difficult to tell which made the most
noise, the artillery of heaven or earth.

1864

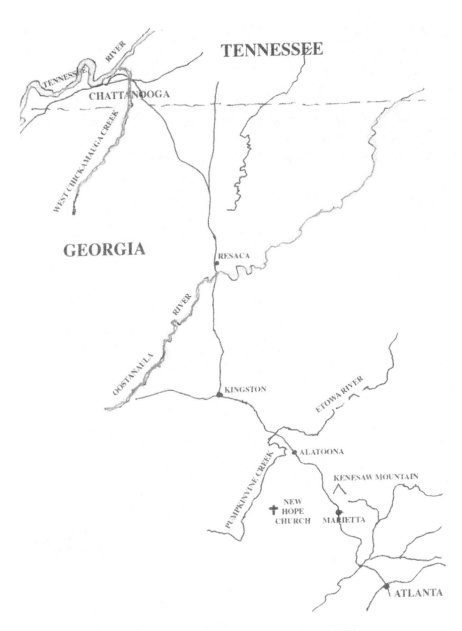

CHATTANOOGA TO ATLANTA

Knoxville, January 8, 1864

My dear Buel,

I got tired of leading an idle life at Chattanooga and started my steamer up the Tennessee on the 4th reaching here last evening. I shall go out to the front tomorrow and join the Regiment. They are now some twenty-miles north east of here.

Longstreet is facing our troops but probably not in great force. Our people are preparing to advance and feel of him but it is not thought that he will fight. It is very cold here and has been for two weeks. The ground is covered with snow and one might easily believe himself in the "frozen north" instead of the "sunnysouth". Our men are suffering greatly from want of sufficient food and clothing and the want of these makes the cold all the worse to bear. We have no tents, but few overcoats or socks, and generally but half rations. I doubt if the stories told of the sufferings of our troops during the winters of the Revolution much exceed the experience of the men now serving in East Tennessee. I have seen plenty of our men without shoes and nearly half their clothing torn from them by the wear of service. This comes not for want of clothing or food but for want of transportation to bring it to us. One little steamer is all that can be spared to run from Chattanooga to this point and that cannot half supply the troops here.

Probably our corps-the 4th will return to Chattanooga soon and go into quarters for the balance of the Winter. The old Regiments are nearly all re-enlisting as veterans and several are on their way home now. The 42nd has re-enlisted entire and I am told the 22nd and 51st have nearly all gone in. I am glad of this for it shows a fine spirit in the men who have suffered so much.

You need not be alarmed about my being kept longer in service, as officers are not held for the new term of service unless they choose.

I do not get letters from any of you although I suppose you write. I have had but three letters from home since I left Chicago November 27th; two from you and one from Mary.

Do write me often and trust to luck for letters getting to me. Direct, "51st Illinois, Chattanooga".

Give my best love to dear Mother, all the others sharing.

Yours ever,

Col

Knoxville, January 16, 1964

My dear Mother,

Your letter of December 8th reached me after I had joined the Regiment having passed me at Chattanooga. I thank you dear Mother for your kind words and wishes. Nothing is dearer to me than your confidence and love and it is my constant wish and effort to deserve it. If I ever win any credit in the world, it will be my chief pleasurethat it will gratify you. I am not ambitious of distinction so that I have the good opinion of my friends as one who has done his duty in his sphere, I am content.

I have been out to the front for a week and received a cordial welcome from Sheridan and other officers. The Army is quiet at present; just watching Longstreet to see that he does not do any mischief. The troops are having a hard time bivouacking without tents and almost without rations.

My Regiment had re-enlisted before I joined them and two days since I got the order for them to return home for a furlough of thirty days to recruit and reorganize. I came in here yesterday intending to return to Chattanooga by way of the river. The Regiment left at the same time and will march to Chattanooga. It will take them a week to reach there and we shall then have ten days good work to get our papers made out and the Regiment mustered and paid. We shall not reach home before the 10 th or 15th of February and we have 30 days after we reach the State. The men are all very happy at the prospect of going home and started on the march in the highest spirit. I shall be very busy while at home reorganizing the Regiment, etc. but shall find time to make you a short visit toward the last of February. The Regiment re-enlisting does not increase my term of service;the officers are "mustered out" at the expiration of their time unless they wish to remain.

I wrote to Rebecca and Buel a few days since and will write to Mary soon. Direct to me at Chattanooga until February 1st. After that to Chicago, care of Munson.

So with the respect of seeing you again soon, dear Mother, I bid you good bye.

With love to all.

Your ever,

Luther

CHATTANOOGA, January 24, 1864

My dear Buel,

Yours of the 16 th came today and the letter of Christmas enclosing Mrs. Livingston's, a few days since. I presume my letters from Knoxville and beyond have reached you so that you will not be surprised at my writing again from Chattanooga.

I left Knoxville one week ago and reached here three days since, coming by way of the River.

My Regiment has re-enlisted as I wrote, and is marching down. I expect them tomorrow when I shall set about the business of re-mustering and in ten days hope to have them on the way to Illinois. You have expressed so many hopes that my Regiment would not re-enlist that I suppose you will be disappointed at the announcement. To me it is a matter of unmissed pleasure. It not only shows the best of spirit among the fine fellows who have seen so much hard service and who re-enlisted when they were half starved and frozen, but it is a compliment to their officers that they are eager to serve another term under them.

There is one thing you do not seem to understand. I do not re-enlist with the Regiment any my status as an officer is not changed in the least. I can go out at the end of my term of service the same as before. The Government makes this distinction between officers and men, rightly considering the latter the most valuable. Nearly all my men who are not disabled will re-enlist. We shall get two or three hundred from the State and during the coming summer a considerable number of Veterans from other Regiments that do not go in entire, so that we have the prospect of soon filling up a full and fine Regiment.

If we reach Illinois early in February as I expect I shall be on East for a short visit sometime during the month. The Regiment will be furloughed for thirty days but I shall have a good deal to do meantime, recruiting and reorganizing.

Col. Davis started for Nashville on the Hospital train day before yesterday. He was much improved having to rid of the pains which have been tormenting him for two months, but still very weak not being able to support himself on crutches. He will stay in Nashville until the Regiment goes home.

You spoke in a late letter of sending me a copy of one of Tibbie's, givingan account of some exploit in Poland. Have not received it yet, neither Lucius or Rebecca's of which you make mention. Tell Rebecca I wrote her from East Tennessee, also Mother and Mary.

I am in very good health with a little of the old lameness in my hip. the girls. Give my best love to Mother and all the family. Regards to Mr. & Mrs. Band

Your,

Col

Chattanooga, February 6th, 1864

My dear Buel,

Your letters of the 18th and 29th January are received. One from Mary and yours of the 15 th. I acknowledged in my last. I have not yet received those from Lucius and Rebecca which I regret as they write so seldom. I have not either had any explanation of that feat of Tibbie's to which allusion is made In your letters; pray enlighten me.

I wrote to Mother and Mary a few days since telling them they might expect me home for a short visit the latter part of the month. My Regiment will "Muster-in" as Veterans tomorrow north with me on the 10th. We shall be detained a day in Nashville and a day in Louisville and reach Chicago about the 15th. I shall go to Springfield immediately on my arri val and may be detained there some time. I will write you as soon as I reach home that you may know when to expect me. I have no doubt what your say of the rudeness of the returned Veterans is all true. War is a rough trade and calculated to improve men in manners or perfect them in the polite accomplishments. Men when removed from the restraints of home and society are but boys of a larger growth. I am sorry your soldiers have carried home their camp manners but after two years of exposure and hardship and self-denial, I am not surprised that they indulge themselves in their newly acquired liberty and wealth. I have little fear of my boys. They are pretty well behaved generally and I shall expect them to keep up the reputation of the Regiment while at home. An officer of the Pay Department who has paid us for the last year said today amonga lot of officers that mine was the quietest and best disciplined Regiment he every saw. So you see what I claim for them may be true.

Your anxiety about Knoxville will be allayed now that I amout of it but you need have no fears for those who remain there if you happen to have any interest in them.

Longstreet has no idea of another siege and our people would welcome a second attack. I couldn't but wish he would try it when we were up there. The place is beautifully adapted for defense, and I think I should like to fight once behind fortifications but having got out of East Tennessee I have no desire to return to it and I sincerely hope our Corps will be ordered back before we return to the field.

I wish you would not cherish forebodings of evil concerning me. I think my good fortune thus far might give you confidence in events if not in a good providence. I have a great mind to send a sweet letter I received from Miss Noble today; really considering her loss and her sorrow, one of the best letters I ever read. She says of Moody "deeply as his loss will be mourned by all of his friends, I do not think there is one who would call him back from the rest he has so nobly won. For myself-in the midst of all my sorrow- there comes a feeling of thanksgiving that hissacrifice has been required of me for the dear land. I think I can truly saythat were it possible to retrace the events of the last two years and I had it in my power to influence in the slightest degree my friend's decision as to embracing a soldier's life, I would say 'Go' even if I foresaw the certainty of what was always a say possibility.· I shall be very certain to call on this lady when I come East and I will show you her whole letter then.

You say something in a late letter ab-pit the recruiting of Negro Regiments in your neighborhood and about the improved social status of the "niggars" generally and intimate that you think the reform is taking a little toorapid a pace. Well it may be. It's the tendency of reforms to go to extremes. You have got to get used to some new notions and habits, however, and you must not be surprised if they are thrust on you a little rudely. It's the penalty we must pay for long years of indignity. I am not a believer in "spec ial providence's" but I do believe in the law of compensations.

Isn't it strange though that this poor despised niggar should be put forward as a champion of freedom, and actually invested with the warriors armor and learned to fight, patted on the back by those who used to cuff him andpromised all sorts of good things if he behaves well; - what a grand up-heaving and overturning of old opinions and prejudices.

It suite me. I do not like war and str ife and bloodshed but I am willing to follow this life a little longer if I can help this poor "niggar" into a position where he can serve God and himself a little while, judging that he hasserved man longenough.

I don't believe in the quality of races but I do believe in fair play and in human rights and I believe all men are entitled to these two things. The capabilities of the black race have always been depreciated and we have something to unlearn in this. Making them soldiers is going to do more to elevate and dignify them than anything else, -more, even, than the elective franchise. War is a manly art and they take to it naturally as white men.

One of these days some "Petione" or "Dessalaines" or "Christophe" will arise and the world will wonder where the deuce he came from. There are some queer developments coming in the future and among them will be that which removes the curse from color.

Write me as soon as you receive this, care of Munson, Chicago.

Give my best love to dear Mother, Mary, Rebecca and the children. Regards to Mr. and Mrs. Baldwin and the "Young Ladies".

Yours ever,

Col.

P.S. - I send photograph of Gen. Lytle killed at Chickamauga, author of the fine lyric "Anthony & Cleopatra".

Anthony and Cleopatra

Lytle's most famous poem, 1858:
   I amdying. Egypt, dying!

Ebbs the crimson life-tide fast,
And the dark Plutonian shadows
Gather on the evening blast;
Let thine arm, oh Queen, enfold me,
Hush thy sobs and bow thine ear,
Listen to the great heart secrets
Thou, and thou alone, must hear.

Though my scarred and veteran legions
Bear their eagles high no more,
And my wrecked and scattered galleys
Strew dark Actium's fatal shore;
Though no glitteringguards surround me,
Prompt to do their master's will,
I must perishlikea Roman ,
Die the great Triumvir still.

Let not Caesar's servile minions,
Mock the lion thus laid low;
"I was no foreman's arm that felled him,
"I was his own that struck the below -
His who, pillowed on thy bosom,
Turned aside from glory's ray -
His who, drunk with thy caresses,

143

Madly threw a world away.

Should the base plebeian rabble
Dare assail my name at Rome,
Where the noble spouse, Octavia,
Weeps within her windowed home,
Seek her; say the gods bear witness -
Altars, augurs, circling winds, -
That her blood, with mine commingled,
Yet shall mount the thrones of kings.

And for thee, star-eyedEgyptian -
Glorious sorceress of the Nile!
Light the path to Stygian horrors
With the splendors of thy smile;
Give the caesar crowns and arches,
Let his brow the laurel twine,
I can scorn the senate's triumphs,
Triumphing in love like thine.

I am dying, Egypt, dying;
Harkl The insultingforeman's cry;
They are coming; quick, my falcon!
Let me front them ere I die.

Ah, no more amidthe battle
Shall my heart exultingswell;
Isis and Osiris guard thee, -
Cleopatra, Rome, farewelll

My dear Buel,

Your letter of the 15th with one from Mary came to hand last night. I wrote a few lines to Mother the other day announcing my arrival here and have been too busy since to write you.

I left Chattanooga wit h the Regiment on the 10th inst. Reached Nashville next day, spent one day there and went on to Louisville and Sunday the 14 th reaching Indianapolis next, thence on to Chicago where we arrived on the afternoon of the 16th. We were very kindly welcomed here. A party of gentlemen came out as far as Michigan City to meet us and a very nice and substantial dinner was provided for the Regiment with a band of music, speeches etc. arrangements had been made to give us an escort through the City, but this was omitted on account of the extreme cold. I furloughed the men on the 17th and started them off to their homes with light hearts and pockets full of money.

We rendezvous here at Camp Fry at the end of thirty days. Meanwhile we are to recruit as far as we can. I went to Springfield on the 18th and received orders to remain on duty here with a part of my officers, the balance being stationed in different parts of the State. I shall not be confined to Chicago but shall have a good deal of running about to do superintendingthe recruiting.

I shall start for the East about the last of March and spend a few days with you. You can expect but a few days for I have plenty of work here and of a kind that must not be neglected.

I brought Col. Davis home with me and he is doing well. He will probably come East with me on his way to Mass. If so, I shall have him stop over a day in New Haven.

He sends kind regards to you all as does Mrs. Livingston.

With best love to dear Mother and all the others. In haste,

Yours ever,

Col.

My dear Buel,

Yours of the 14 th has just arrived. I wrote a short letter to Mother some days ago to tell her of mysafe return. I have been very busy since I got back and am now constantly on the go up and down, getting ready to put the Regim ent in Camp. We rendezvous here tomorrow tho it is not likely we shall get off before the end of next week, on account of the difficulty of gettingtransportation. The large number of troops comingand going keep the roads busy even beyond their ordinary capacity. We go back to the Department of the Cumberland of course.

I see by the papers amongthe probable charges in the Army, the return of Rosecrans to the Army of the Cumberland and the removal of Gordon Granger from the command of the 4th Corps. Two changes I would like much to see. It would seem that Grant was preparing for vigorous work this spring and from his past success, we have a right to expect great results. If he can take the Army of the Potomac out of the "Slough of Despond" in which it has been wading for three years he will have a better title to fame than any he has yet earned. He needn't trouble himself much about one Army; - they'll occupy Georgia when it is wanted. If we have had some checks we have never retrograded.

I did go to see Miss Nolle in Brooklyn. She received me very kindly and I had a pleasant visit. Miss Nolle is not a handsome woman but she is a cult ivated and refined woman, which is better. She talked much of Moody and thoroughly appreciated his fine character.

I am sorry to hear of Mrs. Galpin's sever illness. I remember her very well.

Give my best love to dear Mother, Mary, Rebecca and the children. Will write again soon. In haste,

Yours ever

Luther

Nashville, April 3, 1864

My dear Buel,

We have got thus far on our journey southward. Reached here on the morning of the 1st, three days from Chicago.

Livingston came down with me and will go on to Huntsville to see Mrs. Breck, sister of Mrs. Livingston. Thus far our trip hasbeen very pleasant but the finale does not promise well. Owing to crowd of freight on the Chattanooga Railroad no troops are transported south. All the veteran Regiments are ordered to march through, -151 miles. This will be a tedious and profitless march as it will be without the excitement of a campaign,- just so much ground to be got over. I shall start tomorrow with my own Regiment, the 75th New York and the 77 th Pennsylvania and shal l be 15 or 20 days on the way as many of the men are recruits and it will not do to march them fast. We follow the line of the Railroad and stop at Murphreesboro, Tullahoma and Bridgeport. After reaching Chattanooga we may have to march to London, another 100 miles, so we are likely to have exercise enough, you see.

I met Gen. Sheridan in Louisville on his way to Washington to take command of the Cavalry of the Potomac Army as it is supposed. The announcement is now made in the New York papers and I presume it is correct.

The Army of the Potomac will be strengthened by Sheridans presence, but we shall lose one of our finest officers and I shall lose the influence and companionship of a personal friend. It seems as though it was Grant's policy to break up the old Army in which we have taken so much pride and in which we have done so much hard work. If such a policy is to be carried out I would like to go to some new fie ld myself. It is not known who will succeed to the command of our Division but whoever it is, he can scarcely fill Sheridan's place. We take no baggage on the march I may not have an opportunity to write to you again before we reach Chattanooga. So do not be anxious if no letters come for three weeks. I will write as soon as I can in any case.

The weather is mile and Spring like and we are likely to have a pleasant trip so far as that goes.

Write me at Chattanooga. Give my best love to Mother, Mary, Rebecca and the children. Regards to Mr. and Mrs. B- and the girls.

Yours ever,

Col.

CHATTANOOGA, April 20, 1864

Mydear Mother,

We reached here on the 17th having been nearly two weeks on the way from Nashville. I made very easy marches not to overtire our recruits and they came through in pretty good order. The march was tedious and fatiguing and the weather much of the t time very bad, - rainy and cold.

I am ordered to Cleveland, Tennessee, thirty miles from here and shall go up in a day or two. Am drawing new arms and outfits for the Regiment and shall have them all in good order in a short time.

I found letters here from Buel. I will write you again more fully as soon as I get settled in Cap.

Give my best love to all.

Yours ever,

Luther

Catoosa Springs, Geo.

May 6, 1864

My dear Mother,

We reached here yesterday having left Cleveland, Tennessee on the 24 th . The whole Army is in motion and is concentrating around here preparatory to a move on Dalton.

We have a very large Army, much larger than was ever seen in this part of the country before. Our Corps, the 4th , forms the left wing and McPherson with the 15 th and 16 th Corps, the right, Thomas and Hooker having the centre. The rebels are supposed to be at Dalton but they cannot fight this Army there and I do not believe we shall have a battle before we reach the Coosa, if then. We cannot advance much beyond Dalton now, for want of rations which have to be brought from Chattanooga by wagon. We have got to build the Railroad to Dalton before we can go far South. And this will take considerable time. We are all in fine health and condition and looking forward to a successful campaign.

The weather is pleasant; the country beautiful and the roads excellent. We are without teams or baggage of any kind so that my means of writing are quite limited. I will write again from the next Camp.

Give my best love to Mary, Rebecca, Buel and the children. And with a bountiful share for yourself, dear Mother, I say good bye.

Yours ever,

Luther

Rocky Face Mountain, Geo.

May 11, 1864

My dear Buel,

I know you will all be anxious to hear from me now that the Army is in motion. I wrote to Mother a few days back. We are in front of the rebel army and pressing it at all points. I shall not write you what we have done or expect to do lest the letter go astray. It is enough to say that we have all the force we want and shall beat the rebels if they stand a fight.

Our Brigade has suffered considerably already in taking this mountain which was obstinately defended. "Rocky Face" is the worst piece of mountain I have ever seen, - 2,460 feet above the level of the sea, - and as rough and rocky as it is possible for ground to be. We had to scale the side of the mountain, skirmishing with the enemy and had severe fighting on the top. We are within plain sight of Dalton and expect soon to be in there. Thus far my Regiment has suffered but little and I hope I may be able to bring them out of the battle without such loss as we had at Stone River and Chickamauga. I am yet doubtful whether the rebels will stand a battle here. Sherman is drawing the net around them and if he defeats them here will cut them up badly before they reach the Coosa. Do not worry about me. I shall not be rash in any case in exposing myself, and, I want you all to be hopeful of the result. In case of any injury to myself you shall know it as soon as possible.

We are having a rough time. Our trains are all in the rear and no officer has anything but what he can carry. So we have hard work and poor fare. But it will soon end.

Give my best love to dear Mother, Mary, Rebecca, Lucius and the children.

Yours ever,

Luther

Altoona Mountain, Geo.

May 25, 1864

My dear Mother,

I have written home quite frequently of late in order to quiet your apprehensions for my safety. We have had a good deal of hard fighting and have suffered considerably but have had no general battle and it is doubtful now whether we shall have one.

We are on the highest point of the Altoona Mountains, the last of the high ridges in Northern Georgia. Here we expect to find the rebel army in force but they are gone and have not left even a rear guard to oppose our passage. We are within 35 miles of Atlanta and it is reported the rebels are leaving there for some point farther South. If they do not meet us at Atlanta the campaign will end for the present, I think, as it will not be practicable to pursue much beyond there on account of the difficulty of subsisting the Army.

If we do not beat the rebels in a general battle we at least take a large amount of territory with two of their most important arsenals, besides numerous iron and salt-peter works. We have taken a large number of prisoners and deserters. In one instance an entire Regiment came in with their Officers and surrendered themselves and they uniformly report that there is general dissatisfaction in the army and a desire to get out of it but discipline keeps them in their places as all offenders are short without mercy.

We are strong in the hope that we shall make the campaign an entire success and bring this confounded ware somewhat nearer to a close. At any rate we have circumscribed its limits and in time we shall drive the rebels into the Gulf. We have now been out 22 days without baggage, tents or even a change of clothes. We are ragged, and - not clean and I somewhat doubt if my own Mother would know me if she were to see me.

I find myself very nearly tired out with constant marching, watching and fighting, but I am well and strong enough to go through the campaign. Do not, I beg of you, allow yourself fears concerning my safety. I shall be in danger at times, unquestionably, but I do not believe you would withdraw me from the conflict if you could for fear of harm comingto me. really on your courage as much as on my own.

I hear from you but seldom now as our mail facilities are not the best. In a letter of Buel's she tells me you have been quite sick for a time but through quiet and good nursing are now better for which I am very thankful. Give my best love to Mary, Rebecca, Buel, Lucuis and the children. I will write from our next camp.

Yours lovingly,

Luther

New Hope Church, Geo.

June 4, 1864

My dear Buel,

This is a rainy day and I take advantage of the comparative quiet to write you a few lines to assure you of my safety. I received yours of the 25ᵗʰ May two days since and one from Mary about the same time. I have written as often as was possible up to this time but writing here is not an easy matter. We have now been out a month and have seen our wagons but once in that time. We have nothing but what we can carry on our horses and, of course, not much paper. Our campaign has been successful thus far and weshall push it to a final success. We have had a good deal of hard fighting and considerable losses but we have punished the enemy severely. The 51st has had 35 killed and wounded amongthem one of my best officers, Capt. Tom Lester, killed at Resaca . Our Brigade has lost heavily compared with others, the casualties number over 500 . As usual we have been in all the fighting up to this time and I hope it may be more evenly distributed hereafter.

I am entirely well but very tired. We have no rest night or day and do not expect any until the campaign is ended. I cannot tell you anything of our intended movements now but after the campaign Is over I will give you all the particulars of interest.

I am exceedingly glad that Mother is better. I wrote to her a few days since. Give her my best love and a kiss. The same to Mary, Rebecca, Amie, Tady and the boys. Write often and send me N.Y. Papers occasionally.

With best love,

Yours ever,

Luther

Ackworth, Ga.

June 8th , 1864

Dear Mary,

Your weekly letters come with tolerable regularity, and are very welcome.

I have written home as often as was possible duringthe last month though not as often as you wished, very likely.

We are resting for a couple of days after the late hard work at New Hope. We shall push tomorrow toward the Chattahoochee the last natural obstacle between us and Atlanta. We have had a most difficult and dangerous campaign. You may judge of the part we have taken in it from our losses. Our Brigade has lost 25 percent of its force, killed and wounded, and this without a general battle. Thus far we have been completely successful, obliging the rebels to leave every position where they were strongly entrenched and they are still going south in search of a position where we cannot flank time. We shall have Atlanta soon, with or without a battle, and then I hope the campaign will end for we are all tired out. Thirty-five days of constant marching and fighting are enough to make anyone longfor peace and quiet. For the last twelve days we have not had an hour in the twenty-four without fighting within rifle shot of our main line of works, the men lying in the trenches day and night to escape shots which came over. It has rained often so as to fill the trenches to the depth of half a foot and still we have had to stay in them. Almost every night we have had a flurry to keep us awake half the time, either an attack or skirmish in which the guns, big and little, would join and make a most infernal din. One night we had a sharp fight during a thunder storm and it was a grand affair. We had 20 pieces of Artillery playing with some thousands of rifles and it was difficult to tell which made the most noise, the artillery of heaven or earth. A night battle is impressive.

We are now south of the mountain ranges of Georgia, and the country improves in appearance as we advance. We shall soon have fruit and vegetables of which we are much in need. Our regular diet is coffee, hard bread and bacon without variation. As you are interested in sanitary questions I will tell you that wehave <u>scurw</u> in almost every Regiment and we are trouble to cure it as we have no antiscorbutics.

I have escaped all the ills of camp like as I do generally and am in fine health. Give my best love to dear Mother, Rebecca, Buel and the children.

Regards to Mrs. Patrick.

Yours ever,

Col.

Ackworth, Geo.
June 13, 1864

My dear Mother,

This is a wet, gloomy Sunday. We are laying idle in camp with no disturbance except a little fighting on the picket line and a few cannon shots occasionally from some part of our lines. We move up here from New Hope Church three days since and have fortified a line in front of the new position of the rebels. They are also fortified with the intention of stopping our further advance but the maneuver will fail. A part of our Army is holding our lines while the balance is making a flank march to turn the rebel position and oblige them to leave it and cross the Chattahoochee. Once across the river they are out of the way of troubling our railroad communications and we can follow them at our leisure. We are re building the railroad as we advance. As I write, I can hear the whistle of the train from Chattanooga bringing supplies. The rebels in our front can hear it too and I think it must give them a new idea of Yankee energy and industry for the bridge over the Etowah, which they destroyed, we have built in ten days, and in ordinarytimes it would have taken thirty. One of the features of this campaign is that we have a construction train following the Army loaded with bridge timber and provided with workmen and tools to put up bridges and repair other damages in the quickest time possible. There is always a welcome cheer though the Army when the whistle is heard; the men being specially delighted at the arrival of the "Cracker Wagons" as they call the cars. We are now within 25 miles of Atlanta-a day's march. We shall reach them soon, though not in several days. Sherman is conducting the campaign safely and wisely, I think. More with a view to permanent results and occupancy of the country than fighting heavy battles. Thus far he has maneuvered Johnston out of every position without the loss of men a battle would cost, though of course, we have had a good deal of fighting and considerable losses without a general battle. I do not think the rebels will fight a general battle unless Sherman gives them the advantage of fortified position which I am quite sure he will not do.

They will probably retire before us impeding and harassing our march all they can and saving their army for more promising work.

I hope the campaign will end at Atlanta that we may get some rest for after 40 days of hard work we are sadly in want of it.

The June rains have set in much as they did last year during our Tullahoma campaign. It has rained for four days and promises to continue twenty more.

Last year it rained twenty two days consecutively. I am sorry to hear of Samuel's capture and am afraid he will have a hard time of it. There is little prospect of exchange being resumed soon. With best love to you all dear Mother, and assurances of my constant remembrance.

Every yours,

Luther

Kenesaw Mountain,

June 18, 1864

Dear Buel,

Your letters of May 25th and June 6th reached me safely. The mails come through regularly now and I think all your letters are delivered. I have written frequently to Mother, Mary, and yourself. This campaign is drawing out to such an unexpected lengththat we shall soon be out of writing materials as well as everything else except the bare necessaries which the Government furnishes. We are progressing slowly but surely and shall soon reach Atlanta, the objective point of the campaign. The rebels are contesting our advance with great obstinacy and ability. They have got the whole line of country from Dalton to Atlanta fortified and as fast as we drive them from their positions they retire to new ones already prepared. We have fought no great battle and are not likely to. It is not Johnston's policy to fight us in the open field, nor Sherman's to assault fortified positions with the whole army. We do though assault certain points when necessary to possess them or break the enemies line; the balance of the work is accomp lished by flank maneuvers which render the rebel posit ions unsafe if held, they would have to fight at a disadvantage. This kind of work brings on frequent small battles in which an Army Corps is engaged or general fighting from the main lines of works which are frequently with in 500 yards of each other.

The campaign is more like a huge siege than anything else as we have this same kind of work to do on every new position. It is most wearing work. The fatigue and the strain on the nerves from constant fighting and watching is enough to break down a strong man. Since the 15th of may we have been constantly under fire and three or four times in affairs that may be dignified by the name of battles. Night attacks are frequent and we are often out two or three times to repel them, losing the only chance we have for rest and sleep. For 47 nights past I have not undressed, sleeping on the ground, most of the time "booted and spurred" with my horse saddled near by, ready to mount any moment. For all this I am well and strong so I have no right to grumble and I don't. I write these particulars because you like to know them. We are looking forward to the occupancy of Atlanta as a time of rest and plenty.

The losses in the Army are heavy. My Regiment has lost sixty, which is less than the average in the Division. The Brigade has lost one third its force which is a large loss for any campaign. My best love to dear Mother and all the family. Tell Mother I will write her very soon. I which you would send me a few letter stamps in your next. I am out and cannot get them readily. Kind regards to Mrs. Patrick and Miss Beers.

Yours ever,

Col.

Kenesaw Mountain,

July 1st , 1864

My dear Buel,

We are still here under the shadow of the great Kenesaw in much the same position as when I wrote you last. Our lines of earthworks run nearly parallel with those of the rebels varying in the distance from two to five hundred yards. We are having constant fighting: the work being more like a siege than anything less. Heavy skirmishes, assaults, and artillery duels taking place on some parts of the lines every day. The rebels are very strongly posted and we have got to work them out of their position by slow approaches.

Their works are of such strength that we cannot carry them by assault except at immense cost.

I believe that Sherman is making his movements contingent on Grant's preferring to hold them here rather than bring the campaign to a close when the rebels would to a certainty reinforce Lee.

We are likely to move forward at any time but I do not believe we are to have any great battle. Our losses are already heavy enough without it. Since May 10 thour Brigade has been in three battles and twenty skirmishes losing over 1,000 killed and wounded. My own little Regiment has lost 104 men and 8 officers. I feel heavy hearted and I think of these sacrifices for we are terribly cut up. Day before yesterday the Brigade was ordered to assault the rebel works in our front, three assaulting columns being formed on different parts of the line to charge simultaneously. I did not like the looks of it from the time Harker told me what we were to do and I told him the chances were all against us for we know nothing of the works we were to assault except that they were strong and masked with thick woods through which we could not reconnoiter. I had command of the head of the column, four regiments, the 5151, and 27th Illinois and 3rd Kentucky and 65th Ohio, Harker having the four rear regiments. We moved out at a signal from the Artillery in fine style, entered the woods and soon crossed the ground between the lines, drove in the rebel pickets and took the fire of their guns as we came in sight ascending a hill onwhich rebel works stood. We dashed at that, planted our colors on the works, had a few minutes desperate fightingand were repulsed.

Harker was killed at my side as he was bringing his column up to sustain my shattered regiments. I held on to the ground until I saw the column on our right falling back and that any further effort there was useless and reluctantly gave the order to retire.

It was my first repulse and when I saw Harker's dead body with the hundreds of others stretched on the ground, I felt I would as like to be there with them as not. I don't know how I escaped. I was with the leading Regiment-the 51st - and Salem was badly shot. Brown, commanding my Regiment, Brenan commanding the 3rd Kentucky, Smith of the 27th and Whitbeck, Colonel of the 65th Ohio were all wounded. I lost 27 officers in all, Hall, McCormick, and Cummings of the 51st being among the killed and all the Regiments suffering severely.

Poor Harker! He was as gallant a fellow as ever lived and had just been promoted for gallantry in the field, but had never worn his star. But no death has come so near to as Hall's. He was a splendid fellow in all respects, by all odds the most capable man among us. With talents of the highest order, he had a perfect education and one of the finest tempers in the world. And if every a man was entitled to be crowned for heroism, it was he. His courage was something marvelous for its perfect coolness and steadiness. He fell at the head of the Regiment, pierced by eleven ball.

The 51st did not disappoint me. I placed them at the head of the column because I knew they would go through. They lost 47 in the charge. I now have the Brigade again succeeding to it as at Stone River by the death of its commander. We have but one Colonel left in the Brigade besides myself; Opdyke of the 125th Ohio and many of our best officers have fallen.

Salem has got a bad wound in the body and I am afraid he will not be fit to ride again. I am giving him good nursing and shall try to save him for he is a fellow of great sense and courage.

I received yours of the 20th of June a few days since and one from Mary about the same time. Am much obliged for the picture of Charlie. It is very good. Send me Tady and Lu's if Rebecca has them . I am still well though pretty tired and wanting rest. We expect to drive these rascals across the Chattahoochee soon, and then I think we shall take it easy for a while.

Give my best love to dear Mother, Mary, Rebecca and the children. Remember me to the Breer's and Baldwins when you see them.

Every yours,

Luther

Camp on the Chattahoochee

July 14, 1864

My dear Mother,

I received letters from Mary and Buel a day or two since which give me the comforting assurance of your health and welfare.

I wrote to Buel about the first of the month but have had no chance to write since. About the First of July the rebels left their position at Kenesaw Mountain, our lines being close on to them, in some places less than 200 yards distant. We immediately followed them up on the 4th drove them into a new line of works near the river. We put our batteries in position and had commenced a line of works when, during the night, we say symptoms of leaving and immediately advance and took possession of their works, - fil!lQ!Y, We formed and started in pursuit and before noon had the satisfaction of seeing the last of them across the Chattahoochee. We took a good many prisoners on the retreat, and, I think, demoralized the whole rebel army to some degree.

After resting a day our Division was sent up the river to Roswell, a fine manufacturing town, where were a number of very fine cotton and woolen mills making cloth for the rebel army: these we burned instantly though they had a French flag flying over them, a Frenchman being the nominal owner.

We crossed the river at Roswell fortified a position which we still hold. The Army is crossing at different points where bridges are built and in a few days we shall move on Atlanta. We can see the town plainly some ten miles off, and it looks like a very pretty place with its tall spires and brick blocks. I hope the rebels will not oblige us to destroy it by attempting to defend it and I don't think they will. We are in a better country than we have traveled though of late, some of the towns are extremely pretty and flourishing. Marietta especially would compare favorably with the neatest of our northern villages. The chief attraction is the abundance of foliage and flowers growing in tropical luxuriance; the magnolia being the Queen among them all. The "Cape Jessamine" grow and flowers as abundantly as the rose with us. I frequently have a handful of them, white and yellow, and often think I would like to transfer them to you. I sent you a curious flow I picked from a tree in Rosewell, an African tree, the "Miamosa". It is the prettiest and quite the most curious flowering tree I ever saw; growing to the size of a large apple tree, the leaf being precisely that of the Sensitive Plant and covered with flowers like little tassels of silk, the ends being a deep pink, the balance yellow, and so fragrant that they scent the whole air. The dry flower will show you something of their shape and that is all. You would revel in some of these rebel gardens if you were here and I've no doubt you'd despoil them as we do.

I hope and think the hardest of our work is over. We are so near Atlanta that it cannot be long before we have the town and then, I hope, we shall have rest. A great many of our officers and men are breaking down from sheer exhaustion. I am well as yet.

With best love to Mary, Rebecca , Buel, Amie, Tady and the body,

Ever yours,

Luther

Camp on the Chattahoochee,
Sunday July 17th, 1864

Mydear Mary,

I wrote you the latter part of June and have since written to Mother and Buel.

We have made some progress since I wrote you driving the rebels out of their last line of works north of the Chattahoochee on the 4th and over the river on the 5th. We have had some rest since then awaiting the building of bridges by the Engineers. We forded the river on the 12th and are now camped within sight of Atlanta.

The Army will move in a day or two and I do not think the rebels can keep us out of it many days though there are some considerable obstacles between us and our prize.

The rebel Army is in positi on on Peach Tree Creek about four miles from here where they have a strong line of works. We are all looking forward to the capture of Atlanta , as the end of the campa ign and a time of probable rest. Seventy odd days is a long time in such a life as we are leading with just enough of rest and comfort to keep us from breaking down altogether.

I do not think any Army ever had harder or more harassing work than we have had and I hope never to be engaged on such another campaign. Our service is less agreeable than last year from the fact that we have lost our old Commanders and in their place have a lot of unsuccessful Potomac Generals. None of these come up to our standard.

You ask me how I like Howard. Personally, I like him well enough but I do not like him as a General. He is a gentlemen in manners and has the reputation of being an eminent Christian but he is too ambitious and too reckless of the lives of his men to sustain this character consistently or to be a desirable or popular commander.

Ge. Sherman is an able man but hard, cold and unsympathetic. Thomas is our favorite. He is made up in a large mound; in mind, heart and body. Hooker excites more enthusiasm than any other man among us and he is always cheered when he is seen. His

record as a soldier is good and he is eminently handsome and distinguished in appearance. Schofield of the 23rd Corps; Palmer of the 14th and Logan of the 15th are fine officers and their commands have done well on this campaign. McPherson is over-rated and has too large a command.

I am glad that you have leisure and inclination to minister to the wants of the wounded. It is a patriotic and christian work. Our wounded have less care and attention than they deserve for the reason that we are so far from home. With one single and long line of railroad it is impossible to supply so large an Army as ours with rations and sanitary supplies in sufficient quantity.

We are suffering severely from scurvy owing to want of vegetables, etc. and although the West would willingly supply us they cannot be brought for want of transportation. This scorbutic condition is very unfavorable for wounded men and we lose a good many from this cause.

Will you be kind enough to mail the enclosed letter to Cousin Amelia: With best love to dear Mother, Rebecca, Buel and the others.

Yours ever,

Luther

PEACHTREE CREEK, GEORGIA

JULY 20, 1864

Camp near Atlanta,

July 21, 1864

My dear Buel,

Yours of the 11th reached me yesterday. I wrote you about the 1st of the month and have since written to Mother and Mary. Am still safe and well but longing for rest.

We are now within 3 ½ miles of Atlanta and McPherson on the left is within 1 ½ miles. So you see we have made some advance since I wrote you last and are likely to

go into town any day. We are direc tly in front of the town. That is, it is due south from us and Hooker and Palmer are on our right; McPherson and Scofield on our left. Yesterday we advanced on the rebels at sun-rise and crossed "Peach Tree Creek" under fi re, advancing southward with heavy skirmishing all day until about 3 P.M. When our skirmish line came on the rebel works. Our Division being alone on the road we formed line and commenced fortifying and it was well we did. Just as we had got a litt le pile of rails and dead trees laid up in front of the line, the rebels burst upon us in a perfect storm, having massed Bate's and Walker's Divisions in the woods very quietly, expecting to carry our position with a rush. Hooker joined our right but on the left there was a gap of two miles between us and the other divisions of our Corps; this the rebels soon found out and tried to turn this flank but after three hours fighting we drove them back with very heavy loss, holding all our own ground. It was just such an affair as that of the 27th June in which we suffered so heavily, only here the rebels were the sufferers, no we. The loss in our Division is about 100-Hooker, who had no works prepared lost 1,500. We took a large number of prisoners from Stewart's and Hardee's Corps, showing that both of those Corps were engaged and the ground in our front is strewn with dead and wounded rebels. Gen Stevens of Bates Division was killed Judging by the number of dead their loss must have been very heavy. I send you a notice of Gen. Harker from the pen of Taylor of Chicago. It is very neat and very just. It is singular how he had I were thrown together. I first saw him at Stone River duringthe hottest of the fight when McCook sent me in with the Brigade to check the rebels on the right who were driving our men; we found Harker's Brigade coming out in some confusion and immediately charged a rebel Brigade, relieving <u>him</u> and recovering two cannons which he had lost. He very soon came to me and thanked me for the service rendered and from that time we were friends.

At Chickamauga my Brigade was sent to his relief again. After the campaign was over he was transferred to Sheridan's Division and our Brigades were consolidated. No one welcomed me when I returned more cordially than he and he immediately gave me the command of my old Regiments. Harker was impetuously brave, taking no thought of danger and ambitious of success. His death was unnecessary and if he had listened to my advice on the 27th it would not have occurred. I say as soon as the head of my column had been crushed against the rebel works that they were too strongfor us and told the General this, but he could not brook the idea of defeat and he sacrificed himself and others in a vain attempt to lead the Regiments into the works.

Tell Mother I have more of the photographs like that sent to Cousin Mary. I will send to Chicago and have some more printed and send to you and herself.

Best love to all,

Ever yours,

"Col"

Near Atlanta, July 30th, 1864

My dear Mother,

I have just received notice from Gen. Sherman of my appointment as Brigadier General with the General's compliments.

I write you this at once as I know it will please you and the thought that it will please you, gives me as much pleasure as anything connected with the appointment. My ambition as a soldier is more than gratified in this rank and I hope you will all admit that if I fill this position well, I am doing quite enough.

I am still well and in good heart. We have had a good deal of hard fighting within the last ten days and we have beaten the rebels handsomely at all points. I do not think they can fight us hard again about here for their lossesin recent battles have been fearful; not less than 20,000 in ten days.

On the 20th they attacked our Division with Hooker's Crops in great force, while we were on the march, expecting to catch us at a disadvantage and rout us. They attacked with great fury and disconcerted us a little at first, but we beat them decidedly and completely. I have never been in any fight so satisfactory for everything worked just to our mind and our victory, though complete, was cheap, our loss being very light. I send you a slip giving an account of the engagement. We are drawing our lines around Atlanta and if the rebels do not leave soon, their chance of escape will be small.

I will write again in a few days and more at length. Today I am busy. With best love to all,

Your loving son,

Luther

Near Atlanta, August 2, 1864

My dear Buel,

I have not received a letter from you for some time and fear some of yours have gone astray.

I wrote you about ten days since and wrote Mother day before yesterday telling her of my promotion. This will please you all I have no doubt, and it is pleasing to me, especially for the manner in which it comes, the nomination being made by General Sherman and the appointment by the President without the aid of any outside influence. I am conscious of having earned it by hard and faithful service and I think no man in the Army will dispute my right to it. My friends here are very free in their congratulations and none seem more pleased than my own Regiment. They feel they share in the compliment and they have a right to do so for their gallantry and good conduct won me the Star.

Gen. Newton tells me that the appointment was made in this way. Generals Osterhaus and Hovey went home some weeks since and while on a visit to Washington got promoted to Major Generals. This did not please Sherman and he telegraphed the President that he thought it unfair to promote officers who left the field in the middle of a campaign and neglect those who remain in the front doing the work; that if the President considered Washington the post of honor he would send on some deserving officers. Mr. Lincoln immediately replied to send on his appointments and he would ratify them. Sherman sent on the names of eight Colonels in this Army and the order of appointment was made out.

My commission cannot be issued until appointment is confirmed by the Senate next Winter, but I am entitled to the rank and pay from date of appointment.

We are still in front of Atlanta having more or less fighting all the time; the right wing is doing most of the work and extending well round to the south side of the town to cut off the line of retreat by way of the Mason road. The rebels have been very quiet since the terrible whipping they got on the 25th and I do not thing they'll attack us again.

Hood took hold of the rebel army with great vigor and evidently intended to make a break it. He attacked us in force in the center on the 20th; the left wing on the 22nd; and the right wing on the 25 th and was repulsed with great loss at each point. His losses cannot have been less in the three battles than 20,000 and many of the superior officers of the Army whose opportunities for correct estimates are the best put the number at 25,000.

They cannot fight us in that way and I presume they will hold on to the position until we flank them when they will retreat. They are making a desperate effort to hold Atlanta and the Governor and people, and the Georgia troops, look upon the loss of this as the loss of the State. It is our, however, by right of superior strength as well as abstract right and we'll plant our flags there in spite of all Georgia.

I hope you are enjoying your summer holiday to the utmost. How I wish I could be with you for a few rambles in the woods. Give my best love to dear Mother, Mary, Rebecca, Ami, Tady and the boys.

Yours ever,

General

Thursday Morn, 5 o'clock, August 11, (1864)

My dear Child,

I send a letter which I received from Luther yesterday, announcing his promotion. It is but tardy <u>justice</u> and although I am glad his services are appreciated, still, I tremble lest he should be led into greater danger. But the same kind Providence which has carried him safely through so many dangers, is able <u>still</u> to protect and defend him. <u>To His care</u> we must commend him.

How are you this hot weather? I have suffered very much from heat this week and very much prostrated by it. Hope we shall have a change soon. Rebecca intends coming out to see you in a day or two. Amie goes to North Haven today to stay until Monday. I shall come to Westville next week. I cannot say what day as I want to go and see Mrs.

Heaton before I go out. It has been so excessively warm this week that I have not been able to call upon her as I intended to have done before this. Charles got home on Tuesday evening. His health is pretty good but he has grown old just in the last three years.

I have not said anything of Luther's promotion out of the family. When it is officially announced it will be in time for the world to know it.

We are all as well as we can be this hot weather and send kind love to yourself,Mrs. Ramsdell and Emily.

Your own loving,

Mother

Near Atlanta, August 18, 1864

My dear Mother,

I wrote you the first of the month and have since written to Mary, Rebecca and Buel. Have had no letters from any of you for ten days, the railroad having been out, but we expect trains tomorrow and I hope it will bring letters.

I was greatly shocked to hear of Louie's death. I know how much you must all miss him and I sympathies with you all.

My last from home speak of you as in comfortable health which I am glad to hear. I wish I could be with you for a while to take you about during the pleasant Summer weather. My longing for the sea side is on me again and I thing of it constantly.

We are in much the same position here, as when I wrote you last, - still bombarding and being bombarded in turn. Other parts of the Army, however, are moving to the West and South of Atlanta. The rebels are holding on to the town stubbornly and more as a matter of pride, I think, than for any value the position has. All the peop le are out of it and all the railroads leading from it are out. And we shall soon make it untenable for the Army.

I wrote you of my promotion in my last letter. Since then I have received off icial notice of the appointment from the Secretary of War. I have received a good many congratulationsand no one, I believe, will deny my right to the position.

I want to trouble you to get me some shirts again. Those made when I was home are worn out and it is difficult to get any good ones anywhere about here. I suppose you have the patterns of the last which were right. I enclose some money and would like you to get me some pretty stuff say for four: either a small plaid, light colors or a plain light drab and I would like two patterns. Please have the stuff well shrunk and have the bosoms stitched with different colored silks. Do not bother with these, Mother, more than to get the stuff and cut them out. I would rather you'd get someone to make them and not fatigue yourself by making it a labor of love to do them with your own hands. If the money enclosed is not sufficient, please let me know. I would like them   and when done have them put into a small bundle and sent to Munson. pre-paid, and I will trust to his getting them to me by some one coming to the Army.

I am still safe and well and you may take this comfort in my promotion - that it will relieve me from much dangerous duty such as picketing and skirmishing.

As well as give me a general right to take care of myself.

Give my best loveto Mary, Rebecca, Buel and each of the children.

Your loving Son,

Luther

Camp near "Red Oak", Ga.

Aug. 29th, 1864

My dear Buel,

Yours of the 16 th was duly received but I have hand no chance to write you since it came to hand. I am glad to know you are enjoying, for a little, the quiet of the country, and I wish I could be with you for I could fully enjoy it too. I know, of course., that you are pleased at my promotion and I am gratified that it does afford you pleasure; none are so dear to me as my home friends, and their love and confidence I value above all else: this you know, and you know too, that I will not forget or dishonor your confidence. I send you a few letters received from friends because I think it will gratify you to read them. Also a Memorial of Adjutant Hall, delivered in Dorchester by the Rev. Mr. Fox. Highl y as Hall is spoken of here, it is all true andjust. Hewas in reality a splendid man and I think, all things considered, I have never seen his equal.. In addition to his fine natural capacities he had a most thorough education and the finest temper and temperament. I send you for your collection a fine photograph of him taken last Winter.

Gen. Morgan once told that my Regiment brought intothe field the finest set of Officers he ever saw and I believe he was right. I am proud of them; of their reputations and their memories, and, of my association with them. Whatever reputation I have in the Army is as much theirs as mine and their fine conduct has done as much to win my promotion as any effort of mine.

We left our position in front of Atlanta some days since and the whole Army with the exception of the 20 th Corps is now south of the city. We are on their railroad communication and the rebels must come out and drive us off, or leave. We withdrew from our works around the town in the night, very quietly and the rebels had a general jollification next day thinking we had retreated.

I hope the present movement will end the campaign. Give my best love to dear Mother, Mary, Rebecca, and the children.

Yours ever, <u>General</u>

Atlanta, Sept. 19th, 1864

My dear Buel,

your letters of August 25 th and 29th came to hand some days since. I have not written you for some little time as I had written to Mother and Mary since we returned to Atlanta.

You have seen, of course, that we occupy Atlanta last and the papers have given you some idea of the manner of its capture. I send a very good account of the last flank movement of the Army, which resulted in the capture of the City. Of course, you all share in the general joy at our success. I see by the papers that it excites unusual attention at the North and that Sherman and his Army are handsomely spoken of everywhere. This is all right, -but though you appreciate the fact of the taking of Atlanta- you can never know through what trials, struggles, and hardships it has been accomplished: the long marches, the miles upon miles of earth works built , the battles and daily skirmishes equal to old fashioned battles, the night fights, surprises and repulses; the fording of streams, and bridging those that couldn't be forded, often under fire, building roads through swamps and cutting them through forests: all these, so indelibly impressed on our minds. You can never appreciate, and if it were told to you you couldn't realize it. It seems strange enough to us now that it is over and we are settled down to quiet camp life again: the real work of this campaign, the incidents and dangers, exceed all my former service put together. I think I have been under fire at least a hundred times this Summer: that I have escaped without injury will be a matter of thankfulness to you as it is of surprise to myself.

We are having our much needed rest, recuperating our energies and reorganizing the Army. Where our next campaign will be we cannot tell but Sherman is too restless a fellow to remain idle long. I suppose our future movements will be I influenced by the other Armies; perhaps Canby's Army may unite or co--0perate with ours for the reduction of Mobile, or Savannah and Charleston. I am satisfied we shall have to seek a new base for supplies either at Mobile or Savannah usingthe rivers as channels of communication. Our line of communications at present is too long; too extensive and uncertain and it takes an Army to guard it. If I was in command of the Army though I wouldn't move a foot until matters took a different shape at the North or until the people there decided upon some settled and defined policy as to the objects and conduct of the War.

I don't know whether we see and read the signs correctly, but it seems to us that opposition to the War is getting popular, and we know that treason is talked too openly. If the people of the North want peace and nothing else let us know it at once and stop the further effusion of blood: if peace is to be made with the rebels on their terms and not on ours, then all our losses are cruel sacrifices and further sacrifice will be worse than folly. It is not a pleasant thought that we may be beaten by the treacher y of our own people. It depresses an Army and encourages the rebels. I would like to see an armistice until this miserable half-peace, half-war policy take definite shape one way or the other.

The spirit of the Army is all right but their enthusiasm is damped by the thought that all their sufferings and sacrifices may be wasted by the want of a little pluck in our own people. I am of the same mind I have been from the first: - we can whip these rebels 'till they are satisfied and make our own terms and it will be enough to make a man deny his country if we don't do it.

I am daily hopingto hear from you. I have had no letters from home for some time. I suppose you are back to the school again and I hope it is pleasant. I send you 50 dollars for winter comforts. I have not sent before because you bid me not do it until you wanted it. Tell me if you want more.

Mrs. Livingston is in great affliction for the loss of her favorite sister, Mrs. Woodruff of New York of whom you have heard me speak: she died suddenly while the Livingston's were on a trip to St Paul. She was a beautiful and accomplished women, wealthy and fascinating. Mrs. Livingston has been quite unwell all Summer and is not yet in her usual health.

Col. Davis is in Chicago, unfit for duty in the field and I do not think he will be soon, if ever, be fit for the hard work of active service. I am afraid the Government will oblige him to go into the Invalid Corps which he would dislike very much and I think he would sooner leave the service.

Give my best love to dear Mother and all the family,

Yours ever,

General

Bridgeport.

Bridgeport. Ala., September 28th, 1864

My dear Mother:

You will be surprised to hear from me from my old post-Bridgeport. I left Atlanta on Sunday the 25th on very short notice and arrived here by rail with the Brigade on Monday night.

I am ordered to the command of the Post here and the garrison is increased by my brigade in consequence of the rebel raiders, Foster and Wheeler being out again operating on our communications: and it was thought they might make an attempt to destroy the great bridge over the Tennessee River here. I can hear nothing of them anywhere here and have no idea if they will show themselves where there is a respectable force.

My command extends to Whitesides and I have a force of 11 Regiments and 4 batteries. I do not expect to remain here long after the scare is over and shall probably rejoin the Division, which is coming up to Chattanooga. I should be glad to stay in the rear for a while to give our men the rest they so much need and for the better supplies we are enabled to get here.

There are three German Regiments here and a Dutchier lot of fellows never were seen. One of the Regiments is commanded by the German Prince Salm-Salm who cut quite a figure on the Potomac a year or two since: he is the politest little fellow I ever met if bows and gestures count anything. Another New York Regiment here is commanded by a Pole-Col. Kzryzenouski-. The name looks funny on paper but is harder to pronounce than it is to spell. I am bothered more than a little in meeting my dutch officers, or rather the Prussians and Poles among them for I can't remember their names or pronounce them if I could and as I have to introduce them to my old officers you can imagine what work I make of it. I wish I had "Tib" here to entertain them for they are a very gentlemanly set.

I am in fine quarters built for the Post Commandant; a snug house with four rooms and kitchen, stables, hen-coop, etc. It is very nearly on the same spot where I had my quarters a year ago but the place has changed entirely since we garrisoned it before. Then the only building here was an old saw mill: but making it a Depot of supplies for the Army has built it up into quite a town.

There are four Gunboats here which patrol the river between this point and Decatur: these are officered from the Navy and we have also an Army Gunboat for special use.

We have a fine line of defenses, consisting of four large forts for Artillery and Infantry and two block houses for Infantry alone, so you may consider us perfectly safe here.

I have received notice of my appointment as Brig. General from the Secretary of War and have assumed the rank. I did not intend to assume it until my commission was issued but could not avoid it under the customs which prevail.

Give my best love to all- I have had no letters from home for some time.

Ever yours,

Luther

Bridgeport, Ala.

October 4, 1864

My dear Buel,

Yours of the 25th September and Mary's and Rebecca's letters of similar date are just received having been stopped at Chattanooga and forwarded from there.

I have had a feast of letters, the mail bringing me a dozen besides those from home, among them two from Williams , Major of the "51st" just released from a rebel prison: the poor fellow is as happy as a child at the thought of being free again, and it would touch your heart to hear how he speaks of his old Regiment and of the gallant fellows who have fallen since his capture. He says he was reduced to a skeleton by long confinement and hard fare but his spirit is unbroken and he will join us soon to take command of the "51st", and fight his old enemies with a new hope and courage, convinced from what he has seen of the rebels that they cannot hold out long.

I wrote to Mother a few days since of our sudden transfer to this post and the reason for it. The rebel cavalry are down in the Tennessee Valley where they have done some damage to the Nashville & Decatur Railroad but they have not made any attempt on this road and I have no fear of their coming this way: we are abundantly prepared to protect ourselves and the interests confined to us if they do come. And looking to the interests of the cause only, I wish they would come.

You want to know how I am living. Well, I'm living like a Nabob-a Tycoon if you like that better; indeed, my temporal condition might be expressed in what the Cockney elegantly called "high-jinks". I have a house to live in: a house with paper on the walls and carpet on the floor; and in place of the "army ration", I like on milk and honey, litera lly, for I have both in the house. I have a company of cavalry for escort, and a gunboat to cruise in up and down the river if I wish. The "Head Quarters" are on a bluff overlooking the Tennessee and the town. On the hills nearby are the Forts and Camps with the trim sentries pacing their beat on the parapet of the Forts. When the morning gun fires at sunrise I wake up and thank my stars I haven't got to turn out for a march or a fight.

I thank you for your praise of our gallant General Phil Sheridan: "Don Philip "we call him, the finest fellow in the land. I could not be more pleased at anything than at his success for he is my friend . I have not met him on the field since Chickamauga and I shall never forget how he came to me as I was going off and expressedhis regret for my mishap. Nor shall I forget the pretty compliment he paid us there when we went into action as he slapped his though and said "Oh, for a dozen such Brigades."

God bless him and bring him through safely: Victorious he will be, I know. With best love to dear Mother, Mary, Rebecca, Charles and the Children.

Yours ever,

General

Bridgeport, Ala.

October 12 , 1864

My dear Mary:

I am indebted to you for sundry letters as yet unanswered. Your favors come to me with surprising regularity: as unlike my semi-occasional scrawls as can be and I wish to make you conscious that I receive, and appreciate your constant effort to instruct and assume me. My letters are my chief solace and pleasure and any mail that does not bring me some pleasant messages from the North, brings disappointment, - which is a bad substitute for letters.

My friends, East and West, have treated me very kindly in writing regularly whether I write or not. Yourself and Buel especially have kept me In home news at all times and I have often been gladdened by the sight of your familiar hands when I sadly wanted something to gladden me.

I am back in my old camp in this place after an absence of a year: I find it much changed since I left, having grown into a great depot of supplies and manufacture for the Army.

Our Division was ordered up here to garrison this place and Chattanooga and my command extends from Stevenson to Whitesides. I do not expect to remain here long unless the raiding should be kept up longer than usual. Probably we shall go to Chattanooga or some point South, to remain until the next campaign opens. Hood is trying to break our line of communications and has thrown his forces on to the road in two or three places, doing little damage.

As he cannot hope to check Sherman except by cutting the roads and stopping supplies. He will likely try this, until he is satisfied that it will not succeed.

Most of our Army is stationed along the railroad south of Atlanta ready to concentrate on any point. We are pleasantly situated here having good quarters and plentiful supplies: indeed, we are living well; having for the first time this Summer, soft bread and potatoes.

I should like to remain here if the Army is to lay still for a while but with the inducements for an active Winter campaign and with Sherman's restless activity, there is little chance of that.

I think you mentioned in a late letter that Charles had written me but I have not received the letter. It has probably gone to Atlanta and missed me in consequence of the move. Remember me kindly to him as well as to Mother, Rebecca, Buel and the Children. Enclosed I send some photographs which Buel wished. I send you 100 dollars lately. Did you receive it?

Yours truly,

General

Bridgeport, Ala.

October 18, 1864

My dear Buel,

Yours of the 12th came to hand this morning. I am still here guarding the great bridge over the Tennessee. Hood has made a bold move in Sherman's rear with the intent to break up the railroad and compel him to retreat for want of supplies. The rebels have broken the road badly between Dalton and Resaca and captured some of the small garrisons along there. The breaks are soon repaired, nothing being wanted but rails and labor.

Hood is now apparently trying to escape. Sherman being after him with the whole Army except the 20th Corps left to garrison Atlanta. It was thought yesterday that the rebels were moving in this direction and the 1st and 2nd Brigades of our Division were sent down here from Chattanooga to reinforce. I do not expect to remain here long every probability pointing to a return to the front. What the result of Hood's movements will be we cannot tell. It is a big raid and if he succeeds in getting off it will match Sherman's march to the rest of Atlanta. If Hood cannot out fight us the bests thing is to try and out maneuver us.

I have just received orders to go to Chattanooga with my command and expect to start tonight. I understand they are sending troops south from there and we shall probably join in the chase of Hood. I regret leaving here just now as I had hoped to remain long enough to rest my men and do the work which has accumulated on our hands during the Summer, but if our discomfort will help on the cause, it's all right.

I sent a couple of photographs to Mary in my last letter for Mother and yourself. They are part of a lot Col. Davis has just sent me. You say you'd like to see what havoc this campaign has made on me. You say you'd like to see what havoc his campaign has made on me. Just none at all Madam I I'm as fresh as when you last saw me, a month's rest having dissipated all signs of fatigue. I believe I am well constituted for this work as far

As the fatigue goes for I have never seen the man who could outlast me and I don't allow any one to be more ready to do his paperwork than I am.

I quite approve your project for housing yourself and living in your own home and if I send you any money you do not want to deposit it where it will be available for what may be your paradise and my asylum. I am laying up a penny for myself and my friends and I'll send you some now and then, if I like.

I have just got a situation for Frank Brown in the Quartermaster Department and he is coming out soon on a salary of $1,800 per year. He is to be with Capt. Montandon of the 51st now Quartermaster at Johnsonville, Tenn. Frank has fine qualities and I expect to see him succeed in this new enterprise.

My shirts and the other articles have arrived and suit me exactly. Give love and thanks to dear Mother for all her kindness

yours ever,

General

Athens, Ala.

November 3, 1864

My dear Buel,

Yours of October 17th, also one acknowledging receipt of remittance, with other letters of various dates are received. Some of yours and Mary's with one mentioned from Charles, sent about the time we left Atlanta are lost.

I wrote to you just before leaving Bridgeport, ten days since- and to Mother from Alpine, Ga when I marched from Chattanooga. You say you "cannot find Bridgeport". It is 30 miles southwest of Chattanooga at the point the railroad crosses the Tennessee. Any map should show it to you.

Our Division left Alpine on the 28th October, marched to Chattanooga, fifty miles in two days. From there we came to Athens by cars and marched from here to Pulaski, Tennessee, thirty-five miles due north, where we join the rest of the 4th Corps.

We are no longer a part of Sherman's Army but are sent to Tennessee to form the nucleus of a new "Army of the Cumberland" to be organized by Thomas. This Army will number some sixty thousand and will be employed in Tennessee and look out for Hood, if he crosses the river.

Sherman in the meantime takes the balance of his Army and after destroying the railroad behind him and perhaps Atlanta, pushes out for Mobil, Savannah or any other place he likes in the South, there being no army to oppose him. Hood, after vainly trying to draw Sherman from Atlanta by attacking his communications, has moved his Army up in the vicinity of Decatur for the apparent purpose of crossing the river, this threatening Tennessee and all the points north. Sherman leaves Thomas to take care of Tennessee and will make a separate campaign south with the understanding that Hood can cross the Tennessee if he likes. The rebels have been threatening for some time to transfer the war to the banks of the Cumberland and Ohio and I should not be surprised if they attempt it. They seem disposed to cross the river now but when they find that Sherman is not following they will be disappointed, I think. Thomas will be able to fight them anywhere and if they try this new move they will find it hard to get back to Georgia and Alabama.

My friend, Gen. Ransom, commanding the 17the Corps, died a few days since at Alpine. You will remember my speaking of him and I think you have his picture. He was one of the finest men and finest soldiers in the Army and had a great future before him as a soldier.

I thank you for the particulars you write of Charles, Jr. I am interested in all that interests him. Please give him my kind regards with assurance of pleasant remembrance. Remember me also kindly to brother Charles, and give my best love to dear Mother and the rest of the family with regards to the Baldwins, Beers and other friends.

Will write from Pulaski.

Your ever,

Genl.

Pulaski, Tenn.

November 1 5th, 1864

Direct hereafter "via Nashville"

My dear Buel,

Your letters of October 24th and 29th reached me yesterday. I wrote you last from Athens and wrote Mother from here a day or two since. I am grieved to hear your report of Charles' dangerous illness and shall anxiously look for your letters hoping to hear of some improvement in him though I know his case must be alarming from the particulars you write me even if he should live he may be helpless for the balance of his life. I am glad you can be with him and help to care for him in his infirmities. Give him my love and my best wishes for his speedy recovery to comfortable health.

Do not let dear Mother be worried about him or attempt to take care of him and it will not be well to have her visit him often unless she can do it without exposure or fatigue. I trust to you to take care of my part of the dear woman in my absence.

We have been her some ten days and are already well fortified against attack. Hood is menacing Tennessee and my come up here or make an advance on Nashville: but I am inclined to think that he is trying to scare Sherman and induce him to fall back and give up Georgia, to protect Tennessee. It's a shallow trick of Hood's and when he finds that Sherman has gone off into the heart of the Confederacy with the bulk of his Army, I think he will be less inclined to come north. He may think, howeve,rthat he will catch us now with a small force and try to carry out a favorite purpose:- to transfer the ware to the border. In this he will be mistaken. We have already the 4th and 23rd Corps with about 15,000 cavalry and A.J. Smith's command is on the way from Missouri which with the recruits joining us, will make an army of 70,000, enough to whip Hood and have something to spare. In the event of Hood's falling back we may winter here or somewhere in this neighborhood until a new campaign is laid out but we hope he will remain where he is, on the Tennessee or attempt a northern march if he wishes.

I had a long letter from Sheridan last week, congratulating me on my promotion and telling me of his successes. I am more pleased with his fine performance than with anything that has occurred in the war. I think he will prove one of the most popular men of the war and certainly he deserves all the reputation he has, for a finer or more gallant man never drew rein over a horse. Was it not a fine thing to do, -to gallop from Winchester in the morning, take his beaten Army and whip Early in turn! That is just Phil Sheridan and I can see him as he rode on to the field, his little body swelling 'till he looked the biggest man among them all. I send you a fine thing written by Buchanan Read on the ride from Winchester. I know that black horse well. He is a nobble beast and I have cantered beside him many a mile. Sheridan rode him at Chickamauga and said afterwards he would never ride him into another battle for fear of his getting hurt. Read has made him historical for

"Carrying Sheridan all the way,

From Winchester, down to save the day."

We are all rejoiced at the results of the election as showing that the people of the North are in earnest in supporting the Government in its war policy. The returns as we have then show Lincoln to be elected by a majority so great as to remove any doubt of the temper of the people. I think the result will have a marked influence on the Southern people and set them to thinking seriously of their future. Four more years of war, if they will have it, will leave them little to make a future of. I expect to see their situation more seriously and plainly debated now than ever and the peach party at the South-for there is one here as well as at the North, - will be heard and perhaps heeded.

I am glad to hear that you are getting on pleasantly in school. I would like to look in on you and your pretty flock: some day I may do it, and afterward, take that long walk you spoke of up the "PowerHouse Road ". I remember all the ground well, and that I nearly broke my back there once, long time ago.

Love to Mother and all.

Yours ever,

General

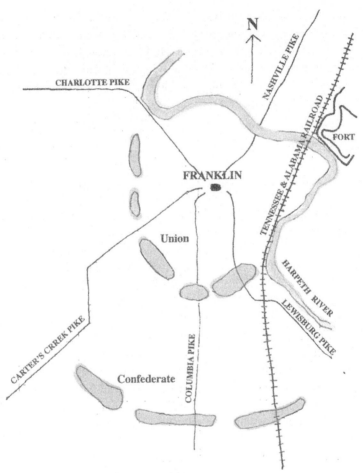

FRANKLIN, TENNESSEE

Nashville, December 7th, 1864

My dear Buel,

Yours of November 24th reached me yesterday. You have heard before this of my mishap. I wrote to Mother three days since telling her how I was getting along. My arm still pains me very severely and is entirely useless from the shoulder down. I have no use of it, whatever. Otherwise I am feeling pretty well.

The doctors tell me it will take weeks and perhaps months to restore the arm so that I can make any use of it. The nerves are always slow to heal when injured and I shall have to apply electricity to start them up again.

I shall start for Chicago in a day or two taking the journey quite easy on the way and shall spend a few days there before coming East.

I hope to be with you at Christmas and New Years.

You have seen in the papers accounts of our retrograde movement from Pulaski to Nashville. It was a success owing to the pluck of the men and the good conduct of the subordinate officers: the Generals Commanding deserve no credit. They nearly lost the Army by their blundering. At Spring Hill and Franklin we had very hard fighting and repulsed Hood handsomely, though he outnumbered us, ten thousand. Our Army is now strongly fortified here receiving reinforcements which will enable it to take the field against Hood.

Will write from Chicago, -With best love to dear Mother and all the others.

Yours ever,

General

Chicago, December 20th, 1864

My dear Buel,

I have not heard a word from home since I was wounded. I telegraphed Lucius of my hurt on the 1st and wrote Mother and yourself soon after. As I did not leave Nashville until the 11th I thought I should get letters there. I wrote Mother from Louisville and Mary from here since my arrival. I had hoped to be home by Christmas but my arm troubles me and pains me to a degree that unfits me for traveling or doing anything else. have no peace with it night or day and get no sleep except under the influence of morphine and but little then. Dr. Isham advises me not to attempt the journey now, so I shall not start until next week by which time I hope to be stronger. If I do not improve in the meantime I shall come home to be with you at New Years. My arm does not improve as yet. I have no use of it and there is no cessation of the pain.

I am with the Livingstons enjoying every comfort and attention possible and but for the pains I suffer from my arm should be as comfortable as need be. I am anxious to hear from dear Mother and all of you; to know how you are. Unless you have already sent letters to Chicago. It will not be worth while to do so as I shall probably leave before they could reach me.

Our Army has gained a splendid victory since I left. The brilliant success atones in part for my hurt and I think I can stand the pain better since our men have shipped Hood. This affair with Sherman's success, settles matters quite to our satisfaction in the South. At one time the prospect looked bad for us owingto bad management; the fight in which I was wounded was the most critical time I have ever seen and if Hood had shown his usual boldness there, I think he would have beaten us disastrously, but he was int imidated apparently by a bold front. By hard fighting we gained time and secured the retreat. Do not have any anxiety about me. I am doing as well as I can considering the nature of my wound and it will come out all right in the end.

With best love to Mother and all the rest.

Yours ever,

Luther

the stayers-at-home have made money
while we have made history, but history
will last the longest

1865

Chicago, Sunday, February 18, 1865

My dear Buel,

Your letter reached me yesterday. It was very good of you to write me so soon and I thank you for remembering me and for all your kind words and wishes.

I wrote Mother on Wednesday, the day I arrived here and, also, from Albany, a week ago today. I spent Sunday there with Captain Hamback, formerly on my staff. He is a fine fellow -one of my favorites- and I could not pass so near without seeing him. He is completing his law studies in the school at Albany. I had a very pleasant visit with him and left Albany for the West at midnight.

I had a tedious journey out without any incident of interest. We were two days and three nights between Albany and Chicago. The trains were all out of time and we were delayed several hours at Buffalo, Erie and Cleveland.

I got along pretty comfortably, my arm being rather quiet. Since I got here the atmosphere has been damp and heavy and as a consequence I have had a good deal of pain. Dr. Isham tells me the arm is doing as well as he expected and advises me to continue the Acetic Ether. I have been to see the examining Surgeon and he advises me to keep out of the field for a while but thinks I could go on light duty safely and has given me a certificate to that effect which I have forwarded to the Secretary of War. I presume I shall get a detail soon for some such duty.

Col. Erskine is here for a week or two, also, Col. Smith of the 88th whose family I visited in New Haven. Waterman is able to get about on crutches. So we are having a fine time together. I expect Col. Davis up here in a day or two and then our party will be complete.

Waterman will go East after a little while and remain until he gets the use of his leg again, when he will join me wherever I may be.

He may be in New Haven before he returns in which case he will see you. shall try and persuade Erskine to make you a call too as he is goingto Maine to see his family.

Mrs. Livingston was greatly pleased with the frame you sent her and wishes me to express her thanks for you kindness. She will write you herself after a while. I had a pleasant time in New York visiting my friends; among others, Mr. Bridgerman, who treated me very kindly. He took me to the Art Building and introduced me to some of the celebrities there. We spent an afternoon with Church and Bierstadt in their studios and it was a great treat to me. They are both pleasant gentlemen and surrounded with everything to please the eye. Church showed me a little bit of landscape about the size of a half sheet of letter paper for which he gets a thousand dollars.

I am glad to hear that Charles is a little better. Give him my love; the same to dear Mother, Mary and Rebecca and the children .

Ever yours,

Luther

Chicago, February 19 , 1865

My dear Mother,

I have not written you for a week or so as I had nothing new to tell you. My arm is about the same as when I left you. Sometimes, I think it is better, then it will take a turn and for days pain me severely. On the whole I think there is a little improvement in strength and gradual lessening of pain. I do not expect to be rid of the pain for a long time yet, so shall be prepared for it more or less severe all the time with a few extra twinges when the weather is bad. For the last week it has been stormy and damp and in consequence I have had a bad week. It has now cleared up and I hope for an easier time .

I have been out to a dinner party the past week at Mr. Kimbark's, where about twenty of my friends were invited to meet me. We sat at the table till midnight and I felt none the worse for the dissipation. Encouraged by this, I went to a large party the next night and came away from it about used up. Since then I have kept very quiet and shall eschew

part ies for the present, though I have a number of invitations on hand. Chicago is very gay this Winter and my friends are kind in remembering me in their invitations.

I shall go to St. Louis in a day or two to spend a few days with Col. Davis as he is unable to come up here on account of his engagements. I shall return here about the 25th of the month, and will then write you again.

I see by the papers that my nomination is confirmed by the Senate so that I shall expect to receive my commission soon.

Am expecting orders from the War Department daily, having reported for light duty. I am convinced I shall feel better for having something to do. Buel's and Mary's letters came to hand last week. I will write them soon.

With best love, my dear Mother and to Charles , Mary, Rebecca, Buel and the children.

Yours ever, Luther

Nashville, March 30th, 1865

My dear Buel,

Yours of the 20th came yesterday, having been forwarded from Chicago by Livingston.

I wrote Mother as soon as I got orders to report here that you might understand why I cam down. I wrote you also the day I left Chicagoand again from Cincinnati and have written Mary since I reached here.

I am detailed here as President of a Military Commission for the trial of Guerrillas and other political offenders. I expect it will be dull work enough but the doctors advise me not to go into the field until the weather gets warm and settled so I am going to be prudent. You must not expect me to remain in the rear long though, - the field is the place for me. I can do the best service and win the most credit thee. I am comfortably quartered in a private house and shall be as well off here as in Chicago.

I feel the greatest interest in all you write me about Charles and shall prizeany relics you choose to set aside for me. I realize less than you the great change his death makes with you. I have seen so little of him for the last ten or twelve years that my recent visit with him seems almost like a dream. I keep thinking of him as being off in some distant part of the world, from whence he will sometime come back to us. It is pleasant to know that his memory is so respected by old friends.

I like your suggestion of fixing up our old burying lot and will be glad to join in anything you think best to do. Let me know whatever expense you go to.

Nashville is looking pleasantly in it spring dress. Peach trees are in blossom. Hyacinths, Crocuses and other spring flowers abound everywhere. The country all about here is delightful in its green dress and the birds are doing their best to give everyone a welcome.

I am taking horse back rides again over the country so often traveled in '62. Love to all - In hast,

Yours,

Gen.

Nashville, April 8, 1865

My dear Mother,

I suppose you are all rejoicing over the good news from Virginia and the prospect of the close of the War.

It seems as though the end was really coming now and out here in Tennessee where the war has raged so terribly for three years we are calculating on an easy time for the balance of the war. I do not expect to see another battle myself- and I hope the remnant of the rebel armies will have the good sense to surrender or disperse and thus save further bloodshed.

With the loss of Lee's Army every chance of success goes and the men who try to prolong the war after this deserve any punishment we can give them.

We are jubilant over Sheridan's success. The gallant little fellow is vindicating our judgment of him for as always claimed that he was one of the best soldiers in the Army and we feel proud that we helped to make his reputation.

Recent news from west of the Miss. shows that the rebel forces there are discouraged and likely to disband soon; they have refused to cross the Miss. And are not to be counted in any estimate of rebel forces. Johnston's Army is the only one we have to cope with and I believe, Sherman will soon dispose of that.

Captain Waterman has joined me here. He is still on crutches and will not be able to walk for a good while. I think he will be obliged to have the leg operated on to remove some splintered bone.

I am on duty as President of a Military Commission. Gen. Thomas tells me to remain here as long as I choose and return to the field when I feel like it.

My arm is getting along very well, I think. I have a little more use of it than when I came down here and it pains me but little generally.

Give my best love to Mary, Rebecca , Buel, and the children.

Ever yours,

Luther

Nashville, April 11th, 1865

My dear Buel,

Yours of the 8th came to hand yesterday and I received the previous letter last week.

Thank you for writing me so fully of all that interests us and all that pertains of Charles' affairs. I am glad that Mary has decided to sell the library. It would be desirable to keep it in the family if we could afford to own so valuable a collection of books but that is not practicable. I have no doubt the College would like to purchase the books and it is natural you should wish them to remain there but I have no idea that Yale College (can at this time give you the value of them.) will give the value of them. ******************** I would very much like a few of the books as keepsakes since you say Mary wishes us to have some. You know perfect my taste in these matters and I leave the selection to you.**************** *********

I am serving here as President of a Military Commission for the trial of offenders of various sorts: - officers charged with peculation's, dishonest Quartermasters, Guerrillas, etc. I have on the Court, Gen. Champion, three or four Colonels and half a dozen officers of lesser rank. We sit from nine to one each day, having but one session. The work is easy enough, but dull enough too. Captain Waterman has joined me here and will be detailed on my Court. He is still quite lame using two crutches and will not have the use of his leg for a long time. There is some chance of an operation being required to remove splintered bone and if this is done it must retard the independent use of the leg for some time. Waterman is so thoroughly fine a fellow that I want him to get well for my own sake as well as his, that we may be together for the balance of the time we are in service.

I hope recent events have removed your fears for my future in the Army. My opinion is that we have fought our last battle in this Department and very nearly our last anywhere. The long looked for crumbling of the rebel armies has commenced and the Confederacy is "played out". Isn't the triumph glorious. The defeat and capture of Lee's Army ends the war practically and we may now calculateon peace. A peace fairly won and an earnest and enduring peace, I believe. My glorious friend and commander, "gallant Phil Sheridan" has done as much toward bringing about this result as any other man almost bears off the palm from Grant himself. He is the very impersonation of Gallantry and all soldierly virtues. No man will come out of the War with a higher or better record. One of the rewards of our service in the field which we shall enjoy after the war is over will be the memories of our intimacies with the great leaders-the men whose names are going down to posterity as the Great Americans of their time. And of all that I have seen or done noting will be remembered with so much pleasure as the marches, battles, and bivouacs with Phil Sheridan.

I do not think the Government will discharge any number of troops except those whoseterm of service is soon to expire, even if peace is concluded at once. All the troops remaining of the 300,000 called into service in 1862 go out in August as well as a largenumber of one year men call out last year. This will reduce the Army as much as will be desirable, I think, as it will be necessary to keep a force in the Southern States for some time until the state Governments are organized again and the state courts prepared to punish criminals.

The 4th Corps is now some 50 miles east of Knoxville and will probably remain there. I do not see any chance of their having any work to to this season. Almost one half of the Corps go out of service in August and they will be likely to rest for the Summer. I shall go up to East Tennessee some time about May 1st, I think.

My arm is improving a litt le and pains me less than it did last month. Out-door life will do me good and you need not fear my doing myself any harm.

Give my best love to Mother, Rebecca, Ami and the little ones.

Every Yours,

General

Nashville, April 20th, 1865

My dear Buel,

Yours of the 10th and Rebecca's letter of about the same date came to hand a day or two since. The letters give me a pleasingly excited account of the rejoicing in our native "burg" over the victories in Virginia. I am glad if the staid people woke up for once and in their hurry to dress at midnight forgot to put on their mantles of propriety. I suspect they all go tight from the accounts and if they did it's all right. No such opportunity ever came to the before and if they didn't celebrate it, I should think worse of them.

Well the war is ended. How do you feel about it? I know you are glad. Everybody is glad, even the bitterly "secesh" here in Tennessee. But you don't know how glad we are who have fought and waited for this triumph. And we are all the more glad because it vindicates our belief often expressed, when others doubted, that oursuccess was sure in due time. We have a right to be glad too, for us there are no more battles, no more wounds and suffering. Whatever, we have suffered in the past is amply rewarded by our glorious successes and we feel more pride today in our scars than the richest Crocesus in the north feels in his money bags. Well the thing is nearly even. The "stayers at home" have made money while we have made history, but history will last the longest. I am ready now to leave the Army and go home, if the country quiets down and the Army is to be reduced. I shall not resign yet but shall wait and see what the South determines on, peace, or further war. My own opinion is that the war is ended and that weshall long have quiet. The only rebel Armies in the field areJohnston's and Kirby Smith's. Sherman will take care of the former and if it does not surrender it must be captured or destroyed. Kirby Smith in Arkansas is ready to surrender or go into Mexico and I think the War Department is arranging to prevent his doingthe latter by sending a part of the forces lately employed at the North into his neighborhood. The 4th Corps is now being concentrated here and will undoubtedly go down the Mississippi if troops are wanted there. If the Corps go, I shall go with it because I am quite well enough for anything likely to turn up. There will be no fighting and the camp work I can get along with well enough. My arm is mending slowly and though I do not expect to get much use of it this year I shall manage to get along very well without it. I ride now as well as ever only I am a little more particular about the kind of horse I ride that I used to be. I have "Robin " here with me having sent to Alabama for him and he behaves very well.

You want to know what I think of "Ward Beecher's Expedition to Sumpter with Lloyd Garrison in tow" and "of Mr. Lincoln's journey to Ric hmond." I think they were both earnest loyal men and that was the kind of men to make a voyage to Charleston harbor to see the old flag raised again. I understand the prejudice that exists against Lloyd Garrison and I think it's time it died out. He has been a true and staunch supporter of the Administration during the war and his unpopularity arose from the fact that he was ahead of public opinion on the slavery question. We have come up to his position for are we not all Abolitionists now?

As for Mr. Lincoln's journey to Richmond, I believe it was prompted as most of his public acts were, by a desire to aid in some way the accomplishment of the great end in view, the ending of the War and the return of peace. What effect his presence had in arousing the dormant Unionism of Richmond we cannot tell. He had an object in going there and that it was a right object no one will doubt now. You eastern people do not know and appreciate Mr. Lincoln's character as we do at the West. He was the one honest and unselfish man of the nation. He had a great good heart, too good, I believe the Government to be entirely just to the enemies

With best love to all,

Yours ever,

General

Camp near Nashville

May 8th, 1865

My dear Mother,

It is quite a long time since I have written you as you no doubt think, but I have written often to the girls and that is much the same.

I am now in camp again and enjoy the open air and the fine Spring weather very much.

Our camps are about five miles from Nashville in one of the prettiest pieces of the country I have seen. We have plenty of shade, fine strings and over the whole country a fine carpet of grass.

The woods are full of mocking birds who keep the air filed with their music.

The Corps is laying quietly here, occupied principally in reviews, preparatory to a part of it being mustered out. All but the veteran regiments will probably be discharged soon and it is the impression here that the Veteran and Negro Regiments will be relied on for garrisoning different points in the South and whatever else they may be wanted for. I do not know how soon I shall go out. If the Government declares the war closed I am ready to go out any time and if they wish to muster me out very well. Otherwise I may stay in the Army until Fall.

There is no prospect of the Corps leaving here at present. The fighting is over and the rest of our work is going to be easy. We all want rest after the wearing work of the last four years and, I don't know but we can do it as well here as any where. You cannot think what a relief it is to know that the War is over and our hard work ended. I look back upon the experience of the last year almost with shudder. I don't know what would tempt me to go through another such year.

My arm troubles me still and since my fall of which I wrote Rebecca, it has been quite helpless and painful. I am thinking after talking with a good many army surgeons that it quite doubtful if my arm is ever of much use to me. The opinion among the best Surgeons is that the nervous action will be but partially restored. I am getting along now very well without it and can ride as well as ever. I have bought a new horse as black as the ace of spades and the most beautiful creature you ever saw. She is as gentle and easy as a lad's palfrey. With the fine roads and beautiful scenery about here, I enjoy my rides very much.

I will write to Mary and Buel in a day or tow. Give my love to all and with a large share for yourself,

Yours lovingly,

Luther

"The horse as black as the ace of spades". From record of horses- "Gipsy" black mare, 8 years old; 15 ½ hands high, long mane and tail; a fine trotter and a very beautiful animal. Bought her of 1st Ohio Calvary in March, 1865. Rode her at the last Review at the close of the war; took her to Chicago and sold her to Mr. Ahern.

Camp "Harker" near Nashville
May 12th, 1865

My dear Buel,

Yous of the 2nd and 8th with one from Mary came to hand today. I ought to have written you before this in answer to your last letter but for the last two weeks I have been very busy and have scarcely written a letter. I joined the old Brigade about ten days since and found plenty of work awaiting me. Matters military and disciplinary not having been managed quite to my satisfaction since I have been gone. Besides drilling and other necessary work we have had two reviews, the preparation for which has taken a good deal of time. I wish you could have been here to see the review of the 4th Corps, the last gathering of the Corps before being disbanded. It was the finest sight, as a pageant, that I ever saw and Gen. Thomas said it was the finest sight he had ever seen. The Corps was out 20,000 strong with 60 pieces of Artillery and all the transportation, consisting of 1,000 wagons -six mules each- and 200 ambulances.

The day was one of the finest I ever saw and nearly all the residents of Nashville were out to see the parade. After the review all the officers of the Corps with Gen. Thomas and Sill went to Gen. Stanley's Headquarters by invitation and spent the afternoon in a general jollification.

Our Corps with the others will soon be broken up under orders to reduce the Army. The regiments enlisting in 1862 will be mustered out very soon, but the Veterans will be retained for some time longer, I think, as the Government will need a large force to garrison all the Southern towns of importance until the country is "tranquilized". There is little prospect of the Corps going to Texas or anywhere else at present. I do not know how soon I shall go out of service. I am ready to muster out whenever the War is declared closed but if we are to remain quiet for a while I would as least remain here as not. I feel the want of rest and indulge myself in Camp as well as anywhere.

My arm troubles me a good deal and from all I can learn from the Army Surgeons there is little prospect of its ever getting well. The best I can expect is to regain partial use of it.

I am glad to know you have heard from Anna Hayman. She is one of the women I remember with pleasure. I wish you would send her the assurance of my remembrance and esteem.

Do not think me indifferent to the home news if I do not speak of it in detail. enjoy it all and wish for more.

About Sherman, -I was as much disappointed as you when we heard of his mistake for it <u>was</u> a mistake and nothing more, but I do not feel like joining in the senseless clamor which denounced him as disloyal and demanded his removal. He has done too much for the country to be sacrificed for one fault and it does not speak well for the Northern people that they were ready to sacrifice their best general for one error of judgment. I do not undertake to excuse Sherman's error and should have been as angry as any one if the terms between him and Johnston had been carried out but I can understand his motive and I believe it was a good one. Sherman is a genius and like all geniuses is erratic. Such men are sure to do queer and unreasonable things. It is only our medium, evenly balanced men that are entirely reliable at all times. Sherman is very quick, hot tempered, original man, fond of striking out new paths and not afraid to travel them himself. He is self-confident, self-willed and still just and generous. Will do a hundred unkind and unfair things from hasty temper and as many generous things from calm judgment. He is just such a man as would make a Cromwell under the same circumstances. After all his mistakes has done no harm. Grant's steady hand soon put him right.

What a grand smash the rebels have made of it! "Didn't I tell you so?" And that we were to have a better Union than ever. The dawn of Peace is the most welcome sight to the tens of thousands of weary fellows in the Army.

After the hardships and perils of the last four years we shall feel entitled to enjoy our "Otium cum dig", when we get home.

Give best love to dear Mother and all the others.

Ever yours,

General

Camp near Nashville

May 29th 1865

My dear Mother,

We are still laying in camp enjoying ourselves and taking our fill of rest. You cannot imagine anything pleasanter than our Camps. They are in a large natural park, comprising hundreds of acres, filled with fine old trees and covered with clean grass from one end to the other. The trees are full of mocking birds as well as numerous other kinds, all singing their best and very pleasant neighbors they are. A little way off the stately magnolias are blooming and the scent of the flower is a common pleasure with us.

I wish you could see this queen of flowers. It is larger than any flower growing at the North, pure white, and very fragrant. Seen on the trees, which is larger than an average apple tree, it makes a very fine show.

We have been expecting orders for the Veterans of the 4th Corps to go to Texas as we hear through private letters that Sherman had applied for them to join his Army to operate against Kirby Smith but as Smith is said to have surrendered, I think there is little prospect of our going South and I am very glad of it. My wish is to get out of service this Summer and I intend to do so unless some obstacle stands in the way. My commands are all Veterans and if they are sent South I shall probably go along but not wish the intention of remaining. I would like to see the country below here and above the Gulf and it would be a fine chance if the Corps goes down there.In any case there would be no fighting. Kirby Smith has never been a fighting man and he'll be less inclined for it now than ever.

If the Trans-Miss Army has surrendered it is probable the Veterans will be mustered out with the other troops, in which case we may get home by mid-summer.

I am in excellent health and but for my arm should not think myself as a campaigner of four years experience. The arm, however, is a constant reminder and I am afraid there is little prospect of its ever letting me forget it.

I see by the papers that Col. Davis has been down into the southern part of Missouri to receive the surrender of the rebel leader, Jeff Thompson, a trip I should think, quite to the Colonel's liking. He is now full Colonel of the 51•t, "vice Bradley promoted by the President".

I have been but one letter from home in a fortnight, - Mary's. I wrote her last week and will write Buel in a day or two.

Love to all.

Yours ever,

Luther

Camp "Harker"

June 1st, 1865

My dear Buel,

Your letter of the 15th and 20th are both received. I thank you especially for the long letter of the latter date. I like you to talk to me about everything in your mind.

As you requested, I will save the stars for you, -the pair I wore at "Spring Hill" if you wish.

I must thank you too for selecting the books for me. Do not lay aside many though. I only want a few for keepsakes. I am very sorry to hear of the death of Major Osborn. I knew him but slightly but he was a fine fellow. I have just had a visit from an old Chicago friend, Capt. Thomas who knew Osborn in North Carolina, and he spoke in the highest terms of him.

We've lost a great, great many noble fellows in this struggle, but thank God, the roll is nearly complete. I have not received the paper with Harrison's speech you speak of. Send it to me.

You want to know what my daily life is. Well, we get up at five, breakfast, sound the "assembly" at six and march out for Brigade drill, maneuver over a fifty acre field, double kicking from one end to the other until about nine when it gets hot and we return to Camp and loaf away the balance of the day under the trees listeningto the birds singing, with the occasional diversion of the visit of a party of friends from town or a gallop across the country . We take our rations regularly, having good camp appetites and in the evening gather round our rustic table in front of the quarters, drink beer, smoke and gossip until bed time.

Now that the War is ended I am quite disposed to get out of the Army and think of resigning. I want a little time to myself this Summer and time to look about for some business to settle down to in the Fall. If our Corps go down the river as seems probable I may go with it but shall not if it is likely to keep me there long. Now that the fighting is over the Army is losing its interest for "we un's" as the poor whites here say.

You misunderstood my remark about Sherman in supposing I said he was like Cromwell. I said he would make a Cromwell under similar circumstances. By that I mean that he is like him as a solider. Cromwell, to be sure, was a cruel old bigot which Sherman certainly is not, but there is no telling what any of us would have been if we had lived in Comwell's time.

With deference to your opinion, I don't think I do much mistake the northern feeling about Sherman. I know there is a kind feeling for him and I think it is sensibly increasing. The Northern Press is a little ashamed of the abuse they heaped upon him and they are now "crawfishing" as the soldiers say. All I complain of is, that the people lauded Sherman to the skies in their intemperate way while he was successful,, making him almost a god and then turned round and wanted to kick him down from the pedestal on which they had set him, because he was only a man. Sherman makes mistakes like other men and he has the same right as another man. What we say is, that a man who has rendered such service to the country should not be denounced and disgraced for one mistake.

I am glad to know that you are hearing often from the Haymans. I would like to see them. Anna Hayman is one of my favorites and it pleases me to know that she is loyal to the North. I have often thought of her since the War has been going on and wondered on which side she had thrown her sensible head. I have always had a fancy I should like that woman if I had a chance to know her well and have a good time together.

With best love to Mother, Mary, Rebecca and the children.

Yours ever,

General

Camp near Nashville

June 14 th, 1865

My dear Mother,

I have received letters from Mary and Buel this week giving me the home news and both speaking of you as not being quite as well as usual. I trust the illness is but temporary and that the fine June weather will help to make you well again.

We are still in camp here enjoying the rest and quiet doing literally nothing. It is the pleasantest country an army ever camped in and we are quite content to be idle in it for a little while. The Corps will leave here soon, however, being under orders for New Orleans and probably Texas. We do not see the necessity for the move as there is no longer an enemy in that section but someone else sees it perhaps which is more to the purpose and more military also. One of the great rules of strategy is to keep your friends as much in the dark as your enemies, - a difficult rule to enforce among our guessing inquisitive Yankees. I do not suppose there will be any action work for our troops in Texas or anywhere on that frontier but the Government probably wants an Army of Observation near Mexico to be ready for any complications that may arise. I did intend to go down the river with the troops but after thinking it all over have decided not to. I have no wish to make the Army my home there is no longer any reason for my remaining in it. The War is ended and the obligation to the Government ends with it. I want to settle down to civil life again and try and make some money. Accordingly, I have sent my resignation to the Secretary of War and as the Government invites resignations there is little doubt that it will be accepted. If the Corps start off soon, I shall get a leave of absence and go to Chicago to await notice from the War Department. If my resignation is accepted I hope to come East sometime in July and shall spend a few weeks about there before settling on any business. I do not know what I shall go at but have no doubt, I shall find something that will pay. I like this state of Tennessee very much and think there is a good chance to make money here. If I can get some of my Chicago friends to put some of their money into the iron or coal mining businesses I shall be inclined to come down here to live. There is any amount of undeveloped wealth in this State and the Yankees have got to unearth it. Already a large number of officers who have left the Army are settled here in professions and trade and it will not be long before there will be a visible change in social and political matters. So far as soil and climate are concerned, Tennessee bears the palm and I believe she will yet be the richest state in the Union.

I will write you again soon. Tell the girls to direct to me after this at Chicago. With best of love to you and all.

Ever yours,

Luther

Chicago, July 12th, 1865

My dear Buel,

I believe I answered your letter of June 27th but I have written so may since my return that I am not quite certain about it. I wrote to Mother last week and received Mary's of July 4th. I am still waiting answer to my my papers from Washington. There is no doubt of the acceptance of my resignation, I think, and if I do not get notice of it this week shall start for the East next week.

Col. Davis is mustered out of service and will com East with me. He did not want to leave the service now as he had a pleasant position in St. Louis but he came under the order mustering out all officers on "detached duty" and so his head comes off. The Government is getting rid of all the unemployed material in the Army and this is right for the expenses of the Army is enormous. I hope they will muster out all but the Negro troops which with the regulars will give us about 150,000, -quite enough for a peace establishment. The 4th Corps has reached New Orleans and is encamped near the old battle ground. I hear they had some difficulty going down the river and that Gen. Elliott is relieved of the command of one Division for mismanagement. This change would have given me the command of the Division if I had remained with it.

I am glad of this change. Elliott is a regular and is not a pleasant man to serve with because he has all the professional prejudices of the old Army in a marked degree. You have no idea how strong the West Point influence is in the Army, although the Army is entirely composed of volunteers, for the regulars don't amount to a handful, either in numbers or weight. Sheridan is the only West Pointer I have known free from the prejudices of his class. The regular Army controls all the higher appointments and manages all war matters, in fact. It is but fair to say they take excellent care of themselves in the distribution of places. This is natural and I have no doubt we should do the same if we had the power.

The leading officers of the Army are West Pointers and we acknowledge their ability and services but we claim that the volunteers have put down the Rebellion and that in the four years race, volunteer officers have beaten the regulars. Considering that the West Pointers have controlled all the Bureaus in the War Department their record is not very creditable for there has been some of the grossest blundering imaginable.

I suppose Tibbie will be home this Summer and Rebecca will have a house full. I would like to take board at your house for a month or so. Cannot you arrange it? I shall be out of town a good deal during the time for I intend to spend some time on the water.

I may leave here in about a week from this date and as there is hardly time for an answer to reach me, you better write me at the Continental Hotel, Philadelphia. I shall remain in Philadelphia two or three days to purchase a monument for Gen. Harker and arrange for putting it up. I may have to go down to Gloucester County, New Jersey where the General is buried before I come home.

I have two of my horses here and spend part of my time in riding. I suppose you are going to the country soon. I shall follow you if you are gone when I get home. Don't let my coming alter any of your plans. I will accommodate myself to your movements in part.

If you will make up a party with Mother, I will take you on a trip to the mountains or wherever you like to go. I have had no leisure or recreation for four years and I mean to indulge myself this Summer before going at any business.

I hope I shall find you all well when I get home and we'll have a good time together.

With best love to Mother, Mary, Rebecca and the children.

Yours ever,

General

CONTENTS

L. P. Bradley

(COPY)

Head Quarters 3rd Div. 4th A.G.
Chatanooga, Nov.5th,1863.

To His Excellency,
Abraham Lincoln,
President of the United States,
S I R : -

During the afternoon of Saturday the 191h Sept., at a very critical moment in the battle of Chickamauga, it was my good fortune to be supported by Col Luther P. Bradley, 51st Ill. Commanding a Brigade in Sheridan's Division. I can bear Testimony and I do it with great pleasure to the very handsome manner in which Col Bradley brought his command into action and to the good service he rendered. At the moment Col Bradley's brigade came into action a very heavy and determined attack was being made, which the brigade very materially aided in repulsing. Col Bradley was very seriously wounded in repelling the attack and was taken from the field. Col. Bradley has earned and deserves promotion and I most heartily recommend him to your Excellency for the grade of Brigadier General.

I am most respectfully,

Your Excellency's Obdt. Servt.

(Signed)

Tbos. L. Wood,

Brig.Gen. Vols.

(COPY)

Headquarters Department of Texas
San Antonio, Texas. May 15'\ 1865.

The
    Adjutant General of the Army,
    Washington, D. C.

Sir:

I have the honor to recommend to the President of the United States for The appointment of Brigadier general, Luther P. Bradley, Colonel 13th Infantry, Brevet Brigadier General.

General Bradley entered the service from civil life in 1861, and served Throughout the war with marked distinction. He took part in all the great battles of the Army of the Cumberland and was three times wounded in battle.

At the action at Spring Hill, 29th of November, 1864, General Bradley commanded the brigade that opposed Hood's advance, and from three in the afternoon until dark defeated the attempts of a force of three Confederate divisions to dislodge him, and though wounded only retired when the enemy was beaten and gave up the attack.

This night and its success, which took place under my eve had consequences in favor of the Union cause no living men can reckon.

Since the war, General Bradley' s services amongst the wild Indian tribes has been almost continuous, and has been marked by great wisdom, firmness and success.

I know of no officer whose record will show more miles marched, more days in tent life, then General Bradley's.

I am, very respectfully, your obedient servant
(signed) D. S. Stanley, Brigadier General
Commanding

(COPY)

TO

    His Excellency
    Abraham Lincoln,
    President of the United States Washington, D. C.

Sir:

    The undersigned desires to present to your Excellency the name of Luther P. Bradley of the 51$_{st}$ Illinois Inf't'y Vol. for the appointment of Brigadier General of Volunteers.

    Col. Bradley has been in the service over two years and for nearly a year in command of a Brigade.

    At Stones River as well as Chickamauga, he distinguished himself by his gallant and meritorious conduct, and has at all times exhibited great ability as a Brigade Commander.

    He is an officer of skill & excellence, devoted to his profession, and will do honor to the service. He has fairly won the appointment

    I am sir,

Very Respectfully,
Your Obdt. Servant
P. H. Sheridan,
Maj.Gen!.

(Signed)

(COPY)

Head-quarters Military Division of the Tennessee.
Nashville, Tenn., Dec. 18ᵗʰ 1865.

Circular.

By direction of Major Genl. Thomas Comdg & c I have the honor to respectfully request that you will reward to those Head-quarters,to my address, at as early a day as possible, a complete summary of your military history from the breaking out of the rebellion up to the present time.

This is desirable in order that it may be forwarded with the proper recommendationfor your appointment and promotion in the Army of the U.S., upon its reorganization and increase.

The Major Genl. Comdg. desires that this matter be kept strictly confidential, for the reason, that if made known, it will subject him to an unpleasant necessity of declining to give like recommendations to many who would thus be induced to apply, and who do not deserve this consideration.

I am very respectfully,
Your obt Servt.
Robt. N. Ramsey
Bvt Col and **A A** Genl.

General L. P. Bradley,
Chicago, Illinois.

(COPY)

Head-quarters Military Division of the Tennessee.
Nashville, Tenn., Dec. 18th,1865.

Circular.

By direction of Major Genl. Thomas Comdg & c I have the honor to respectfully request that you will reward to those Head-quarters, to my address, at as early a day as possible, a complete summary of your military history from the breaking out of the rebellion up to the present time.

This is desirable in order that it may be forwarded with the proper recommendation for your appointment and promotion in the Anny of the U.S., upon its reorganization and increase.

The Major Genl. Comdg. desires that this matter be kept strictly confidential, for the reason, that if made known, it will subject him to an unpleasant necessity of declining to give like recommendations to many who would thus be induced to apply, and who do not deserve this consideration.

I am very respectfully,
Your obt. Servt.
Robt. N. Ramsey
Bvt Col and A A Genl.

General L. P. Bradley,
Chicago, illinois.

(COPY)

Headquarters Division of the Missouri,
Chicago May 16th 1885

The
    Adjutant General
    U. S.Army
    Washington, D. C.

Sir:

I have the honor to recommend Colonel Luther P. Bradley, 13th Infantry brevet Brigadier general, as eminently worthy of appointment to the rank of Brigadier General in the Army, on account of his very gallant and distinguished services, high personal character and great merits as an officer.

General Bradley served with great distinction as a brigade commander in numerous battles of the late civil war; especially, in the battle of Spring Hill, Tenn., on the 29th of November, 1864, where his brigade gallantly bore the brunt of the enemy's attack, and with the two other brigades of Wagner' s division, gained the victory which was essential to the success of that day's operations and to the complete victory gained by the Army on the following day.

General Bradley was severely wounded at Spring Hill while gallantly leading his men.

General Bradley's services in the Army since the civil war have been marked by conspicuous merit and he is yet fully qualified for active service, though near the period of retirement on account of age. His promotion before retirement would be only a just reward for services rendered.

Very respectfully,
Your obdt. servt.
(signed) J.M. Schofield
Major General.

HEADQUARTERS
Department of Mississippi
Vicksburg, Mississippi. August 8th, 1886

To the   Hon Secretary of War
          Washington, D C.

I desire most respectfully, yet most earnestly, to recommend Brig. Genl. Luther P. Bradley U.S. Vols. for appointment to the grade of colonel in one of the new regiments, either of Cavalry or infantry, to be added to the army on its reorganization under the act lately passed by Congress.

It was my good fortune during the war of the rebellion to serve a long time and to get well acquainted with Genl. Bradley; and I may say truly the memory of that service and acquaintance will be among the most pleasant of the whole war.

When I first became acquainted with Genl Bradley he was colonel of the 51st Illinois Volunteers, and commanded a brigade in Sheridan's division of the 20th Corps.

On the bloody field of Chickamauga, while his brigade was supporting my division, then terribly engaged with the enemy, Genl. Bradley received a ghastly and frightful wound, from which he was an invalid for months. Returning to his brigade before the opening of the grand, brilliant, and successful Atlanta Campaigne, Genl Bradley participated in it throughout, with much usefulness to the country and distinguished honor to himself.

During that campaign he was promoted from Colonel to Brigadier General of Volunteers.

In the affair at Spring Hill, Tenn. Nov. 29th 1864, just before the bloody battle of Franklin on the following day, GenJ Bradley was again seriously wounded, much to the regret of his comrades in arms, who thus lost his valuable services in the battle of Franklin and Nashville.

Genl Bradley resigned his commission in the volunteer service at the close of the war.

He would be an honor to our military establishment, and I most earnestly ask his appointment to the grade named, viz: Colonel.

I am Sir,

> Very respectfully,
> Your Obdt Servt
> Th: J. Wood,
> Maj Genl Vols
> Comdg.

House of Representatives U. S. Washington.
Washington, D. C. Jan. I I. 1904

Gen. L. P. Bradley
Tacoma, Washington

My dear General:

While in the barber shop at the Capitol a few days ago, it was my pleasure to meet an old and dear friend of yours, Mr. Henderson, of Illinois, who was for many years the Representative in Congress from that State. During our conversation he said a great many flattering and complimentary things regarding you, and asked to be remem bered to you. One thing in particular I recall that he said was, that you "were one of the men whose Military honors and promotions were received as the just reward of your military service, and without the influence of any political pull or backing"

In such a military record you are certainly entitled to feel a great degree of honorable pride, and I am not sure but that I am guilty of feeling some degree of pride in that I am permitted to number such a man among those whom I count as my friends.

I send you my very kindest personnel regards,

Cordially yours,
Francis W. Arshman

Diet. M.E.P.

Civil War Career

of

Brigadier General Luther P. Bradley

as shown in

Official Records

and in

Memoirs of Maj-Gen. Phillip Sheridan

Luther P. Bradley - In Sheridan's Memoirs.

Stone River

"A lull followed the third fierce assault, and an investigation showed that, with the exception of a few rounds in my brigade, our ammunition was entirely exhausted. - - I was satisfied that I could not hold on much longer without the danger of ultimate capture, so I prepared to withdraw as soon as the troops of Rousseau's division, - - - came into position. - - Roberts brigade (L.P.B. second in command) offering such resistance as its small quantities of ammunition would permit, was pulled slowly in toward the Nashville pike, - - Thus far the bloody duel had cost me heavily, one-third of my division being killed or wounded. I had already three brigade commanders killed, a little later I lost my fourth. - - -

When we came into the open ground (near the above mentioned Nashville pike) McCook directed Robert's brigade - now commanded by Col. Luther P. Bradley - to proceed a short distance to the rear on the Nashville pike, to repel the enemy's threatening attempt at our communications. Willingly and cheerfully the brigade again entered the fight under these new conditions, and altho it was supplied with but three or four cartridges to the man now, it charged gallantly and recaptured two pieces of artillery which the Union troops had had to abandon at this point."

Luther P. Bradley - In Sheridan's Memoirs

"Upon arrival at Lee & Gordon's Mills (Chickamauga) I found the ford over Chickamauga Creek temporarily uncovered, thru the hurried movement of Wood to the assistance of Davis' division. The enemy was already present in small force, with the evident intention of taking permanent possession, but my troops at once actively engaged him and recovered the ford with some slight losses. Scarcely had this been done when I was directed to assist Crittenden. Leaving Lytle's brigade at the ford, I proceeded with Bradley's and Laiboldt's to help Crittenden, whose main line was formed to the east of the Chattanooga and Lafayette road, its right trending toward a point on Chickamagua Creek about a mile and a half north of Lee and Gordon's Mills. By the time I had joined Crittenden with my two brigades, Davis had been worsted in an attack Rosecrans had ordered him to make on the left of that portion of the enemy's line

-1-

which was located along the west bank of the Chickamauga, the repulse being so severe that one of Davis' batteries had to be abandoned. Bradley's brigade arrived on the ground first and was hastily formed and thrown into the fight, which up to this moment had been very doubtful, fortune inclining first to our side and then to the other. Bradley's brigade went in with steadiness, and charging across an open cornfield that lay in front of the Lafayette road, recovered Davis' guns and forced the enemy to retire. Meanwhile Laiboldt's brigade had come on the scene, and forming it on Bradley's right, I found myself at the end of the contest holding the ground which was originally Davis' position. It was an ugly fight and my loss was heavy, including Bradley wounded."

-2-

Bradley, Luther P.   8, 16, 17, 20, 23, 30, 32, 38, 39, 45, 49, 52

S1, V8, P 109 - By Brig. Gen. E. A. Paine, Fourth Div. Army of Miss. 4-16-62

"The Second Brigade, commanded by Col. G. W. Cumming, consisted of the 22nd Illinois Regiment, Commanded by Lieut. Col. Hart, and the 51st Illinois Regiment, commanded by Lieut. Col. Bradley, followed, with orders to send small parties upon the road leading from our lines of march and report the position of the rebels if found".

Refers to the attack on Island No. 10.

S. I. Vol 16 Part 1, P 841.

Report of Lieut. Col. Luther P. Bradley, 51st Ill. Infantry, Decatur, Ala. 8-7-62

"Wires cut, so I cannot telegraph you. The convalescent train from Tuscumbia was attacked this A.M. about 5:30 near Moseley's plantation, about 2½ miles from here. There were over 200 men in the column, and of those one-half are missing. One hundred came in, and we have two killed and two wounded.

The attack was made by some 250 rebel cavalry. They came from their camp, some nine miles south of here, last night, and crossed over to the Courtland road before morning. Their designs were to attack and cut off our patrol, and if they had not fallen in with the convalescents would have done it without doubt. Major Koehler turned out promptly as soon as we heard of it and took the road after them. He followed them to Silses' plantation, near Minty, across the railroad and nearly to the foot of the mouhtains, but could not overtake them. I do not think they have taken a large number of prisoners. Most of the missing men are probably scattered through the woods and will come in today or tomorrow. You will see from this that the rebels are showing some little enterprise. It is already unsafe to send foraging parties over two or three miles out and when Col. Starkweather leaves (he is already under marching orders) you may expect to see a part of your command in trouble. Unless we are re-enforced we cannot protect this part of the line. They can run us into our defenses any day and keep us there if they choose.

Capt. Rose sent out a corporal and four men yesterday to repair telegraph. Returning they were fired upon by a band of fifty rebels. One man mortally wounded, one slightly, and one missing.

L. P. Bradley,
-3-   Lieut. Col. Commanding

S.I Vol 17. Part II   Page 147

Mentioned in Table of Organization, Army of Mississippi, Brig. General

Wm S. Rosecrans, First Division, 51st Illinois, Col. Luther P. Bradley.

S.I. Vol XX Part I. Page 176   Stone's River Campaign - Table of Organization.

51st Illinois, Col. Luther P. Bradley, Third Brigade, Third Division,

Brig. Gen. Phillip H. Sheridan, Right Wing, under Maj. Gen. Alexander Mc D. McCook.

Page 200

Stone's River Campaign - 12-31-62

"Effective Force" --- Third Brigade, Col. L. P. Bradley

Strength	Killed & Wounded	Percentage
1520	443	29.14

Page 203

"Names especially mentioned for important services"

Bradley - Col., 51st Illinois Volunteers --- "especially commended for skill
and courage."

Page 209   Return of Casualties

Col. Luther P. Bradley, 51st Ill.

            1 officer killed
            6 enlisted men
            4 officers wounded
           37 enlisted men
           9 enlisted men captured or missing

Page 256

Report of Maj. Genl. A. M^{C}D. McCook.

Re: Murfreesborough - "On arrival at the pike, I found Col. Harker's Brigade,
of Wood's division, retiring before a heavy force of the enemy. I immediately ordered
Robert's brigade, of Sheridan's division, to advance into a cedar wood, and charge the
enemy and drive him back.

Although this brigade was much reduced in numbers, and having but two rounds of
cartridges, it advanced to the charge, under the gallant Col. Bradley, driving the
enemy back with the bayonet, capturing two guns and forty prisoners, and securing our
communications on the Murfreesborough pike at this point."

-4-

Page 351

"On the death of these officers ----took command of ---- and Col. Bradley of the
51st Illinois of Roberts Brigade. These officers behaved gallantly through the day."

Page 357

Col Bradley commanding the Third Brigade   1-15-63

Page 362

Camp on Stone's River   1-7-63

Report of Lieut. Col. Wm. B. McCreey, 21st Michigan Infantry.

"The next morning we were ordered to recross the creek, and took position on the
right of the pike and to the left of the 24th Wisconsin, in support of Col. Bradley's
Brigade, where we remained without action until the next morning ----."

Page 369

Report of Col. Luther P. Bradley, 51st Illinois Infantry, commanding Third
Brigade, 3rd Division Right Wing, 14th Army Corps.   1-3-63

Sir: I have the honor to report, for the information of the general commanding,
the part taken by the Third Brigade in the operations before Murfreesborough, ending
Jan. 4.

On the morning of Dec. 30, 1862 the brigade, under command of Col. G. W. Roberts, advance
on the Winchester pike, having the right of the column. About 9 o'clock we came on the
enemy's skirmishers, engaged with a regiment of Gen'l Negley's division. The 22nd
Illinois was thrown out on the left, and the 42nd on the right of the pike as skirmishers, and soon forced the enemy back.

Houghtaling's battery was sent to the high ground, just in the edge of heavy timber
on the right, and the 27th and 51st Illinois formed in line of battle to the rear of the
reserves of the 22nd and 42nd, and on the left of the battery. We had active work with
the enemy's skirmishers all day, the battery occasionally shelling them, but they were
generally out of range. At noon the 51st Illinois relieved the 42nd Illinois, and
occupied the right of the brigade line of skirmishers for the balance of the day. About
dark the skirmishers were withdrawn, and the brigade bivouacked on the field. The losses
for the day were 7 killed and 35 wounded.

-5-

On the morning of the 31st, the brigade was under arms at daylight, and soon after formed line of battle. The enemy's columns opened out from the opposite woods, and Col. Roberts ordered a skirmishing force to advance and fire the timber on our left. Companies A & B, 27th Illinois, were thrown out under Major Schmitt, the balance of the regiment being held in reserve, its left resting on the pike.

About 8:30 A.M., Col. Roberts ordered the 22nd, 42nd, and 51st to charge the enemy's columns, and gallantly led them in person. The 42nd and 51st charged in line, with the 22nd in rear of the 42nd, at battalion distance. These regiments went forward at the double-quick, and cleared the wood in front of our lines, the enemy giving way before we reached him. The line was halted and opened fire in the timber. After some ten minutes, the line on our right giving way, we were ordered to retire to the lane leading nearly right angles with the pike, and take a new position.

Very soon the whole brigade was moved to the left and rear, and formed in the cedar woods on the pike, east of the hospital. Houghtalings battery was posted so as to sweep the open ground and timber the brigade has lately occupied. The 42nd and 22nd were thrown to the left and rear of the battery, and the 27th and 51st formed on the pike, fronting south. The whole command was soon hotly engaged with the enemy, advancing on the east and south. The 27th changed front to rear on first company, and the 51st moved by the right flank, so as to form an angle with the 27th Illinois Company K, 51st Illinois, under Lieut. Moody, was thrown out in advance of the battery to the east, to skirmish the woods, and remained there until driven in. Houghtaling's battery was worked with great spirit and vigor during the whole action; it as well as the regiments of the brigade, was exposed to a cross-fire from rebel batteries situated at the brick-kiln, and at the point occupied by Houghtaling on the 30th, as well as a heavy fire of small arms.

There the brigade met its chief loss; 400 killed or wounded in two hours. Colonels Roberts and Harrington fell about 10:45 o'clock. At this time the ammunition of the battery and of the infantry was nearly exhausted. Being hard pressed by a superior force, and nearly surrounded, it was thought necessary to retire.

At about 11 o'clock I withdrew the 51st in concert with the 27th, under Maj. Schmitt,

-6-

232

both regiments moving by the right flank in good order. Houghtaling's battery was left upon the field, after firing the last round of ammunition and losing more than half the horses; being outflanked on both sides, it was impossible to bring it off in its crippled condition. I was not informed of the fall of Colonels Roberts and Harrington until after the 22nd and 42nd had moved. These regiments, after suffering a loss of half their numbers, retired towards the Nashville pike, striking it near the grounds held by General Palmer's division, and being separated from the brigade, reported to him.

The 27th and 51st were the last regiments to leave the ground, the regiments of General Negley's command having already retired. As soon as I was informed that the command of the brigade devolved on me, I sent Capt. Rose, of Col. Roberts staff, to report to General Sheridan for orders, and fell back thru the timber toward the pike.

Not being able to find General Sheridan, I reported to General Davis, who ordered me to re-inforce Col. Harker's brigade, then engaged with the enemy, who was endeavoring to turn our extreme right and get possession of the road. I took the 51st in line of battle, just as our troops were falling back in some disorder, and after delivering a volley or two, charged a rebel brigade of five regiments, routing them completely and taking some 200 prisoners. This was the final effort on the right. About 1 P.M. we stacked arms and supplied the men with ammunition, the 22nd and the 42nd joining soon after.

On the morning of Jan. 1st, we stood to arms at 3 o'clock, expecting an attack, and after daylight built a breastwork in front of the brigade line. In the afternoon a brigade of the enemy issued from the timber opposite our position and advanced on our line. As soon as they were in range, I opened with small arms and shell, driving them back in disorder.

Observing that a part of them had skulded in the rocks, I sent out a strong line of skirmishers, under Lieut. Hauback, of the 27th Illinois, and captured two lieutenants and 117 men, mostly of the Third Confederate. The brigade occupied the same position on the 2nd and 3rd and 4th of Jan, skirmishing with the enemy every day.

-7-

233

The entire loss of the brigade is 3 commissioned officers killed, 12 wounded; 58 enlisted men killed, 328 wounded; 161 missing; making a total of 562.*

This loss occurred on the 30th and 31st. I think there is a considerable number of wounded men in the hands of the enemy, who are now reckoned among the missing; but having no positive knowledge of their condition, we account for them in that way.

I cannot forbear to express the sorrow felt by the whole command at the loss of its senior officers, Col. Roberts and Harrington. They had served with the brigade since last April, and had each been in command of it for a considerable time. Long service had made the command familiar with them, and inspired them with confidence in their judgement and skill. They fell in exactly the line of their duty, and each met a soldier's death, bravely.

L. P. Bradley

Colonel, Commanding Brigade

*The revised figures for 3rd Brigade, 4 officers killed, 58 men; 15 officers wounded 328 men: 3 officers captured or missing and 158 men, a total of 566.

* Series I. Vol. XXIII. Part 1 Page 407

Mentioned in report of Maj. Gen'l. W. S. Rosecrans --- "while General Sheridan sent Bradley's brigade, of his division, on another (scouting expedition) for the same purpose"

Page 414

Listed as Colonel Luther P. Bradley, Commanding Third Brigade, composed of 22nd, 27th, 42nd and 51st, all Illinois regiments.

Report of A.M^cD. McCook to Brig. General James A. Garfield, Chief of Staff, Army of the Cumberland. 7-10-63

"Sheridan's division marched from Millersburg to Hoover's Gap on the 26th inst. except Bradley brigade, which was ordered to follow the baggage wagons of the corps, and, owing to bad roads and the detention caused by the trains, did not arrive there until the morning of the 27th.

* Middle Tennessee Campaign

-9-

S. I. Vol. XXIII Part i Page 515

Report of Maj. Gen. P. H. Sheridan.

"June 30, (1863) I advanced Col. Bradley's brigade 2 miles in front of my position, and made a reconnaissance to within 3 miles of Tallahoma, finding the enemy in force at that point."

On the morning of July 1, with Colonel Watt's cavalry and five companies of the 39th Indiana Mounted Infantry, under Col. Harrison, which had joined me the evening previous, and two regiments of Col. Bradley's Brigade, I advanced cautiously in the direction of Tallahoma, driving the enemy's pickets, until I reached the open space in front of their fortifications. I here became satisfied that there was nothing left there but a small covering force of cavalry, and directed the cavalry to charge them. This was very handsomely done by Colonel Harrison and Lieut. Col. Watts. I found in their works three heavy rifled siege guns, the carriages of which had been burned; also some 3 or 4 new cassions and a quantity of commissary stores in the town were saved, that the enemy were about setting fire to. In the meantime I had ordered all of my division to the front, and encamped it in Tullahoma that night, the cavalry continuing in pursuit of the enemy, and bringing in numerous prisoners. ----

I take great pleasure in bringing to the notice of the commanding general the zeal and energy displayed by my brigade commanders - - and Col. L. P. Bradley, Third Brigade, and the cheerful fortitude with which all the officers and men endured the vicissitudes and exposures of the march from Murfreesborough to the place."

-10-

S. I. Vol. XXIII   Part I   Page 519

Report of Col. Luther P. Bradley, 51st Illinois Infantry, Commanding Third Brigade

July 6, 1863

Captain:

I have the honor to submit the following report of the operations of the Third Brigade, under my command, since the division left Murfreesborough.

The brigade left camp at 6 A.M. on the 24th of June, and marched on the Shelbyville pike, having the advance of the division. Five companies of the 39th Indiana Mounted Infantry, under Lieut. Col. Jones, reported to me, and were sent in advance of the brigade. My orders from Maj. Gen. Sheridan were to proceed as far as the cross road leading to Christiana, post the brigade so as to protect the road, and await orders. The cavalry commenced skirmishing with the enemy soon after crossing the Knob, 3 miles from Murfreesborough, and drove them back beyond the cross road. I advanced the brigade thru the timber, and took position on the east side of the pike, the cavalry driving the enemy's skirmishers to the foot of Marshall's Knob, about a mile distant. The skirmishing becoming brisk, and the enemy opening on us with a heavy gun, I relieved the cavalry skirmishers with 5 companies of the 27th Illinois and put Wright's battery in position. By direction of General Sheridan, the battery did not reply to the enemy fire. About 2 P.M. Brigadier General Brannan's division came up, and relieved my skirmishers, when the brigade moved on the road to Millersburg, reaching there about 5 P.M., and going into camp.

The brigade remained in camp at Millersburg on June 25th.

At 8 o'clock on the morning of the 26th, the brigade left camp, being in the rear of the division, but were halted by the order of Major General McCook, and directed to remain at Millersburg until further orders. The brigade remained under arms thru the day, and camped at night near Gen'l McCook's headquarters.

I received orders from Gen'l McCook to march at 4 A.M. on the 27th, and join the division at Hoover's Gap. I took the road at daylight, and crossed the mountain, overtaking the first and second brigades, reaching the gap with them about 9 A.M. and reported to Gen. Sheridan. Was ordered to issue rations to the men, and, after resting

-11-

an hour, marched to Beech Grove. After a short halt, moved with the division to Fairfield. Left Fairfield between 4 and 5 in the afternoon on the road to Manchester, the 42nd Illinois as train guard. Colonel Walworth, of the 42nd Illinois, found near Fairfield a train of some 8 or 10 wagons, without guard, belonging to General Rosseau's division which he took charge of. Went into camp about 9 P.M. on the mountain, 6 miles from Manchester.

Marched at daylight on the 28th and reached Manchester at 9:30 A.M. Went into camp, and devoted the day to washing.

Left Manchester at 8 A.M. on the 29th, having the advance of the division. Camped, early in the afternoon, on the stream about 6 miles from Manchester.

On the 30th, by direction of Maj. Gen. Sheridan, I sent out the 22nd and 27th Illinois to examine the country toward Tullahoma. They were put into camp about 2 miles out, the balance of the brigade joining them at night. About 10 A.M. on the 1st of July, General Sheridan ordered two regiments forward in the direction of Tullahoma.

The 43nd and 51st Illinois, were sent out, and advanced cautiously in support of the cavalry, entering Tullahoma at noon. Details from these regiments were on guard in the town during the day. The 22nd and 27th Illinois and battery joined the brigade early in the afternoon, and camped at Tullahoma.

Marched at daylight, July 2, in rear of the division, the 22nd and 27th Illinois as a train guard. Reached ford on Elk River about 4 P.M., and halted while First and Second brigades crossed. I camped on north side of the river by orders of General Sheridan.

On the morning of the 3rd, I crossed the Elk at 4:30 o'clock, and marched on the road taken by the First Brigade. Reached Winchester at 9 A.M., having halted a considerable time outside the town. Two miles beyond Winchester halted again. Resumed the march in the afternoon, and reached Cowan at 5 p.m.

The brigade was in camp at Cowan July 4 and 5.

Private William Sullivan, Co. C. 27th Illinois, was wounded in the leg while skirmishing on the 24th June. This is the only casualty I have to report.

--

My brigade train came through, under charge of Capt. James E. Montandon, brigade quartermaster, without loss of an animal or breaking a wagon.

Respectfully,

L. P. Bradley

Col. Commanding

S. I. Vol. XXIII Part 2

University

Capt. George Lee, Asst. Adj. Gen. tonSheridan

Captain: I have 20 of Colonel Ray's men here, sent back when he left Sweeden's Cove,
because their horses were used up. I suppose they should join their regiment soon.
Shall I send them to Cowan? A good many of the people living on Battle Creek and
a Tracy City are leaving their houses to escape the guerrillas. I have allowed them to
pass on to Cowan and other points where they have friends.

I saw last evening a scout employed by Gen. Rosecrans, who came from Chattanooga
on the 14th. He says Baggs forces are mostly at or near Chattanooga, and that none
had crossed he river, as was reported, below here. The report was current when he left
that Charleston had fallen, and that Buckner had been defeated in East Tennessee.

I send in 3 deserters. Signal officers from corps headquarters have established
a station within 1 mile of our camp, on a high bluff looking toward Cowan.

Respectfully,

L. P. Bradley

Colonel, Commanding

* *

Hdqtrs 3rd Brigade 3rd Division

Aug. 2, 1863

Lieut. Denning.

Act. Assist. Adj. Gen, Third Division

Your communication of last evening was received at 11 P.M. We have had no firing
with the enemy since we came here, and none will be allowed from my men unless they are
annoyed by the rebels.

My instructions from Gen. Sheridan are to place my battery so as to command the
bridge on the opposite side, and to protect it. The guns cover it perfectly, but we
cannot protect it without taking possession of the island, for the rebels can burn it
any night in spite of us.

Respectfully,

L. P. Bradley

S. I. Vol. XXX Part I Page 44

Table of Organization, Army of the Cumberland, Gen'l Rosecrans,

Battle of Chickamauga, Sept 19 & 20, 1863

Twentieth Corps Maj. Gen'l A. M^cD. McCook

Third Division, Maj. Gen. P. H. Sheridan

Third Brigade, 4 Illinois Infantry Regiments, and 1st Illinois Light Artillery,

Battery C. Commanding Officer Col. Luther P. Bradley.

S.I. Vol. XXX Part I Page 83

Inclosure in report of Gen Rosecrans

"Col. L. P. Bradley, Fifty First Illinois, Third Brigade, Third Division,
Twentieth Army Corps.

"Major General Sheridan speaks of him as having been twice severely wounded in the
action of the 19th, and greatly distinguished himself as commander of the Third Brigade
of his division, and recommends him for promotion, in which Maj. Gen. McCook joins him."

S.I. Vol. XXX Part I Page 175

Maj. Gen'l Sheridan lists him among wounded of Sept 19th.

Gen'l McCook in reporting action of Sept 19.

"Gen'l Davis' division fought on the right of Widow Glenn's house against vastly
superior numbers, maintaining the conflict gallantly until near nightfall, when it was
relieved by Bradley's brigade, of Sheridan's division, which was hastily thrown forward
and gallantly drove the enemy from the open ground and across the Chattanooga and
LaFayette road, after a sanguinary engagement, recapturing the Eight Indiana Battery,
which had been previously captured by the enemy, and capturing also a large number of
prisoners belonging to Hood's division, of Longstreet's Corps. Darkness coming on
the battle closed."

-15-

241

S.I Vol. XXX   Part I   Page 492

Report A.M^CD. McCook, Maj. General

"Col. L. P. Bradley, 51st Illinois, commanding 3rd Brigade, of Third Division,
and - - - are strongly recommended for promotion by General Sheridan."

S.I. Vol. XXX   Part I   Page 493

Col Bradley's Brigade has total casualties of 547 at Chickamauga.

S. I. Vol. XXX   Part I   Page 579

Gen'l Sheridan makes same report of the Third Brigade at Chickamauga as does
Gen'l McCook, then adds:

"In this engagement Colonel Bradley received two severe wounds while gallantly
leading his brigade." - - - "Col. Bradley, commanding my Third Brigade, who had greatly
distinguished himself, was twice wounded in the action of the 19th."

S.I. Vol. XXX Part I   Page 594

Report of Col. N. H. Walworth, 42nd Illinois Infantry, Commanding 3rd Brigade.
(after wounding of L. P. Bradley)

"Col L. P. Bradley, of the 51st Illinois Infantry had command of the brigade until
about 4 P.M. of the 19th, when he fell gallantly leading it against the enemy. At that
time the enemy had attacked a brigade of Gen'l Wood's division and driven it from its
position, compelling them to leave 4 guns and 2 caissons on the field.   In pursuance
of orders from Gen'l Sheridan, Col . Bradley formed his brigade in 2 lines as follows:
The 27th Illinois on the right and the 22nd Illinois on the left of the first line,
with the 42nd Illinois on the right and the 51st on the left of the second line.   In
this manner he ordered the brigade forward to attack the enemy. The brigade moved
steadily forward across a piece of open, level ground and ascended a gentle slope,
when the enemy opened with a most withering fire of musketry, which cut down Col.
Bradley and Lieut. Moody, his acting assistant adjutant-general, at the outset.   I
had command of the second line, and seeing that the first line wavered under the

-16-

242

deadly fire of the enemy, who were posted along the whole front and in the woods to the left, I ordered the second line to pass the first. This was splendidly done, and I retired the firstline to the shelter of the rising ground. The enemy could not withstand the steady fire of the 42nd Illinois (Lieutenant Colonel Hottenstein) and the 51st (Lieutenant Colonel Raymond) and quidkly retired in great disorder and with heavy loss, leaving the captured battery (the 8th Indiana) inour possession. This battery was subsequently turned over to its officers."

                            * * * * * * * * *

Other officers of the 3rd division in reporting on the Chickamauga campaign make references in a few places to having received orders from Colonel L. P. Bradley on routine matters.

S. I. Vol. XXX Part II   Page 203

Bridgeport, Aug. 28, 1863

Maj. General Sheridan:

Colonel Hunter has reported with two regiments of Brannan's division. He has not brought axes.

L. P. Bradley,

Colonel

S. I. Vol. XXX Part II   Page 286

H'dq'ts. 3rd Brigade, 3rd Div.   Sept. 1, 1863

Capt. George Lee,

Asst. Adj. Gen'l. Third Division:

Captain:

Colonel Hunter thinks he will have all the timbers of the bridge down tonight, and if he does this, will lay the plank during the night. I will not be ready to cross until tomorrow forenoon.

Respectfully,

L. P. Bradley,

Colonel, Commanding

S. I. Vol. XXX Part II   Page 916   Chattanooga
                                                     Sept. 28, 1863

General Order No. 69

II. "Colonel N. H. Walworth, 42 Illinois Infantry Volunteers, is assigned to the command of the Third Brigade of this division during the absence of Col. L. P. Bradley, wounded in action Sept. 19, 1863.

By command of General Sheridan:

Geo. Lee

Asst. Adjutant General

-18-

244

S. I. Vol. XXXII   Part III   Page 552

Table of Organization "Troops in the Department of the Cumberland, Major General

George H. Thomas, U.S. Army, Commanding, April 30, 1864.

Brigadier General Charles G. Harker, Commanding Third Brigade 51st Illinois,*

Col Luther P. Bradley -

* Returned from veterans furlough

S. I. Vol. XXXVIII Part I Page

Organization of Forces of Maj. Gen'l W. T. Sherman, Atlanta Campaign

May 3 - Sept 8, 1864

Fourth Army Corps, Maj. Gen'l O. O. Howard

Second Division, Brig. Gen'l John Newton

Third Brigade

      Brig. Gen'l Chas. G. Harker, Killed June 27, 1864
      Brig. Gen'l Luther P. Bradley

S. I. Vol. XXXVIII Part I   Page 203

Report of Maj. Gen'l O. O. Howard: - "The brigade commanders, Brig. Gen'l Kimball,

Colonels Bradley and Blake, are highly complimented for gallantry" - - .

Page 290

Brig. Gen'l Newton from Peach Tree Creek 7-21-64 reports position of "Colonel

Bradley was along the road perpendicular to their (?) but apparently at right angles to

other Union brigades previously mentioned) position in order of march."

Brigade Gen'L Newton, reporting work of 4th Corp around Atlanta, Sept 1864.

Page 294

"June 15th the corps was ordered to attack the enemy in his new position(Pine Mts)

my division to lead. Division was formed in column of attack, preceded by three

regiments deployed as skirmishers, under command of Col. Bradley, 51st Illinois, who

conducted the advance with great skill. The enemy's skirmishers were steadily driven out

of skirmish pits in strong positions, and forced back to their main line of works,

-19-

245

the strength of which, in the opinion of Gen'l Howard, forbade an attack by my main force."

Ibid: Re. Kenesaw - June 22, Skirmish line was reinforced, and, under command of Colonel Bradley, advanced, driving the enemy's skirmishers from their pits into the main line. The enemy's position behind a strong line of works was plainly determined by this advance. Our skirmish line lost very heavily this day."

Ibid: "It is no injustice to the claims of others to state that General Kimball, commanding First Brigade; Colonel Bradley, commanding 51st Illinois; Colonel Opdycke, commanding 125th Ohio Volunteer Infantry, and Colonel Lane, commanding, 97th Ohio Volunteer Infantry, distinguished themselves by their conduct on this occasion."

Ibid: Page 297 Division crossed Peach Tree Creek, on road to Decatur and Atlanta, placed temporarily under command of Gen'l Thomas. "Colonel Bradley (Third) Brigade formed along the road, nearly perpendicular to the other two brigades. The formation was as near as possible that of a T, Bradley's Brigade forming the tail of it."

In this formation the division started on advance but was checked. Ordered by Gen'l Thomas to dig in and hold line. Division was outflanked - - "Colonel Bradley, from the road, threw forward some of his regiments to the support of Blake's left, connecting him with the road upon which the rest of his brigade was. The enemy advance quite near the road, but were repulsed by Bradley's Third Brigade, who employed their leisure time in throwing up a barricade along the road. The first attack lasted about 30 minutes before it was finally repelled." - - - Among those who highly distinguished themselves on this day I mention the names of General Kimball, Colonel Bradley, and Colonel Blake" - -

Ibid: Page 300 "I have been ably and zealously seconded by the brigade commanders, Gen'l Kimball, Wagner, and the lamented Harker, Gen'l Bradley, Cols. Sherman and Opdycke."

Ibid: Newton's report of casualties in Second Division, Fourth Corps, from 5-3 to 9-8 the Atlanta Campaign shows a total of 2659 officers and men, 1022 of whom were in the Third Brigade.

-20-

246

Report of Brig. Gen. Luther P. Bradley, U.S. Army, commanding Third Brigade.

Hdqrs. Third Brig., Second Div., 4th Army Corps,

Near Atlanta, Ga., September 12, 1864

Captain: I have the honor to submit the following report of the operations of the Third Brigade during the recent campaign from the 3d of May to the 8th of September, 1864, inclusive. The report is incomplete in many respects, as I have not kept the run of the operations of the entire brigade for the whole campaign, having been in command since the 27th of June:

The brigade--composed of the Twenty-second, Twenty-seventh, Fifty-first, and Seventy-ninth Illinois Infantry, and the Sixty-fourth and One hundred and twenty-fifth Ohio Infantry and the Third Kentucky Infantry, numbering about 2,000 muskets, under the command of Brig. Gen. C. G. Harker--left Cleveland, Tenn., with division at 1 p.m. May 3, 1864, marched to Red Clay, ten miles, and camped. We broke camp at 6 a.m. of the 4th, marched about twelve miles, halted at 3 p.m., and went into camp about dark near Catoosa Springs. On the morning of the 5th instant we adjusted our lines and built a strong line of earth-works. The Forty-second Illinois Infantry and Sixty-fifth Ohio Infantry joined the brigade on return from veteran furlough on the 6th instant, and we remained in the same position until the morning of the 7th instant, when we marched for Tunnel Hill, reaching camp near that place about 3 p.m. The Brigade numbered today 2,325 muskets. On the morning of the 8th we marched at 6 a.m., and halted about one and a half miles out, near the mountain named as Rocky Face. General Harker directed Colonel Opdycke, One hundred and twenty-fifth Ohio Infantry, to scale the side of the mountain and try and effect a lodgment on the ridge, supposed to be in possession of the enemy. Colonel Opdycke carried the ridge very handsomely, after an hour or two of severe skirmishing, and drove the enemy half a mile along the ridge into his defenses, which were too strong to be carried. The Sixty-fifth Ohio ascended the mountain with the One hundred and twenty-fifty Ohio as a support, and the Fifteenth Wisconsin, of General Willich's brigade, was sent up after we had carried the ridge and were put into position by Colonel Opdycke to protect his flank. At noon the Brigade moved on

-21-

the mountain and relieved the regiments occupying it. On the 9th the brigade was under arms at 4 a.m. and skirmishing briskly. We brought up two 3-inch rifle guns, the men dragging them up the mountain, and opened upon the enemy's fort, but their sharpshooters prevented their being worked with any effect. Heavy skirmishing continued all day. At 5 p.m an assault was ordered, the regiments engaged being the Third Kentucky Infantry Sixty-fourth and One hundred and Twenty-fifth Ohio Infantry, and Twenty-seventh and Seventy-ninth Illinois Infantry. After a severe struggle, they were repulsed with heavy loss. At dark the brigade was relieved by General Wagner's brigade, and retired about a half a mile, where it bivouacked. We lay in the same position during the 10th and 11th. The Twenty-second Illinois, which was detailed at Cleveland as train guard, rejoined the brigade to-day. On the morning of the 12th moved off the ridge with division and marched to the left to occupy a pass from which the Twenty-third Corps had retired, formed, and went into camp. About noon threw up works, expecting an attack; Lay under arms all day, and camped at dark. Marched for Dalton early on the morning of the 13th, the enemy having evacuated in the night. Halted at Dalton an hour at noon, and marched about eight miles in afternoon and camped. May 14, marched at 5:30 a.m.; halted at 9 and formed in line of battle; brigade in reserve; moved to the front and left, and about 5 p.m. were ordered to relieve a portion of the Twenty-third Corps, then engaged in front. Advanced in two lines, coming under fire of the enemy's guns several hundred yards before going into action, and suffered severly. We relieved a brigade of Cox's division, and immediately became hotly engaged. General Harker was severely wounded soon after going in, and turned over the brigade to me. I directed Colonel Opdycke to take charge of the front line, and he put his own regiment into action, very gallantly going over the breast-works to a rise of ground nearer the enemy, and getting severely wounded, obliging him to retire from the field. We held the position until 5 p.m., our ammunition being exhausted, even that in the boxes of the dead and wounded, when we were relieved by Sherman's brigade, and went to the rear to replendish ammunition. At dark we took up position on the ridge, in rear of the battle-ground, and camped. On the morning of the 15th instant we changed our lines

-22-

248

to connect with General Wood's line, and fortified. May 16, advanced at 6 a.m. and took possession of the enemy's works, and at 8 a.m. marched for Resaca. Reached there at 10 a.m., and halted three hours to repair the bridge over the Oostenaula, partially burned by the enemy. Continued the march in afternoon with heavy skirmishing, having the Twenty-seventh and Forty-second Illinois in the skirmish line, supported by Third Kentucky and Sixty-fourth Ohio. Reached Calhoun at 6 p.m. and camped. Marched at 6 a.m. of the 17th and reached neighborhood of Adairsville at 4 p.m., formed line of battle on left of division, and bivouacked in same order at dark. Left camp at 6 a.m. of the 18th instant in advance, the Twenty-second Illinois as skirmishers. Reached Adairsville at 10 a.m., and halted until noon. Marched down the railroad about six miles and camped. May 19, marched at 7 a.m. and reached Kingston at noon. Halted two hours, when we marched out and formed line of battle on a range of hills looking south. Moved from here about 4 p.m. and formed about two miles from town, where we camped. On the 20th we moved back to the mill on Movine Creek and camped, remaining here until 1 p.m. of the 23rd, when we marched south, crossing the Etowah at dark, and camping about six miles south of the river late in the night. May 24, marched seven miles and camped on Raccoon Creek. Left camp at 8 a.m. on the 25th and reached the crossing at Pumpkin Vine Creek at 4 p.m. Advanced to the support of the Twentieth Corps, which was engaged with the enemy. Formed line of battle and advanced half a mile, then moved in column to position on left of Twentieth Corps, near New Hope Church, and bivouacked. At daybreak of the 26th we adjusted our lines, and after driving back the enemy's skirmishers, advanced the lines and built two lines of strong breast-works. From this date to the 5th of June we occupied this position, with some immaterial changes, being constantly engaged in heavy skirmishing and sham attacks.

The enemy having evacuated the position at New Hope, we moved on the 6th to within two miles of Acworth and camped, remaining until the morning of the 10th, when the brigade moved with the division in the direction of Lost Mountain, and after halting through the afternoon, formed on the right of the Fourteenth Corps and fortified. The Twenty-second Illinois Infantry left for the rear to-day to be mustered out of service.

-23-

249

On the 11th Instant we moved two miles to the left and formed on the right of Baird's division, Fourteenth Corps, and fortified, and the 12th, 13th and 14th were passed in skirmishing. On the 15th we marched at 8 a.m., and halted some hours near Pine Mountain. At 2 p.m. formed with the division in column of attack, expecting to assault the enemy's works, some distance in front. I was ordered by General Newton to form a strong skirmish line, advance, and develop the enemy's line. The Forty-second Illinois Infantry and Fifty-first Illinois Infantry were put on the skirmish line, with the Third Kentucky in support. This work was done very successfully, capturing 2 very strong lines of rifle-pits, and driving the enemy inside the main works. The brigade camped within half a mile of the enemy's works and fortified. On the 15th that part of the brigade on the front line was relieved by regiments of the First Brigade, and moved a short distance to the left, where it rested for the day. June 17, advanced and occupied the enemy's works at 8 a.m.; camped, and afterward moved forward a mile with sharp skirmishing; formed line of battle and bivouacked. On the morning of the 18th moved out in line of battle and crossed Mud Creek in a very severe storm; Heavy skirmishing in front by Second Brigade. Relieved Second Brigade, occupied a line of rebel works, and had heavy skirmishing all day. June 19, advanced at 8 a.m., the enemy having left his works; formed line of battle about one mile out, and changed position from one to another until 3 p.m., when we formed in front of Little Kenesaw. On the 20th we adjusted our lines and fortified; Had heavy skirmishing all day, and suffered from the fire of the enemy's batteries; at dark were relieved by Carlin's brigade, Fourteenth Corps, and retired about a mile to the rear, where we bivouacked. June 21, marched at 5 a.m. one and a half miles to the right and relieved a brigade of the Twentieth Corps; advanced the lines at 2 p.m., Third Kentucky skirmishing, and took up new lines near the enemy and fortified. From the 21st to the 27th we occupied this position, having constant skirmishing and losing heavily. On the morning of the 27th the brigade moved out at 6 a.m. and formed in column of attack in front of Stanley's division; between 9 and 10 were ordered forward to assault and carry the enemy's works in our front. The brigade advanced steadily and attacked in spirit, but found the works

-24-

too strong for them. After a short and sharp fight, and the loss of a large number of officers and men, the brigade was retired by me, bringing off most of our wounded. General Harker, the very gallant commander of the brigade was shot in the endeavor to carry the men up to a second charge. The brigade retired to its position behind the works, where it remained without material change until July 2, when we moved 500 yards to the left and occupied the ground vacated by one of General Wood's brigades. On the morning of July 3 advanced the skirmish line at daybreak, and took possession of the enemy's works, which we found deserted. At 7 a.m. marched for Marietta, and after a short halt, then continued the march about six miles, camping in front of a new line occupied by the enemy. July 4, we moved out about 9 a.m., and took possession, after considerable skirmishing and commenced fortifying. Discovered signs of the enemy withdrawing in the night; we advanced the picket at daylight in the morning, and found the works deserted. Marched at 8 a.m. of the 5th and took the line of railroad, following Wood's division. The enemy crossed the Chattahoochee, and we camped near Vining's Station, where we lay until the morning of the 7th, when we moved two miles to the left and camped. On the 9th marched at 6 a.m., in advance of the division, fourteen miles to Roswell; after a short halt forded the Chattahoochee River and relieved Minty's brigade of cavalry. Next day, 10th, formed connection with the First Brigade and fortified. Were relieved this p.m. by a brigade of the Sixteenth Corps, and on the 11th crossed the Chattahoochee and camped.

July 12, returned to old camp near Powers' Ferry and camped about three miles out, putting brigade in position in two lines and constructing works From this time to the 18th remained in this position, sending regiments to the river every day for fatigue duty. On the morning of the 18th marched at 6 a.m. on the Atlanta road, having the advance of the corps; met a brigade of rebel cavalry with four pieces of artillery, on the road, and skirmished all day. Colonel Opdycke, with the Sixty-fifth and One hundred and twenty-fifth Ohio and Third Kentucky, drove them all day, crossing Nancy's Creek under fire, and pressing them back to Buck Head, where we went into camp. July 19, sent out Sixty-fourth Ohio and Seventy-ninth Illinois to picket roads, and marched

-25-

251

about dark, and camped on Peach Tree Creek. On the morning of the 20th we moved at
6 a.m. and crossed two regiments over the creek, relieving a part of Hazen's brigade,
and occupying their works. About noon crossed over the balance of the brigade, and
at 2 p.m. advanced, following the First and Second Brigades on the Alanta road, where
they formed across the road about half a mile from the creek. My brigade was massed
in column of regiments in rear of Kimball's brigade, the men resting. About 3 p.m.
the enemy made a furious attack on the front and left flank of the division. I
formed immediately and sent three regiments to re-enforce the front line, one to
General Kimball and two to Colonel Blake, directing Colonel Opdycke, with the remaining
four regiments of the brigade, to move into the timber on the east side of the road
and protect the left flank. Returning from the front line soon after I found the
enemy working around to our left and immediately withdrew Colonel Opdycke and formed
on the Atlanta road, facing east. We had a sharp fight here of half an hour's
duration, and successfully repulsed the attack on our part of the line. The Twenty-
seventh Illinois, which had been sent to the First Brigade, and the Forty-second and
Fifty-first Illinois sent to the Second Brigade, remained with those brigades until
next day and did good service. We remained in position until the morning of the 22nd,
when we advanced toward Atlanta, and come on to the enemy's works on the north side of
the city, formed line of battle, and made breast-works of rails. In the p.m. I was
ordered by the general commanding to occupy a high ridge on the right of the road and
fortify. We took position connecting with the Twentieth Corps on the right, and
commenced building a strong line of works; we were under a heavy fire of artillery from the
enemy's forts all day. From this time to the 25th of August we were confronting the
in his works, strengthening our own defenses, and having frequent demonstrations on the
lines. At midnight of August 25 the brigade marched out with sixty rounds of cartridges and three days' rations, moving to the rear and right, being on the left of the
corps. The Twenty-seventh Illinois went to the rear to-day to be mustered out of
service. After a tedious night's march, we halted about daybreak for breakfast.
Formed line of battle at 8 a.m. and commenced fortifying. Moved to the right soon

-26-

252

after; marched eight miles and camped on Utoy Creek. August 27, marched at 2 p.m.
ar rear guard, made about five miles and crossed Camp Creek, going into position on
right of General Wood's division; occupied two hills in advance of the line and
fortified. Marched at 4 p.m. of 28th about four miles, and camped near Montgomery
railroad.

On the 29th advanced our lines about half a mile and fortified. August 30,
marched at 6 a.m. and crossed the Montgomery railroad near Red Oak. Moved east
about six miles and formed line of battle on left of Kimball's division. On the
31st advanced several miles toward Macon railroad, formed line, and fortified three
times. About dark (took) position on right of Grose's brigade, and camped. September
1, marched at 7 a.m. and struck Macon railroad near Battle Station; commenced tearing
up track and burning rails. Continued at this until afternoon. At 4 p.m. moved on
toward Jonesborough, and at 6 p.m. took position on the left of the division,
forming in three lines; in accordance with instructions from the general commanding,
advanced, and made connection with First Brigade. Just before dark I was ordered to
move forward to attack, keeping connection with Colonel Opdycke. Advanced about one-
quarter mile my front line, capturing a rebel hospital, with 2 surgeons, and about
150 wounded. It now being dark, I was ordered to halt and fortify. Moved up the rear line
to supporting distance, and fortified.

On the morning of the 2nd went into Jonesborough and halted until 10 a.m., when we
marched south, striking the railroad a few miles out, and following until afternoon,
when we came on the enemy strongly fortified near Lovejoy's; formed line of battle on
left of First Brigade, and advanced half a mile. At 5 p.m. the general commanding
ordered me to advance to the attack, in connection with the First Brigade, and to go
forward till I could go no farther. I advanced with General Wagner on my left, passed
General Wood's line, but, as the First Brigade did not come up on the right, and as
General Wood did not advance, I did not think it prudent to go farther. September 3,
changed position to connect with First Brigade, and fortified. Third Kentucky left
for the rear to-day to be mustered out of service. Remained in same position until

-27-

253

the night of the 5th, when we withdrew at 8 p.m., and retired to Jonesborough, camping soon after midnight. Left position near Jonesborough, the morning of the 7th and marched ten miles, camping near Rough and Ready. September 8, marched to Atlanta, and camped two miles east of the town.

The total loss of the brigade during the campaign is 1,040, as per accompanying report. I regret that I cannot give the losses by date, but I have no record of those details.

The brigade has captured and turned over 148 prisoners during the campaign.

I cannot close this report without paying a word of tribute to the memory of the late gallant General Harker, who commanded the brigade for the first half of the campaign, and who fell in trying to retrieve one of its disasters. No more gallant soldier has fallen in the war. Conspicuous for gentleness and generosity as well as courage, he won the confidence and respect of all who knew him, and was everywhere recognized as a true gentleman and soldier.

I desire to return my thanks to the officers of the brigade for their ready and cheerful performance of duty during the late arduous campaign, and especially to Colonel Opdycke, of the One hundred and twenty-fifth Ohio, for the very gallant and skillful manner in which he has performed the various duties devolving upon him since the opening of the campaign.

Very respectfully, your obedient servant,
L. P. Bradley,
Brigadier-General, Commanding.

Report of casualties during the recent campaign, commencing May 3 and ending Sept. 7, 1864

Date	Killed		Wounded		Missing		Total		
	Officers	Men	Officers	Men	Officers	Men	Officers	Men	Aggregate
May	5	76	16	386		9	21	471	492
June	11	64	32	320		19	43	403	446
July	1	9	3	47		5	4	61	65
August . . .	1			14			1	14	15
September .	1	2	1	11		7	2	20	22
Total	19	151	52	778		40	71	969	1,040

S.I.   Vol. XXXVIII   Part I   Page 888

Journal of the Atlanta Campaign, kept at Headquarters of the Fourth Army Corps, by Lieut.-Col. Joseph S. Fullerton, Assistant Adjutant General.

"June 27, 5:30 a.m. (In front of Atlanta) The country is so thickly wooded, and the topography is such that it is almost impossible to tell anything about the enemy's works. It cannot be done by a reconnaissance, as such would be almost fatal as an assault. The works cannot be seen before we get right upon them. We are about to make an assault upon works we know little about." (Third Brigade 4th Division made it) 9:30 - "Colonel Bradley, in command of Harker's Brigade, sends word by Col. Opdycke that Gen. Harker has just been mortally wounded, shot from his horse, while he was within 15 paces of the enemy's works, and that the brigade can not move any further, tho he is trying to work his way up; that he is on the same hill the enemy's works are on, but the head of his column is all smashed up and disorganized.

July 4th "6:30 p.m. General Newton reports that Colonel Bradley has taken the rifle pits of the enemy in his front, and that the others in front of his (Newton's) division vacated , all save one, which seems to be the end of a covered way to the house on the high hill in his front, which is easily re-enforced, and that there would be no advantage in taking it; further, his (Newton's) skirmishers are well posted and occupy the most favorable ground in his front. Lost in killed and wounded today about 130. Took 90 prisoners. Day very hot and bright."

S.I. Vol. XXXVIII Part V   Page 52

Headquarters 3rd Brigade, Second Div. 4th Corps.   7-5-1864
                                                          2:15 a.m.
Brig. Gen. Newton

2nd Div. 4th Corps

General: Colonel Opdycke and Lieut.-Col Moore, of the 125th Ohio Infantry, both report the enemy retreating. They report trains moving off—artillery, baggage and railroad trains. The enemy still keep up a slight firing from their skirmish line. Both Cols. Opdycke and Moore seem confident that the report they bring is correct.

                         Very respectfully, your obedient servant
                               L. P. Bradley
                               Col. Commanding

-29-

255

Ibid P 289 Headquarters, Military Division of Mississippi, In the field near Atlanta, Ga.

7-29-1864

Col. James A. Hardie,

Inspector General, Washington, D. C.

In compliance with your dispatch of the 28th, I now send you the names of eight colonels who are recommended by their immediate and superior commanders for promotion, and I earnestly recommend that they be appointed brigadier-generals - - - Colonel L. P. Bradley, 51st Illinois, - - -. Three of them are from each of the armies of Cumberland and Tennessee and two of the Army of the Ohio, and are all at their posts doing good service.

W. T. Sherman

Major General

Ibid Page 300   War Department

Maj. Gen. W. T. Sherman   July 30, 1864

Commanding &c, before Atlanta, Ga.

Cols. William Grose, 36th Indiana; Charles C. Walcutt, 46th Ohio; James W. Reilly, 104th Ohio; Luther P. Bradley, 51st Illinois, John W. Sprague, 63rd Ohio; Joseph A. Cooper, 6th Tennessee; John T. Croxton, 4th Kentucky and William W. Belknap, 15th Iowa Volunteers, were this day appointed Brigadier Generals of vo/unteers.

The appointment will be forwarded without delay.

Jas. A. Hardie,

Colonel and Inspector General

S.I. Vol. XXXIX Part II   Page 545

Table of "Organization of troops in the Department of the Cumberland, commanded by Maj. Gen. George H. Thomas, U. S. Army, Sept 30, 1864"

Fourth Army Corps, 2nd Division, Third Brigade Brigadier General Luther P. Bradley commanding six regiments.

S.I. Vol. XXXIx Part III.   Bridgeport, Oct 17, 1864

General Schofield, Chattanooga:

I have just heard from Coperton's Ferry by gun-boat and scouts sent from

-30-

Stevenson, No news of the enemy. I shall receive all news from scouts and couriers, and will forward to you immediately. Gun boats are patrolling from Coperton's down.

L. P. Bradley

Brigadier General
****
Ibid P. 354   Bridgeport, Oct. 18, 1864

Maj. Gen. Schofield:

I have information from gun boats that scouts sent out by General Granger from Decatur report a force of the enemy moving this way from the west; also that the enemy is picketing the south bank of the river between Coperton's Ferry and Guntersville.

L. P. Bradley,
Brigadier General

****

Ibid Page 57   Chattanooga, Tenn. Oct 3, 1864

Brig. Gen. L. P. Bradley, Commanding at Bridgeport:

The enemy were threatening at Dalton yesterday. I have sent three of my regiments there.   G. D. Wagner
Brig. Gen., Commanding
****

Chattanooga, Tenn. Oct. 5, 1864

Brig. Gen. L. P. Bradley,

Commanding at Bridgeport, Ala.

Colonel Opdycke has gone south with six regiments. You will relieve his regiment at Whitesides with one of your own and order it to report here. Fighting at Allatoona.

G. D. Wagner,
Brig. Gen. Commanding

-31-

257

S. I. Vol. XXXIX Part III   Page 214

Chattanooga, Oct. 11, 1864   11:30 p.m.

Brig. Gen. L. P. Bradley

  Commanding at Bridgeport, Ala:

  It is reported that Wheeler is at Villanow and intends to attack Dalton tonight; that one corps of Hood's infantry were in Mill Creek Valley this afternoon, marching in the direction of Tunnel Hill, and would encamp at Villanow tonight. Later dispatches from Colonel Johnson, at Dalton, dated 9:30 p.m., state that cavalry has attacked his pickets and were in front of his line.

Geo. Lee
Asst. Adj. General

****

Ibid Page 235 Headquarters 2nd Div. 4th Army Corps

Chattanooga, Tenn. Oct 12, 1864   7 p.m.

Gen. Bradley

  Bridgeport, Ala.

  From telegram just received from Gen. Thomas I am informed that the enemy is moving in the direction of Chattanooga and Bridgeport, and he desires that all the cavalry scout well to the front, and find the enemy if possible and report promptly any information received. Have you any news?

G. D. Wagner
Brig. Gen. Commanding

****

Ibid Page 299   Chattanooga, Tenn. Oct. 15, 1864   9 a.m.

Brig. Gen. Bradley

  Bridgeport, Ala.

  General Schofield has ordered Gen. Steedman to relieve your command. As soon as relieved you will repair to this point.

G. D. Wagner
Brig. Gen. of Volunteers, Commanding.

-32-

Ibid   Bridgeport, Oct. 17, 1864

Gen. Schofield,

    Chattanooga:

    I have just heard from Caperton's Ferry by gun boat and scouts sent from
Stevenson. No news of the enemy. I shall receive all news from scouts and couriers,
and will forward to you immediately. Gun boats are patrolling from Caperton's down.

               L. P. Bradley

               Brigadier General

               ****

Ibid Page 354   Bridgeport, Oct. 18, 1864   12 no.

Maj. Gen. Schofield:

    Cavalry just in from Caperton's Ferry; scouted the south side of river to
Racoon Creek; bring a report that a force of the enemy, with 800 wagons, is moving
toward Gunterville from the south.

               L. P. Bradley

               Brig. Gen.

-33-

259

After reporting back at Chattanooga, Gen. Bradley with the Third Brigade, Second Division under Brig. Gen. Geo. D. Wagner was sent to Alpine, Ga., as he is mentioned in Wagner's dispatches from that place as being expected to report there.

****

S. I. Vol. XLV Part 1   Report of Maj. Gen. D. S. Stanley, 4th Army Corps.
Campaign in North Ala and Middle Tenn.   Nov. 14, - - Dec. 1, 1864

(This campaign was part and counterpart of Hood's effort to draw Sherman out of central Georgia. The campaign culminated in the Battle of Nashville and ended the last northward drive of a Confederate army and in the destruction of Hood's Army.)

This report covers Union efforts to meet hood's advance from Atlanta to Nashville. The Fourth Corps including Gen. Bradley's brigade was sent out to meet Hood's advance on Columbia, during which - "The second division was pushed on, and, attracted by the firing east of the village, (Spring Hill) double-quicked into place and deployed the leading brigade as they advanced, drove off a force of the enemy's cavalry which was driving our small force of cavalry and infantry and would very soon occupy the town. General Wagner was ordered to deploy his division at once; Opdycke's and Lane's brigades to cover as much space about the village as would serve for room to park the trains; Gen. Bradley's brigade was sent to occupy a wooded hill about 3/4 of a mile east of the pike, which commanded the approaches from that direction.

Up to this time we thought we had only cavalry to contend with, but a general officer and his staff, at whom we sent some complimentary shells, were seen reconnoitering our position, and very soon afterward General Bradley was assailed by a force which the men said fought too well to be any dismounted cavalry -v- - we were threatened and attacked from every direction, and it was impossible to send any re-enforcements to Bradley's brigade, which had become quite severely engaged, lest in so doing we should expose the train and artillery park to destruction. The enemy made two assaults on Bradley's position, and were severely handled and repulsed; but finding his flank the 3rd time they overlapped him on his right, and the General receiving a severe wound whilst encouraging his men, his brigade was driven back to the outskirts of the village, where we rallied them and again formed them in line. The enemy attempted to

-34-

260

follow up his advantage, but - - - they fell under the fire of at least 8 pieces of
artillery, at good range for spherical case shot and receive a fire in flank from a section
of a battery which had been placed on the pike south of the village. A part of the rebel
force making the charge fled to their rear, and a portion ran down into a ravine between
their own lines and ours, and concealed themselves in the bed of a small stream, neither
able to crawl forward or go back until night-fall. General Bradley's brigade had lost
150 men in killed, wounded and missing. We now know that the enemy lost, according to the
statement of one of their surgeons - - 500 men. Our greatest loss was the disabling
of so intrepid an officer as General Bradley." Nov. 29, 1864.

Page 122

General Thomas J. Wood reported this action:-

   "Brig. Gen. Bradley's brigade was formed on the right, with its right slightly
refused, but not sufficiently to rest on the road. Skirmishing was kept up during the
afternoon, without, however, serious result until 4:30 p.m. Then the enemy appeared
in front, and on the flank of Bradley's brigade, with a strong force (it was Cleburnes's
division, of Cheatham's Corps) and made a vigorous attack. As Bradley's brigade was
heavily outflanked, while pressed in front, it was forced from its position and its
right doubled back on the road and into the village. A few prisoners were captured
from us, including the assistant adjutant general of the brigade. But the heaviest
loss was in the serious wounding of the gallant brigade commander, Brig. Gen. L. P.
Bradley. While nobly attempting to stay his brigade under the tremendous assault
which was then being made on it he received a serious wound (fortunately for the
country and the military service it was only a flesh wound), which compelled him to
relinquish command of his brigade and leave the field."

Ibid P. 267   General Bradley's report of above action:-

                          Operation Nov. 22 - 29, 1864

   Headquarters 3rd Brigade, 2nd Division 4th Army Corps.

   Sir: In obedience to orders from the general commanding the division, I have
the honor, very respectfully, to submit the following report of operations of my

                              -35-

brigade since leaving Pulaski, Tenn., Nov. 22, 1864 to 5 p.m. of the 29th inst.

At 8 a.m. of the 22nd my brigade consisting of (6 regiments listed) broke camp near Pulaski, Tenn., and moved north on the Nashville turnpike in the direction of Columbia, via Lynville; reached Lynville at 2 p.m. and went into camp. We remained at Lynville until 4 a.m. of the 24th, when we took up line of march on the Nashville turnpike, moving north toward Columbia. We reached Columbia at 10 a.m., and went into position on the south side of the town, fronting south. We here built a line of works and remained in camp near them until 7 p.m. of the 25th instant, when we changed position to the west side of the town and built a line of works; remained in camp near them until 9 p.m. of the 27th, when we broke camp and moved across Duck River, and at 12 p.m. bivouacked on the north bank. We moved from there 8 a.m. of the 28th, crossed Rutherford's Creek, moved to the left about 1½ miles and went into position on the north bank of Duck River; built a line of works and remained in that position until 8:30 a.m. of the 29th, when we broke camp and moved north on the Nashville turnpike in the direction of Spring Hill. My brigade on this day was the rear brigade of the division. When about 2 miles from Spring Hill I received an order from Gen. Wagner, commanding division, thru Capt. E. G. Whitesides, of his staff, to pull out of the road and let the artillery pass. According to the instructions I immediately moved to the right of the road, and let the artillery, consisting of two batteries, pass. I then moved on and reached Spring Hill about 2 p.m., and went into position on the east side of the village, fronting east, and immediately threw out the 64th Ohio Infantry as skirmishers. I put 4 regiments on the line, the 65th Ohio on the right, the 15th Missouri Infantry on the left of the 65th, the 51st Illinois Infantry on the left of the 15th and the 79th Illinois on the left of the 51st. I then had one regiment, the 42nd Illinois, in reserve. I then received orders from Gen. Wagner, commanding division, to advance my skirmishers. I immediately sent orders to have them advance. They had not advanced more than 300 yards when they became engaged with the enemy's skirmishers, but we drove them steadily before us for about 3/4 of a mile, when I sent orders to Lieut. Col. Brown to halt, as he was getting too far advanced.

-36-

In the meantime I had got the men to carrying rails with which to form some shelter in case we were attacked by a superior force. The men were busily engaged in the work when my skirmish line was attacked by superior numbers and driven back within 300 yards of my line of battle. I immediately got my men in line ready for an attack, and rode down to the skirmish line and found that it had been attacked by dismounted cavalry. The officers on the skirmish line reported to me that the enemy was massing troops in front of my right. I immediately rode back to my line, and as I had no connection on my right or left, I was fearful that my flank would be turned, and believing that an attack would be made on my right I formed the 42nd Illinois (my reserves) on the right of my line of battle and at an angle of about 45 degrees to it. The 64th Ohio Infantry, which formed the skirmish line, had by this time got entirely without ammunition, and as they were being steadily pressed back I ordered them in. When they had got in and reformed again and supplied with ammunition, I sent the regiment over on the right of the line in support of the 42nd Illinois. As soon as the regiment had got into position as directed, a heavy column of infantry was seen approaching my line, threatening my front and right flank. We were soon furiously attacked in front and on the right flank, a brigade of the enemy swinging completely around the right of the 42nd Illinois and the 64th Ohio. We gave them a very destructive fire and somewhat staggered them in front, and had we had some support on the right, and the right flank not been turned, we could have held our ground. After firing about 10 minutes, the right and center were compelled to give way, and in some disorder, owing to the fact that over one-half of the men of these regiments were recruits and drafted men who had never been under fire, neither had they been drilled. The brigade fell back about ¼ of a mile where it was rallied and placed in position by Gen. Wagner, commanding the division. The subsequent movements of the brigade will be reported on by Colonel Conrad, who then assumed and is now commanding the brigade.

The following are the casualties of the brigade: Commissioned officers - wounded 5; wounded and missing 5. Enlisted men - killed 17; wounded 109; Missing 62 - total 198.

I am, captain, Very respectfully, your obedient servant,

L . P. Bradley
Brigadier General

****

Ibid Page 230   Brig. Gen. G. D. Wagner wrote of this action (Spring Hill)

"General Stanley directed a brigade to be put into position on the east side of the
road, about 2 miles south of Spring Hill, to protect our flank at that point until the
artillery could get post. General Bradley's brigade, having been assigned to that duty,
did not reach Spring Hill until the first attack of the enemy had been repulsed.
Finding the enemy's cavalry posted on the crest of a ridge overlooking the town, and
enabling them to overlook our whole movement, I directed Col. Lane to advance his
brigade and drive off the enemy and occupy the ridge, which orders was promptly obeyed,
and the enemy driven off behind the ridge more than a mile from town. Gen. Bradley's
brigade having by this time come up, General Stanley directed me to place it in position
in a point of woods to the right of, and somewhat detached from Col Lane's brigade, and
about $\frac{1}{2}$ mile from the turnpike along which our train was passing. This brigade had been
but a short time in position before the enemy's cavalry appeared in its front and
assaulted his line, but was promptly repulsed.

It was near sundown when the enemy again appeared in Gen. Bradley's front, but this
time with infantry, and in very strong force. Seeing that his right flank was in danger, I
placed 2 pieces of artillery and my only reserve regiment, the 36th Illinois Veteran
Volunteers, Lieut. Col. Olson, well out on his right flank. These dispositions were
scarcely completed before the enemy was upon us in heavy force, his lines outflanking
ours by great odds, which compelled Gen. Bradley's right to fall back after a hard
fight. His left flank being also turned was giving, seeing which he went in person to
that flank to assist in checking the enemy in that position, but while doing so was
so severely wounded by a musket-ball in the left arm near the shoulder that he had to
be carried from the field. Gen. Bradley's brigade being now outflanked and outnumbered,
retired and reformed at the edge of the village, taking such a position as to protect

-38-

264

our wagon train, part of which had reached Spring Hill just before the last attack commenced." - - - Each of the brigade commanders, General Bradley, - - - and and Colonel Conrad, who succeeded General Bradley in the command of the 3rd brigade after the former received his wouund at Spring Hill, acted most gallantly and efficiently in every particular during the action."

Page 275   Major F. A. Atwater, 42nd Illinois Infantry, who was to cover Gen. Bradley's right at Spring Hill:-

"On the morning of 29th Nov. at 6 o'clock we marched to Spring Hill, arriving at 2 p.m., and were soon placed in position on the extreme right of the Third Brigade, and distant to the right about 150 yards, and, by order of Gen. Bradley we threw up a barricade of rails in our front as best we could with one line of a rail fence, and sent out a line of skirmishers, which were very soon driven in by the enemy advancing in force; we were ordered to hold said line as long as possible, but having 350 entirely new recruits, who had no drill at all and never were under fire, I did not expect to hold such a line very long. The enemy soon struck us in our immediate front, he having three lines of battle plainly fisible and moving well to my right. I ordered my men to reserve their fire until the enemy came within very short range, which they did; then we poured a deadly volley into them, which caused them to retire their first line and reform, the second line advancing while the first line moved by the flank and under cover of a hill completely past the right of my regiment, when they commenced firing rapidly into our right and rear, and being advised twice by my superiors, the field officers of the 64th Ohio, I finally ordered my regiment in retreat."

S.I. Vol. XLIX Page 568

                                          Headquarters

                                          Dept. of the Cumberland

Special Field Orders   5-2-1865

       No. 115

X "Brig. Gen. L. P. Bradley, U. S. Volunteers, is hereby relieved from duty as a member o

of general court-martial convened to meet at this place by Special Field Orders, No 42,

Paragraph 12, current series, from these headquarters, and will report to Maj. Gen.

D. S. Stanley, commanding Fourth Army Corps.

     By Command of Major General Thomas."

     Ibid Pages 965-966   June 7, 1865

                      Headquarters Fourth Army Corps.

                           Nashville, Tenn.

- - - "The troops of the corps whose terms of service does not expire before the

1st day of October will move toward New Orleans as soon as payment now progressing

is completed."

     "Second Brigade, Second Division, Brig. Gen. L. P. Bradley."

S. I. Vol 52

     Supplements and Reports of Union Correspondence, same going back to early 1862

Page 266   Tuscumbia, July 30, 1862

General Rosecrans:-

     I forward dispatch just received from Lieut. Col. L. P. Bradley, commanding at

Decatur:

     The cavalry have scouted the country thoroughly for 10 miles out and find nothing

alarming. Refugees from the mountains report that nothing has been seen but scattered

bands of guerrillas, Colonel Starkweather, of the First Wisconsin, is here. General

Buel has sent him with his regiment and a battery to Mooresville, five miles from here,

on the other side of the river, with orders to protect our lines if attacked in force.

                                -40-

                                   266

Colonel Starkweather has telegraphed for permission to cross to this side."

L. P. Bradley

Ibid Page 270   Aug. 8, 1862

"Letter forwarded by train today from Lieut. Col. L. P. Bradley, commanding
at Decatur. Guerrilas are very active upon that portion of the road." - --

****

Ibid Page 415

Headquarters 3rd Division, 20th Corps

Cowan, Tenn. 7-19-63, 1 a.m.

Maj. Gen. McCook;

I do not know of any rebel cavalry having crossed the Tennessee River. I have no
information of any on this side of the river except that which is contained in the note
from Col. Ray sent you this evening. I communicated with Col. Bradley, who had no news.
I believe the rebels will burn the Crow Creek bridges near Sturnson unless steps are
taken to give them better protection than they how have. I directed Col. Bradley to
make a reconnaisence tomorrow morning with 2 regiments and a section of artillery to
head of Sweeden's Cove.

P. H. Sheridan
Maj. Gen. Commanding

****

Headquarters, 3rd Division, 20th Army Corps

Cowan, Tenn. 7-25-63   10:45 p.m.

Brig. Gen. J. A. Garfield,

Chief of Staff, Dept. of Cumberland, Nashville, Tenn.

General: Your telegram just received. Colonel Bradley at University, reports 500
cavalry in Sequatchie Valley. - - -

P. H. Sheridan

-41-

267

General Garfield:

    I have the honor to forward a copy of a dispatch just received from Colonel Laiboldt, commanding at Bridgeport. Colonel Laiboldt has been ordered to remain and occupy Bridgeport, and, if possible, protect the remaining portion of the bridges there. Colonel Bradley will reach there tomorrow with his brigade.

P. H. Sheridan

****

Winchester, 7-29-1863

Colonel Laiboldt:

    I have ordered Col. Bradley to move down via Sweeden's Cove and occupy Bridgeport. You need not return to Stevenson tonight, if you consider it safe to stay at Bridgeport or vicinity. Col Bradley will reach Bridgeport tomorrow. - -

P. H. Sheridan

****

Winchester, 7-29-1863

Colonel Laiboldt:

    Bradley will move tomorrow at daylight, one day later than I supposed. Order two regiments to report to him at Bridgeport on his arrival. - - -

P. H. Sheridan

****

Winchester, 7-29-1863

Brig. Gen. Lytle:

    Order Col. Bradley to move down via Sweeden's Cove and occupy Bridgeport. He should have at least 3 days rations for the movement, and can be supplied at Bridgeport by rail. The movement to be made immediately if he has rations on hand; if he has not, send them to him in division wagons, to save time, unless he has the brigade wagons at your camps. Additional instructions will be forwarded for Col. Bradley. Start Bradley today if possible.

P. H. Sheridan

Maj. Gen. Sheridan:

    Immediately on the receipt of your order it was signaled through to Col. Bradley, and he was instructed to report by signal the earliest hour at which he could move. No answer has yet been received, but one is momentarily expected. The written instructions have gone forward by courier.

W. H. Lytle
Brig. Gen.

****

Ibid Page 422   Headquarters, 3rd Division, 20th Army Corps.

Cowan, 7-29-63

Maj. Gen. Sheridan,

    Dispatch just signaled from Col. Bradley. He moves tomorrow morning at daylight. Could not get off sooner, having to wait for rations. - - -

W. H. Lytle

****

Gen. Lytle:-   7-29-1863

    Your dispatch just received. The movement you describe all right. - - -

P. H. Sheridan

****

Ibid Page 423   Headquarters, 3rd Division, 20th Army Corps.

Cowan, 7-29-1863

Maj. Gen. Sheridan,

    Commanding 20th Army Corps.

    Bradley reports that a brigade of Brannan's Division is at University and will remain there.

W. H. Lytle
Brig. Gen. Commanding

-43-

Ibid Page 429   Hdqtrs, 3rd Division

Stevenson, Aug. 3, 1863

Col. Thurston, Asst. Adj. Gen.

Following, by courier from Col. Bradley, just received:

A private of the 7th Indiana, late of prisoner of war in Chattanooga, entered
my lines this morning, having escaped from prison in Chattanooga yesterday a.m. He
crossed the river at Kelley's. Reports about 20,000 men around Chattanooga, and that the
enemy have no bridge laid, but have pontoons tied to shore. They are throwing up heavy
works on the east and north, but have no defenses on this side. He reports also that
2 Mississippi regiments mutinied and stacked their arms 3 days since. All quite in the
neighborhood. - - Bridgeport.

W. H. Lytle
Brig. Gen.

****

Ibid Page 658   Headquarters, U. S. Forces

Pulaski, Tenn. Nov. 13, 1864

General Orders

No. 3

The following are announced as the names of the works composing the defenses in
and around Pulaski:

6. The works on the cluster of hills, spurs and ridges, fortified by General
Bradley's brigade, to be called Bradley's Intrenchments.

****

The Official Records are notorious among historians for their poor organization.
The above is the last mention I find of Brig. General L. P. Bradley in the Records,
tho you will note that chronologically the last mention should have been June 7, 1865
when the Second Brigade, Second Division, Fourth Army Corps starts from Nashville,
after pay day, enroute to New Orleans.

H. L. A.

-44-

Historical Sketch of The Bradley Family

The surname Bradley is ancient and prominent in the English Towns
of Yorkshire, Lincolnshire and Staffordshire.
Robert de Bradeleye was living in Cambridge in the year 1273.
In the Yorkshire pollTax of 1379, we find Willelmus Brodlegh,
and Agnes de Bradelay.
From the record made by Luther P. Bradley in the "Family Histories".

The first record of any of our family of Bradley is found in the
"Harleian Manuscripts" in the library of Yale University

It is a derivation of the Old English "brad" and "leah" and signifies the
"Broad-lea". Record of the name is found as early as 1183, when
Lord Hugh, Bishop of Durham, caused a list to be made of all
revenues of his Bishopric. The survey of Hugh Pudsey, called
Bolton Duke, mentions Roger de Bradley, who held forty acres at Bradley.

William Bradley, then mentioned lived in Sheriff-Hutton, Yorkshire Co.,
England about 1560.

His son William Bradley lived in Coventry, Warwick Co., and in Bingley,
Yorkshire Co., England.

His son, the third William Bradley, was born in Bingley. He came to America
and settled in New Haven, Conn. In 1644 where he acquired large tracts of
land,and is recorded as the first landowner of that place. This William Bradley
was the founder of the family in America. He married Alice Prichard February 18,
1645, whose family came to America on the Mayflower. He was the great, great,
great, great grandfather of Luther P. Bradley.

William's son Abraham was born in 1650
Abraham's son John was born in 1674
John's son Phineas was born in 1714
Phineas' son Phineas was born in 1745
Phineas' son Luther was born in 1772
Luther's son Luther P. was born on Dec 8, 1822

Family history sent to Prentice Bradley Feb. 4, 1946

(otorod in a computer file byRobert Dewey Bradley, Feb 24, 2015)

Luther Prentice's son William Dewey was born on Nov 9, 1869
William Dewey's son Prentice was born on June 10, 1906
Prentice's son Robert Dewey was born on Mar 16, 1935
Robert Dewey's daughter Kirsten was born on May 29, 1969
Kirsten's child Max Ellery was born on Aug 9, 2003

Max' s great great great grandfather is Luther Prentice Bradley, known as

The General, was appointed by Abraham Lincoln, President of the United States
In 1864.

THE BRADLEY COAT OF ARMS

A coat of arms is an emblem or a device which is displayed by titled persons of royal blood, and their descendants. Coats of arms were originally used for purposes of identification and recognition on the field of battle.

Heraldry, as we know it today, did not become of much importance until soon after the invasion of England by William the Conqueror in 1066. Heraldry became of general interest at the time of the Holy Crusades.

The Bradley coat of arms as shown on the attached sketch is described in Burke's "General Armory", and other reliable works of heraldry. It has been used for generations by many American branches of the Bradley Family.

The Bradley shield has a background of red, the chevron is silver, and the Boar's Heads are gold.

The chevron is one of the so-called honorable ordinaries, "Likened Unto the Roof of a House," is emblematical of protecting defenseless people . The Boars' Head is a symbol of hospitality.

Bradley

REFERENCES

The Illustrated Battle Cry of Freedom, The Civil War Era, James M. McPherson 2003, 1988

War for The Union, 1861-1862, 1862 - 1863, 1863 - 1864, The Improvised War, Allen Nevins 1971

Untold Civil War, Exploring The Human Side of War, James Robertson, National Geographic

Civil War Dictionary, L. C. Mark M. Boatnen III , 1959

Stones River, Cozzens, Peter, *No Better Place To Die,* noted author and historian, University of Illinois, 1990

Stones River Debacle, Cozzens, Peter, America's Civil War Magazine, May 2016 Pp. 22-31

The Battle of Stones River, Stevenson, Alexander

Campaigning with Uncle Billy, Girardi, Robert, Trafford Publishing, 2008

The Official Atlas of the Civil War, 1958, Library of Congress 5/8_3 Compiled by Capt. Calvin D. Cowles

Federal Records Centers; National Archives and Records Administrations, 51st Illinois Infantry Regiment, Journal by L. P. Bradley, Lt. Col. 1861 -1862

Library of Congress, Bibliographic information, resomce, maps and Civil War History

51st Illinois Infantry Regiment, Volunteers, Chicago Legion, Army of The Cumberland, 1861 - 1865, "episodes in its history", Edward Leroy Tabler Papers 2006 William Edward Henry

ABOUT THE AUTHOR

Robert D. Bradley, Luther's great grandson, is an architect in Boston and has practiced for over fifty years. He graduated from the College of William & Mary and the Graduate School of Design at Harvard University. Robert spent three years in Germany in the U. S. Army and was promoted to Captain and honorably discharged from the reserve.

His continued research of the Bradley Family led him to chronicle the events of the civil war from 1861 to 1865 through the letters that General Bradley sent to his family during the conflict.

Made in the USA
Coppell, TX
22 July 2021

59324751R00154